Introduction

List of Illustrations

Constantine The Great
Credit: The Metropolitan Museum of Art
Bequest of Mrs. F. F. Thompson, 1926

St. Augustine and Monnica
Credit: The Bettmann Archive

Innocent III
Credit: The Bettmann Archive

Sir William Blackstone
Credit: The New York Public Library

Lucretia Coffin Mott
Credit: The Bettmann Archive

A Suffragette Trio From Illinois
Credit: The Bettmann Archive

Sylvia Pankhurst
Credit: British Information Service

Mrs. Oliver H. P. Belmont, Mrs. J. B. Battelli and Miss Elsie Hill
Credit: United Press International Photo

WOMAN:

PRODUCT OF HER PAST—A PROMISE OF PROGRESS

Woman of the Western World is pursued by her past, by man's sophistry as to her proper functions in society, by century-old concepts of her role in life. This background constantly yet deceptively reflects itself in present thinking on woman and retards her acquisition of full equality with man in our existing culture, especially in the economy and in the law.

The origin and evolution of the beliefs sanctioning discriminations against women are exposed in the first part of this book. This exposure, and with it the tracing of woman's fortunes and ill-fortunes, is a patchwork history as we move rapidly from one place and age to another, viewing only lands and periods of major distinction and significance. However, the patches are colorful and their quilted pattern gives, at a glance, what has transpired for woman during the 6000 years of recorded history.

The history of present Western civilization comes from Rome as directly influenced by Greece and Israel. The Greek influence was mainly cultural, the Israelite, religious. Before Greece and

Israel, and through them also influencing Rome and the West, was the ancient Near East: Mesopotamia, Egypt and Mediterranean Asia. We will consider these early great civilizations through the fall of the Roman Empire, then the civilization of the Middle Ages, but only insofar as they are a part of the background for the status of modern Western woman.

Next, women of the United States will be observed: first, those of the early nineteenth century, among the most morally strong in history; then those of today, daughters to this morality, and among the most progressive women in history. Present-day laws are examined such as the "married women's acts" and other favorable modifications of the English feudalistic common law which stripped the wife of most of her legal rights by transferring them to the husband. Also considered are coming laws, such as the proposed Equal Rights Amendment to the federal Constitution which will eradicate, regardless of the attitudes of the various states, all remaining discriminations against women *of a legal nature*. However, the more subtle non-legal discriminations, as the withholding of equal opportunities for women's advancement in business, are not covered by the Amendment. They are discussed separately, and objectively.

In the United States today one of every three members of the work force is a woman, and one of every two women in the population is in the force for some period during her life, hence facts and figures are given on the working woman. Much of the data about her is revealing, often surprising. For instance, contrary to common assumption, woman's employment, not her devotion to domestic duties, is a prime cause of the substantial increase during recent decades in the popularity of marriage. In 1890 only 56.4 per cent of the male and 65.9 per cent of the female population fourteen years of age and older were or ever had been married — percentages so low that they are startling. As women workers increased, marriage appealed to more couples, was less avoided by each of the contracting parties, and by 1959, 75.1 per cent of the male and 81.3 per cent of the female population fourteen and over were married or once married. Furthermore, from 1890 to 1959 the median age of marriage dropped almost four years for men and almost two for women. The American man likes the working girl, and is more anxious to marry than ever before. His nature has not changed over the last seventy years; the modern girl is simply a better and more advantageous partner and associate than the girl of earlier periods.

In the United States, woman's improvement by working outside the domestic realm started in the early nineteenth century, so I re-tell that era's now "forgotten episode" of the Ladies of Lowell and their contribution to the economy of our young nation — a narrative of the working girl which should be a treasured tradition of a grateful people. Also, Lowell has its lessons for modern industry employing women. The Research Institute of America, Inc., in a 1959 pamphlet entitled *How to Handle Women,* stated: "There is considerable statistical evidence that women work better and produce more if they can socialize." The Lowell story vouches for this and demonstrates other basic aspects of working girls.

Reviewed are the two modern innovations, unparalleled in history, primarily benefiting women. One is economic, the other biological. Life insurance during recent decades has placed in the hands and under the control of women billions of dollars, cash dollars, with far reaching effects both in the national economy and in the family security. Artificial insemination now gives motherhood to thousands of women who would otherwise be denied children of their own. In the United States alone, 20,000 fertile brides annually marry sterile husbands, and there are already an estimated 100,000 living persons in this country conceived by artificial insemination. There is a paucity of reliable popular information on the process and the medical and legal discussions as a rule are limited to circulation within those respective professions. Unfortunately, many of the current attitudes on artificial insemination are the result of traditional thinking and should be eliminated. This thinking is seldom exposed though it casts its realistic shadow over the advancement in both medicine and law.

We know that a knowledge of history gives a better understanding of the present, and this is especially true for woman's sociolegal status. While concepts from the past as to woman's proper place in society are usually the basis for opposition to an increase in her rights, regardless of the sundry reasons given therefor, few studies have been made of this underlying stratum. As a result there still exist potent misconceptions harmful to woman. Often religion is invoked to support them. I essay to expose the current major misconceptions by showing their actual origins and evolutions in the hope that this will hasten their rejection, if not by those of ossified opinions, by the flexible-minded. Comprehension of a particular subject – or education generally for that matter – is often thought to be the result of the affirmative acquisition of knowledge through presentation to the reader or student of correct data, properly correlated and interpreted. This is not, however, the whole process; first must be neutralized or overcome any conflicting fixed ideas, and the breaking down of these mental barriers can be the most difficult task. Many persons will strive to retain an erroneous opinion in the face of positive proof of its falsity.

The young do not absorb new ideas faster than the mature because of better or more efficient mental processes, but because they are not hampered by contrary views. An idea presented to a free mind will take root immediately. Though false or partly false, it will have its effect if presented with a little logic and by one in authority, as by parent to child, or teacher to student, or priest to parishioner; and its constant repetition will insure results. Often the mere postulation of an idea as self-evident, though evidence be entirely lacking, will convince the credulous, and the realist is not always immune to off-tangent methods of persuasion.

Perhaps the most widespread illustration of a misconception relating to woman's rights which has arisen from the process of authoritative repetition is that the church through the centuries has sponsored woman's equality with man. Typical claims are that the church "following the maxims of the Gospel and of St. Paul, proclaims woman the peer of man in origin and destiny" and that the church is "the savior of her sex."[1] Clergymen and influential laymen long have iterated this theory, hence many believe it in some nebulous form.

Those who do may be reluctant, may even stubbornly refuse, to accept the truth that the church, relying upon the express provisions of the Bible, especially the admonitions of St. Paul, always took an adverse attitude toward woman's equality until recent times; even today, it is only certain Protestant denominations which sponsor her complete equality. The spiritually powerful and secularly influential Roman Catholic Church still cleaves to its age-old position that the husband is dominant over the wife.

Pope Pius XII on September 30, 1957, at Rome, in addressing a congress of the World Union of Catholic Women's Organizations (said to represent 63,000,000 women), first praised the advancements women had made, then expressed a reservation as to the modern tendency to regard woman as man's equal in all aspects of both public and private life. He failed to specify in what particulars woman should be denied equality, but he did quote to the ladies these words of St. Paul:

> Wives, submit yourselves unto your husbands, as unto the Lord . . . Therefore as the church is subject unto Christ, so let the wives be to their own husbands. (Ephesians 5:22, 24)

In the United States, in the 1959th year of Our Lord, the doctrinal committee of The Lutheran Church — Missouri Synod, recommended to the Synod's 44th triennial convention at San Francisco that women not be allowed to vote in church affairs. Again, the authority was St. Paul:

> Let your women keep silent in the churches: for it is not permitted unto them to speak; but they are commanded to be under obedience, as also saith the law. And if they will learn any thing, let them ask their husbands at home: for it is a shame for women to speak in the church. (I Corinthians 14:34-35)

Often those with contorted thinking on woman's rights are free of other common prejudices. The Lutheran delegates at San

Francisco condemned racial prejudice in this effective tone: "It is a violation of God's will for any man to treat his fellow man with contempt or to despise any particular race of man."

In spite of Paulism and the male's need for build-up, today the two sexes are considered equal by most men and women in countries such as the United States. In these lands even the husband's being the head of the family is merely an attitude of social amiability and psychological pleasantry; however, it is the custom to narcotize the husband by mentioning that he is the family head when calling on him to shoulder extra responsibilities or to bestow undeserved favors.

One aim of this book relates to the future. If a knowledge of the past aided only in an understanding of the present, the lessons of history would be ephemeral and often shallow. Fortunately, the socially minded person who observes a historical trend will use his knowledge to encourage the trend if he considers it beneficial or to oppose the trend if he believes it harmful; and thus history serves its highest value.

In the chapter on Rome the reader will see that, during the centuries after Christ, the Roman woman acquired (for all practical purposes) equal legal rights with man, which was the first time in history when woman enjoyed this equality. The Roman woman proceeded to exercise one of her newly acquired equal rights, that of divorce, with such freedom and abandon that dissolution of marriage became a major evil of the Empire. Divorce plus the high percentage of sterility caused an alarming reduction in the birth rate; the various laws of Augustus encouraging marriage and discouraging divorce, designed to increase the birth rate, failed to accomplish their purpose.

The reader will readily compare conditions in Rome to those in modern United States where women again possess virtual legal equality, where divorces are freely obtained, and where ten to fifteen per cent of all marriages are involuntarily barren. He will also apply his conclusions to the future of our society. A conclusion, which will be contrary to the assumption of many, may well be that laws are without practical value in reducing the divorce rate and that some other approach to this problem is necessary. Neither marriage dissolution nor sterility are presently the evils they were in Rome, but they are nevertheless serious and of vital concern to the future.

As a preface to examining the early civilizations and cultures from which comes the background of present-day woman's rights, I impress on the reader that their individual members were basically the same as ourselves. Therefore a familiarity with woman's status among them is of value to us, and often most revealing. There is a greater variety among peoples on the earth today than between many modern and ancient folk. Biologically, man has not changed since he became *homo sapiens,* perhaps 100,000 years ago. Once there occurred the great transition from superior animal or near-man to man, there has been no appreciable evolution in man's physical processes or structure, in his emotions or intelligence. This is aptly expressed in a recent work of the illustrious French biologist, Jean Rostand: "Already at the origin of the species man was equal to what he was destined to become."[2]

The exact biological change which produced the great transition is not known, and may always remain speculative; but the results were a much greater intelligence and, more important, a much higher creativeness or inventiveness. The new intelligence was of sufficient degree to give man an awareness of his own existence as an individual and of the finiteness of that existence on earth; and his creativeness was of such an order as to enable him to believe in a hereafter and in a god or gods for himself. As clans and tribes developed there were gods for the group, and later for races; as the races grew and separated, gods for their branches, and in time came the belief in one God for all mankind, a universal God.

Regardless of the form which religion took, man realized

that unless there was a hereafter, death ended his existence. For early man, constantly subject to sudden and violent death, the ever-present fear of the end was — unlike the Anguish of Heidegger — more a reality than a philosophy. The continual imminence of disaster bred superstitions in the fog of ignorance which surrounded this early man. These superstitions commingled with his religion to produce customs and taboos, which in time became traditions; and while the superstitions eventually disintegrated, the traditions often remained to cloud man's thinking. Gone is the superstition that woman is responsible for the sins of the world, a concept which was once a basis for assigning her an inferior role in life, yet the tradition of her inequality still manifests itself.

Religious beliefs are fundamental to mankind. There is no record of a culture without them, and there is evidence of their existence long before records were kept. It is not true religion which hampers woman, but the traditions resulting from superstitions which were grafted onto religion in the distant past. Such is the source, as we shall see later, of the quoted views of Paul. While he is the ranking Christian next to Jesus, his views on woman's proper status are not attributable to Jesus, as we shall also see.

Although there have remained constant the two important factors of the existence of religion and the absence of biological change in *homo sapiens,* the reader may think that a study of ancient societies loses much of its value in the belief that fundamental environmental changes have made entirely different today's life from theirs. What if the wife's dowry in Hammurabic Babylonia was carefully protected against encroachment from the husband, or the family woman of Periclean Greece sank to little more than a breeder while the courtesan gained full intellectual freedom with man? Of what practical value is a knowledge of these facts and their causes to women of today in our new environment and different way of life? But false is the premise of a new environment and a different way of life.

If we divide man's 100,000 years into the two periods during which he recorded his history and during which he did not, we find it was within the earlier period that he made the great discoveries which brought the profound changes in man's existence. All civilizations of the 6000-year recorded era have lived in the same basal environment passed on to them by earlier man. These civilizations have improved immeasurably the discoveries made by earlier man and extended vastly their uses, but this has been of degree and not of origin.

It was earlier, pre-record man who harnessed fire, invented the wheel, developed syllables, language and intelligent communication, established the family unit, and learned to live in organized groups and to govern himself — the dominant pattern of society ever since. He not only developed words for objects but words for abstract ideas, essential aids to intelligent thinking. During the recorded era man has merely enlarged the vocabulary and the number of abstractions, but their natures remain the same. Early pre-record man learned the value of vegetables and milk as foods and added them to his main diet of wild meat and fish. He domesticated animals and discovered that grain is reproduced from seed, and both domestication of animals and development of agriculture in turn changed his world — changes by which we still live.

Our meat we continue to get from animals, our grain and vegetables from soil, sun and rain, and our fish from the sea. We avail ourselves of no new basic methods of food production on land, nor do we cultivate the water. We merely mimic pre-record man in countless ways. He first salted and froze his meat for later use, wove fibers and skins to clothe himself, supplemented his hands with tools and weapons, and traded with neighbors what each could better produce or acquire.

The improvements during the record era of all pre-record man's great discoveries have been tremendous. There is a vast difference between the footlog and the Brooklyn Bridge, yet none in purpose and principle, and it was pre-record man who realized he could span a stream without having to enter upon or into it. The distinctions are pronounced between a boat of animal skins and the Queen Elizabeth, but both involve the same principles of construction and displacement and serve the identical purpose of transporting man by water. These illustrations of fire, language, organized society, domestication of animals, agriculture, and wheel are some of the paramount discoveries which, by putting them to practical usages, changed the very nature of man's existence on earth. We live today in the environment wrought by these discoveries.

It is almost certain that woman played the primary role in many of the great environmental changes. She was no doubt the first to guess the process of vegetable reproduction and to try her hand at agriculture by planting seed near the camp while the men stalked the game. Man would take over agriculture after he realized it was worth his while, but woman pointed the way. She must have been the first to realize that cooking vegetable matter, which broke down its starches and cellulose, would enlarge the number of edibles. Surely it was she, when her own milk was inadequate from food shortage, who demanded of her mate that he rob some animal mother of its milk to quiet the hunger cries of her own young. It is likely she was the first to domesticate animals, perhaps a litter captured after their mother was killed for meat, which she kept around the camp as watchdogs since they would react in a set way — bark, growl, hide, become intent — on picking up a strange sound or odor, thus warning her and her children to escape danger in the absence of the men. She was the first doctor — as nurse for the family and midwife for her neighbor in labor.

It must have been woman on whom dawned the connection between sex and birth, a realization which did not come readily because of the lapse of time between intercourse and the signs of pregnancy. With man's beginning came no cave-dwelling biologist to relate cause and effect in the cycle of life, no pelt-girded Sappho to sing of labor as "Love with his gift of pain"; but woman would sense passion's purpose. Without dispute around earliest woman evolved family life, still our social structure for daily living and continuance of the race.

Since man's basic environment was already established for him when he began to record the events of his life only six millennia ago, and since there has been no change during those millennia in his nature, or in his fundamental belief that his existence does not end with death, it follows that his thinking, his philosophies, his worldly aims, his problems, his very life must be comparable throughout that short period. Romans and Carthaginians warred for the same causes as do modern nations; the Babylonian worshipped the beneficent sun with the same spirit of reverence as the Christian does God; the Egyptian youth and maiden mated with the same emotions as do the twentieth century couple.

The civilized woman 2000 years before Christ was not a stranger of the distant past or of a faraway land. She lived yesterday, around the corner. She loved, married, looked after her home, and bore the children who would follow her. She is the sister of every woman, and her history is within all women of today.

This book will demonstrate that the continual intellectual advancement of a society is the controlling influence in the elimination of differences in the sociolegal status of man and woman. Since social progress is of such importance to woman, what holds the future in this respect? Whatever the causes be which pressure a civilization to arrest its progress, to disintegrate, to disappear from the face of the earth, they are not innate to man. It therefore follows that these causes can be prevented. I do not say they will be. It is easy for a society to become corrupt and decay from within, to become soft and fall to aggression; hard to arrest the historic cycle of birth, hardship, strength, progress, prosperity, then ease, indifference, weakness and death. Yet regardless of particular civilizations, advancement for man will continue long into the immeasurable future. The great transition from near-man to man endowed *homo sapiens* with the nature to move onward, with the mental capacities for continual creative achievement.

This does not mean the human brain does not have an outside limit, the same as other bodily organs, but the progress to be made with its present capacity, from where we stand in time, may be considered boundless. This is so to a great extent because of the cumulativeness of acquired knowledge. What man learns is passed on as social heritage. Witness our debt to pre-record man, and following chapters will reflect what we owe to the long extinct civilizations of the Near East. Conant defines science as "that portion of *accumulated knowledge* in which new concepts are continually developing . . ."[3] (emphasis supplied). Each generation, with the same limitation of thinking capacity as those which preceded it, moves forward by building on the knowledge from the past.

Sustained progress in the future, therefore, does not depend on another biological increase in intelligence and creativeness, not on the superman of Nietzsche's *Zarathustra*. We have barely started on the progress we can accomplish with the known abilities we have and need not a higher intelligence to advance. Let us say that without it our progress must one day reach a dead end, but what is to happen a million years from now is of little pragmatic concern today. If woman applies herself only to what may occur during the lives of her children and grandchildren, she will have ample latitude for her mental talents. Yet insofar as her sociolegal status depends upon the intellectual progress of mankind, she is assured for eons to come.

Since history indicates that the forward momentum of her particular culture may slacken, cease, and reverse, the lesson is plain. To gain needed rights, even to guard acquired ones, in her existing society, woman should lend her efforts to its constant advancement. For those efforts to be effective, she must remain strong and not become an addict to moral indifference as has repeatedly happened in history; nor allow herself to sink in the mire of idleness into which the matron of the past has often succumbed; nor ever wear the shabby cloak of ignorance. Woman did not acquire, and will not retain, her present sociolegal status by courtesy, but by merit.

What is the foreseeable future of our American civilization, in many aspects now a world civilization? I do not heed those who fear it is soon to abort in chaos. Reflection on only this one phenomenon will serve to convince that our advancement is to be accelerated as never before: *intelligence is soon to become commonplace*. We now enter the very decade when we must prepare for a drastic revaluation of that revered human quality.

The spark of creativeness in man has enabled him recently to build "thinking" machines which substitute for his own intelligence. Though cybernetics is in its infancy – it was only given a name in 1947 – the machines already work, in fractions of a second, the most complicated problems. In some fields they accomplish in hours what would be a lifetime task for the expert. In the oil industry, for example, giant computers with "memory" units not only calculate thousands of monthly royalty, overriding royalty and working interest checks, but also compute such factors as the optimum production rate to extract the most oil from a given reservoir, the most economical refinery run for each month's production, and the most efficient locations for lift stations along extended pipeline routes. Such machines in the future will turn out thousands of times more intellectual work and with greater accuracy that can man.

Intelligent man, as distinguished from creative man, and "thinking" machine will together perform the mental routine of the future. They will be the clock punchers and pencil pushers of progress, while the creative man will continue to steer it. Many consider Einstein, the discoverer of general relativity whose theories were not chained to this planet, to be the greatest scientist of all. It is said that he could not always solve the involved mathematical problems the answers to which he needed, that he got others to do this for him. Notwithstanding, he knew the answers he needed and what to do with them. The machine, being devoid of creativeness, will know neither, yet when "fed" the necessary data it will surpass even the mythical superman in intellectual results and physical endurance – to serve the Einsteins.

As the machine relieves man of many hours of wearisome mental toil, we can expect an intellectual revolution similar to the Industrial Revolution. The economy in mental work may be visualized by considering the difference between the making by hand and the manufacture by machine of any item in general use: the simple can opener for example, or the cloth for a dress. Heretofore most intellectual work has been "by hand," hereafter it will be by machine. Whether the "thinking" machine will develop beneficial "conditioned reflexes" or can win at chess must at this stage be left to a Wiener;[4] and though the machines never become "human," at least, as expressed by Uttley, tedious thinking, calculating, counting and checking will no longer make "machines" of humans.[5]

Certainly an intellectual revolution is at hand, and I have selected the "thinking" machine from the numerous causes of our coming accelerated progress because it will be women primarily who will "feed" and operate them, as women now "feed" and operate the typewriter, comptometer, and other office equipment. Women are presently an integral and essential part of our economy, among other reasons, because of their virtual monopoly in the handling of paper work and the equipment necessary to turn it out. In such handling many not only type and file but serve on a higher level, discreetly exercising judgment outwardly attributed to the executive. The sudden removal of women from office work in a country such as the United States would disrupt the flow of business; the bewildered and impatient male would bog in detail, his very thinking impaired.

More essential to male efficiency than present secretaries will be the office woman of the future who methodically controls the machines' intellectual productions. The handling, processing and organizing of paper work enters into the final result and gives one an insight into the ultimate accomplishment. The "thinking" machine, which will associate woman closer than ever with intellectual material, will increase her value and status. Furthermore, woman's present principal role in the economy of assisting the male is temporary; already many take the primary responsibility in jobs from clerk to president, and those at the top beckon for others to follow.

As the tempo of intellectual activity increases multifold and the society advances as never before, woman will close the final gap of inequalities in all aspects of life, and her status of full equality will be perpetuated so long as her society progresses.

With a promise of progress for the future, we turn to our engaging product of her past: this Eve, who was so willingly persuaded by the ancient symbol of fertility to partake of the forbidden fruit; this maid, to whom Isis gave the instinct to understand her lover; this mate, who to man has been wife, companion and mistress; who has reigned as queen and toiled as slave; but who, during the span of time, has been, most of all, a woman.

---

[1] Gibbons, James Cardinal, Archbishop of Baltimore, *Our Christian Heritage,* p. 361, 368. John Murphy Company, New York (1889).

[2] Rostand, Jean, *Can Man Be Modified?* p. 76. Basic Books, Inc. New York (1959).

[3] Conant, James B., *On Understanding Science: An Historical Approach,* p. 98. Yale University Press, New Haven (1947).

[4] Wiener, Norbert, Professor of Mathematics at Massachusetts Institute of Technology.

[5] Uttley, A. M., Superintendent of Electronics Division, National Physical Laboratory of England.

Historical

MESOPOTAMIA

The People and the Land — The Code of Hammurabi — Types of Marriage — Dowry — The Family and the Wife — Slander and Adultery — Divorce — Characteristics of the Society — Conclusion

THE LAND OF THE TWO RIVERS, CIRCA THE EARLY PART of the seventeenth century before Christ, was ruled by Hammurabi,[1] King of Babylon, a Semite. The civilization of the valleys of the Euphrates and the Tigris was already two millennia old. Hammurabi was perhaps the greatest lawgiver of all time, and his famous Code of Laws granted the women of Mesopotamia more legal rights than were enjoyed by the women of Europe and America eighteen centuries after Christ. The Mesopotamian woman did not have full equality with man, and was subject to her father and husband in many respects. Yet she possessed valuable personal and economic privileges, was respected and protected, and played an important role in the society and in the economy.

The first civilized settlers of this land, the Sumerians, were neither Semitic nor Indo-European and probably originated to the East. For centuries they maintained an agricultural civilization stabilized by extensive and efficient networks of irrigation. Their women shared in the progress and were not considered as having in life only the two purposes of childbearing and giving pleasure to man, a belief typical of most Eastern races. By the twenty-first century B. C., the Sumerians possessed a written code setting forth comprehensive rules of law governing their society.

Early in the second millennium B. C. nomadic Semites of little culture began moving into Mesopotamia and they were able to conquer and settle various parts of the land. The virile Amorite branch, probably during the latter part of the nineteenth century B. C., established a kingdom at Babylon. Hammurabi, the sixth king of the Amorite First Dynasty of Babylon, brought under his sway the entire area of Mesopotamia or Babylonia. Unity increased the general prosperity and soon business, commerce and trade rivaled the older agricultural and pastoral pursuits. There was great wealth, consisting of expansive grain fields, grain storage facilities, large flocks and herds with professional shepherds, branders and veterinarians, wool weaving concerns, fishing industries, shipping trades with boats, docks and wharves, commercial and mercantile establishments, investment and lending houses, and slaves. Canals and irrigation ditches criss-crossed the area between the Rivers and business activity characterized the towns.

In addition to the king and his family, there were three classes in the society: the ruling class, the freemen, and the slaves. The ruling class was composed of the military leaders, the priests and the governmental officials. The freemen, or middle class, were farmers, herders, fishermen, merchants, shippers, professional men, and laborers. The slaves formed a substantial category in the society; in the economy they comprised much of the wealth. While owned by their masters, they were not wholly comparable to slaves in other lands; they had defined rights permitting them to own property (including other slaves), to earn money, to purchase their freedom, to marry (even a freeman or freewoman), and to participate generally in the daily life. Each of the three classes had its own privileges and duties, and the higher the class the greater were its duties as well as its privileges.

THE CODE OF HAMMURABI

Hammurabi undertook the codification of many of the customs and laws regulating the society, including those of property ownership, land uses, agriculture, commerce, debts, price fixing, wages, military, marriage, family, inheritance, adoption, divorce, and slavery. The Code restated numerous important Mesopotamian common law rules, amended others, and no doubt included some merely because they needed publicizing. It did not purport, however, to cover all laws, and it was not called a code by Hammurabi. For instance, the rights and duties of the priests were not dealt with. This important portion of the law was well established, was familiar to the priests and was not changed. The priests and the scribes handled virtually all legal matters; there were no professional lawyers as a distinct class.

The Code was a fusion of the Sumerian and Semitic laws and reflected the fusion of their societies and their joint progress. It established many wholesome legal principles such as the payment of damages in certain cases for the negligent injury of a person in lieu of "punishment by retaliation" (an eye for an eye). Another great forward step advanced by the Code was the enlargement of women's rights including the mitigation of the control of the husband over the wife. Hammurabi did much to elevate woman. Before reviewing some of her specific benefits under the Code, a word about the Code itself.

It contained a prologue, the law sections and an epilogue, and was written in cuneiform on a stela of black diorite over seven feet high. It was discovered in 1902 by DeMorgan, a French explorer, and is now in the Louvre in Paris. At the top of the stela is a picture of Hammurabi receiving the Code from Shamash, the Sun God, who, among other attributes, was the God of Law, and whose two children were Right and Justice. This God's morning rays drove away the night, the cover for law breakers and evil doers. The prologue sets forth that the gods had foreordained the supremacy of Babylon, that Hammurabi should bring justice to the land, and that he should destroy the wicked so that the strong might not oppress the weak. It named certain accomplishments of Hammurabi and pointed out that he had established laws of right and justice in the language of the land and thus promoted the welfare of his people. The law sections, plainly and simply worded, were well arranged pursuant to a planned structure and grouped according to subject matter. The penalties were harsh, and the laws contained little flexibility, little mercy; yet they applied alike to all within a recognized justifiable classification, as must modern laws in order to be constitutional.

In theory, the Code was of divine origin as were most ancient legal pronouncements; the ruler knew that if the laws of his realm came from above, the people would more readily obey them. Yet the Code of Hammurabi provided for the administration of justice by secular judges rather than by priests. The king of course could render personal justice, either original or appellate, but ordinary litigation was handled by professional judges who sat at the gates and in the market places of the cities. There was a court of appeals at Babylon. The enactment of laws and their administration are two different phases of the legal process; the manner in which Mesopotamian laws were administered was itself a great advancement. The trained judges rendered decisions in strict compliance with the law; a merchant could get his due against the ruler of a city, a slave against the freeman, and a wife against the husband. There was government of laws, not of men who determined on their own what was right or wrong in a particular case.

The Code contained many specific rights and obligations of the Babylonian woman, and their very inclusion in this monumental work of the times indicates the importance which Hammurabi attached to woman's place in the culture.

TYPES OF MARRIAGE

First marriages were usually negotiated before the girl was old enough to enter upon the discharge of that relationship.

Various procedures existed for the initiation and completion of these early marriages. A frequent initiation was the bridegroom's delivery to the bride's father of two gifts called the betrothal gift and the bridal gift, both of which were retained by the father. The betrothal gift was probably to pay for the marriage expenses including the feast, but the bridal gift was net to the father. Upon the delivery of these gifts an inchoate marriage arose, a status unknown today and which may be described as a relation somewhere between a betrothal and a firm marriage. The bride remained in her father's house until she was of suitable age; she was then delivered by her father to the bridegroom, which delivery completed the marriage. One variation of this procedure occurred when the bridegroom was too young to act for himself, in which case his father did the negotiating and delivered the two gifts to the bride's father.

If a man raped an inchoate bride while she lived in her father's house, and she was a virgin, the penalty was death. This may not appear singular to the modern reader, but it was a protection afforded the girl of few societies throughout history; the drastic death penalty reflects a high respect in the society for her person.

Another procedure for the marriage of a young girl was by contract between the fathers of the couple whereby the bride came to live in the house of the bridegroom's father. This was in the nature of an adoption of the bride by her future father-in-law and she was referred to by one word, *kallatum,* a term with the connotations of both bride and daughter-in-law. It is believed this "adoption" method was followed in cases where the bride's family was of low income.

Whenever the bride came to the father-in-law's house, he was prohibited by heavy monetary penalty or death from molesting her.

> If the man has chosen a bride for his son and his son has not known her and he himself lies in her bosom, he shall pay her ½ maneh of silver and further shall make good to her anything that she has brought from the house of her father, and a husband after her heart may marry her. (Section 156)

> If a man has chosen a bride for his son and his son has known her, (and if) thereafter he himself lies in her bosom and they catch him, they shall bind that man and shall cast him into the water. (Section 155)

Marriage was an encouraged union which it was hoped Ishtar, the goddess of motherhood and of the fertility of all nature, would bless with children. Ishtar was often referred to as The Holy Virgin or The Virgin Mother. This was, however, because she was not wedded to any particular god; her inspiration for reproduction was for all life: human, animal and plant. Ishtar was called Ashtoreth by the Hebrews, and Astarte by the Greeks. She was later to be identified with the Egyptian Isis, the Grecian Aphrodite and the Roman Venus. Ishtar was the brilliant Venus of the heavens and the exalted goddess of love and bounty as well as of fertility.

DOWRY

With the wife went a dowry of property which was a gift for life to her from her father. If the father was dead the Code specified, "Her brothers shall bestow a dowry on her according to the capacity of the paternal estate and shall give her to a husband." (Section 184)

If the husband wished to divorce his wife because she had not borne him sons, he must "make good to her the dowry which she has brought from her father's house and divorce her." (Section 138) If he wished to marry a second wife because the first was suffering from "ague" — probably some fever accompanied by chills which, when not fatal, was incapacitating — the husband could do so, but he could not divorce his first wife; she had the choice of remaining in his house or leaving. If she decided to leave, he must "make good to her her dowry which she brought from the house of her father and so she shall go." (Section 149) It will be noted that the husband could not divorce the wife pursuant to 138 until he had first given her the dowry. Also, if she left his house pursuant to 149, she got the dowry first. No credit arrangement was allowed the husband insofar as the law was concerned. If the wife with ague elected not to leave her husband "she shall dwell in the house which he has made, and he shall continue to maintain her so long as she lives." (Section 148)

The one word "ague" no doubt covered any fever, disease or illness which rendered a wife unfit for married life. If so, it well illustrates the economy in wording found in the Code sections. The Code was carved on exceptionally hard stone, only about 3600 lines would go on the pillar, and it was for reading by the public in a public place. Brevity was therefore essential.

A modern lawyer in lieu of "ague" would say "any fever of whatsoever kind, type or nature, including but not limited to malaria, typhoid, yellow or parrot, whether or not accompanied by ague, chills and/or other symptoms, and any other sickness, illness or disease, similar or dissimilar to said fevers, which disables a wife from performing the usual, ordinary and customary marital relations, duties and/or obligations; provided, however, that such disability is permanent and not of a temporary nature." But his words would not be carved on diorite, and no doubt all this was understood by "ague," chills being the principal visual symptom, and therefore the name, of the incurable fevers which sapped the strength and interest of the inhabitants of the lowlands of the Tigris and Euphrates.

It is patent from the quoted sections that the wife's dowry was carefully protected for her benefit during her life and for her sons thereafter and was readily available to her in most cases of divorce or separation. Certainly it was more diligently guarded against a designing husband than is a married woman's property today.

THE FAMILY AND THE WIFE

The primary purpose of marriage was to perpetuate the family. No civilization in history, not even the Romans before Christ, considered the family unit and its continuance of such importance as did the Babylonians. A wife was expected to bear children including sons; if she did not, there was a good chance she would be divorced. She could reduce this chance by furnishing her husband a fertile concubine, and in such case the law protected the wife against the concubine's replacing her as mistress of the household — regardless of the husband's inclinations. If the wife was a priestess and the concubine "goes about making herself equal to her mistress, because she has borne sons, her mistress . . . may put the mark (of a slave) on her and may count her with the slave-girls." (Section 146) The wife, however, could not sell the concubine if the latter had borne sons by the husband.

The husband also had children by his slave girls if he wished. A girl born or taken in slavery contributed her body as well as her services to the master; no legal or moral contraventions existed against this practice. Actually a slave girl overlooked by the master would have been chagrined, especially among her friends. If the master formally recognized the sons of the slave girl in the manner prescribed by the Code, they inherited from him along with the sons of his wife. Even when not formally recognized, the children of the slave girl became free on the master's death and "the sons of the first wife shall make no claim to the sons of the slave girl for slavery." (Section 171) The slave girl was also freed by the death of the master where she had borne him children.

Childless couples not divorcing nor having a concubine or slave girls virtually always adopted children, so strong was the desire to continue the family. The Code contained provisions for the protection of adopted children and, in turn, required them to respect and obey their foster parents. Penalties were imposed on an adopted son who went back to his natural parents without cause; yet, if a child were adopted in infancy, and "it persists in searching for its father and mother, that adopted child shall return to its father's house." (Section 186) Where a child was taken by a craftsman for bringing up in a craft and was not taught the craft, "that adopted child may return to its father's house." (Section 189) Adoption was made beneficial for the child in many ways so that parents with numerous children would be encouraged to release one or more to barren couples.

Throughout marriage absolute chastity was demanded of the wife although prior to marriage or between marriages she enjoyed more sexual freedom than would today be considered proper. A girl not a virgin at the time of her first marriage was not "disgraced." Regardless of the premarital morals in a society, as men or families acquire property in their individual capacities — as distinguished from tribal or community property — there arises an additional reason for denying extramarital relations to the wife, which is to insure the husband that the family estate will not pass to spurious issue.

The Babylonian husband was free to do as he pleased in matters of sex so long as the woman consented and was not married. If a man was caught with a married woman he was subject to the penalties of being her paramour, but he was not guilty of adultery. That offense applied only to women. (The same distinction was also made in the later Hebrew and many other laws, including the early Common Law of England. It was the Ecclesiastical Law which enlarged our own concept of adultery to include men.) Adultery by a wife was a legal offense against the husband; but a husband's relations with another woman, married or single, was not a legal offense against the wife. She could not prosecute him nor obtain a divorce or other relief on that ground.

In spite of the chastity expected of a wife, the Code placed her maintenance ahead of her faithfulness in certain circumstances, a concept which reflected the economic rights of the wife in marriage and the duty of the husband to maintain her. For example, if the husband took a journey to a foreign land and his return was prevented or delayed by illness or capture and he had not left "the means of eating in his house, his wife may enter another man's house; that woman shall not have a punishment." (Section 134) Should the first husband later return he could reclaim the wife, though any sons by the second husband remained with the latter.

It was expected that the adequately maintained wife of a husband absent without fault from the city was to remain chaste. "If that woman has not guarded her body but enters another man's house, they shall convict that woman and cast her into the water." (Section 133b) She was an adulteress.

A Babylonian wife was not permitted to persist in foolish

conduct and neglect her family and home; the penalty was divorce or reduction to a slave girl at the election of the husband. However, he could not on his own determine if his wife was guilty; she had to be convicted in court before his election arose. Upon conviction, if the husband chose to reduce her status, she remained in his house; he could not sell her.

> If a married lady who is dwelling in a man's house sets her face to go out and persists in behaving herself foolishly wasting her house (and) belittling her husband, they shall convict her and, if her husband then states that he will divorce her, he may divorce her; nothing shall be given to her (as) her divorce-money (on) her journey. If her husband states that he will not divorce her, her husband may marry another woman; that woman shall dwell as a slave girl in the house of her husband. (Section 141)

"To go out" is used in the sense of leaving home for improper conduct. The Babylonian woman definitely was not restricted to home life and domestic duties as has been the case with wives in many societies. The above quoted section of the Code applied to a wife "dwelling" in her husband's house; she was permitted more freedom if living elsewhere.

It can be concluded from this and other sections that the husband had no right of corporal punishment or chastisement over the wife, a right characteristic of most ancient societies. If the husband could have physically punished the wife for misconduct or have restrained her person by compelling her to stay at home, there would have been little point in the legal remedies of this section. Hammurabi apparently removed all despotism of the husband over the wife.

SLANDER AND ADULTERY

Slander of a married woman often pertains to her relations with a man other than her husband. Idle gossip in this respect was discouraged by the Code in a rather practical way:

> If a man has caused a finger to be pointed at a highpriestess or a married lady and has then not proved (what he has said), they shall flog that man before the judges and shave half his head. (Section 127)

The woman was also given the benefit of the doubt where accused of adultery unless actually caught in the act, as appears from the following two sections.

> If the husband of a married lady has accused her but she is not caught lying with another man, she shall take an oath by the life of a god and return to her house. (Section 131)

> If a finger has been pointed at a married lady with regard to another male and she is not caught lying with the other male, she shall leap into the river-god for her husband. (Section 132)

Thus if accused only by the husband, all the wife had to do was to swear she was not guilty and thereupon return to her home, her innocence being formally established. If others than her husband (who might be unduly suspicious) accused her, more than an oath was required to clear her; she must invoke the River God's judgment by leaping into the river. If the wife was innocent, the River God would permit her to return to the bank, and no doubt she used her best discretion as to how far she should "leap."

Circumstantial evidence was never sufficient among the early Semitic societies of the Near East (Babylonian, Assyrian and Hebrew) to convict a woman of adultery. There had to be a witness to the act. The Bible student will recall that this rule prevailed among the Hebrews as late as Jesus' time; when the adulteress was brought to him by the scribes and Pharisees, the first thing they explained was that she "was taken in adultery, in the very act." Had she not been caught in the act itself her guilt would not have been established.

If the Babylonian adulteress was caught, it was the river again for her, but this time she was not permitted to leap; she and her paramour were bound, cast into the water, and drowned. However, a loving or forgiving or indifferent husband could spare the wife, and if so, the king spared the paramour. This is one instance of mercy in the Code:

> If a married lady is caught lying with another man, they shall bind them and cast them into the water; if the husband wishes to let the wife live, then the king shall let his subject live. (Section 129)

This is the only Code section, among several providing for a woman to be cast into the water, which required that she be bound. No chance was taken on an adulteress escaping if the husband wished her death. Actually, escape was most unlikely even for an unbound woman thrown into water over her head. Virtually none could swim; the skill is of modern origin for women as well as for most men.

DIVORCE

A Babylonian wife could refuse conjugal relations to a husband whose philanderings were such that they "belittled" her, could even leave him for this reason. Hence the husband's extramarital activities, if scandalous, did not have to be endured by the wife even though under the law they were not adulterous. This was a dignity allowed the women of few early civilizations.

> If a woman has hated her husband and states 'Thou shalt not have me,' the facts of her case shall be determined in her district and, if she has kept herself chaste and has no fault, while her husband is given to going about out and so has greatly belittled her, that woman shall suffer no punishment; she may take her dowry and (go) to her father's house. (Section 142)

Under this section the wife had to establish before the court two things: first, that she was a chaste and good wife, and second, that her husband was guilty of serious misconduct; then she could leave him. However, it was unfortunate for her if, after having denied her husband his ancient privilege of enjoying her at will, it turned out she was also "given to going about out." Code section 143 specifies: "If she has not kept herself chaste but is given to going about out, will waste her house (and) so belittle her husband, they shall cast that woman into the water."

The legal privilege of a wife to leave her husband because of his misconduct, or for any reason, is a right — and at one stage in a society an innovation — the fundament of which is hard to realize today. In most older societies the woman was tied for life to the husband even though he beat and abused her, failed to maintain her, and indulged in the grossest misconduct. He could be a scalawag and a drunkard, still his wife was his chattel and her body his for the taking. In a society where a wife is chained to such a husband she is usually denied other basic civil rights, and that was the fate of most Asiatic women. In actual practice few wives in Babylonia found it necessary to pursue their right under the Code to end the marriage; the average Babylonian husband was a stable family man sincerely interested in the welfare, advancement and happiness of his wife and children. Divorce was no evil.

CHARACTERISTICS OF THE SOCIETY

In order properly to comprehend woman's position in Babylonia one must know (in addition to the foregoing familial data) that the society was permeated with three characteristics: it was highly capitalistic, was thoroughly business-like, and had a scientific legal system administered by professional secular judges.

Prior to Hammurabi the capitalistic system was already the way of life in Mesopotamia, and under him it further developed. A definite factor of the economy was that money was entitled to make money, and it was the money lenders of this general era who inaugurated in everyday business practices the payment of interest on capital. Also in extensive use was the limited partnership between the man with money and the man with need therefor whereby both shared in the profit or loss of a particular undertaking. In case of loss, however, the investor's share was limited to his original contribution. Venture capital and equity capital were important factors in the Babylonian economy.

Perhaps the most striking example of the capitalistic attitude was that freedom itself was an asset with which the owner could bargain. A man owing a debt could discharge it by giving himself or a member of his family into slavery to the creditor for a stipulated period, or to a lender in return for needed capital. The practice affected women as they could in this manner become slaves, or, to borrow a term of our own colonial days, bond-servants. It must be remembered that slavery was not necessarily abject. Actually the slave of a well-to-do master or alert businessman was often better off than a poor freeman or freewoman. As a matter of public policy there was a limitation of four years during which slavery of the bond-servant type could last. The purpose of the maximum period was to protect the freeman against himself and to retain this valuable class in the society without permanent impairment. Thus, any person who was not a slave always had, as a capital asset, four years of liberty of himself and family which he could sell.

Numerous other instances could be given of the capitalistic attributes of the economy; suffice it to say that what a man acquired was his and was not easily lost except by his own mismanagement. There were no exorbitant taxes; and capitalism, work, fertile lands, systematic business practices, and good laws made Babylonia for many centuries one of the most prosperous lands which the world has ever known.

Business, commerce and trade under Hammurabi reached high levels. Precious metals took on the attributes of a medium of exchange which materially reduced barter. Silver was used extensively and, in less degree, gold, copper and lead. These metals retained the basic quality of a commodity (rather than a medium) in that their weight and purity had to be determined between the parties at the time of exchange. Silver, for instance, was not in bars made standard by either law or custom. Nevertheless, from a practical standpoint, metals served as does money today. The lack of standardization in the metals used, and the absence of coins, created a situation encouraging the best of the bargain for the merchants, traders and money lenders, who were familiar with precious metals and had their own scales. No doubt they were satisfied with the system as it was. Because the door was open for cheating, the Code carried strict penalties therefor.

Tavern keepers, who in most cases were women, seem to have given particular trouble along this line. These taverns, where beer was sold and girls usually available, were considered unsavory by the law. They enjoyed a thriving business. The farmers when they came to town did substantial trading at the taverns, often on credit until their crops were gathered. The Code had a specific provision against an "ale-wife" shorting a customer in the exchange of beer for grain. Since beer and brunettes increased the opportunity to cheat the innocent male under their influences, the Code went far to protect him; it provided drowning for the guilty "ale-wife." She was also subject to this same fate if she failed to report to the police any ruffians or suspicious characters at her inn. They could be spies, especially in the border areas, gathering information for raids, even for major conquests, against which the state was on constant guard. Madam could operate within the law, but she must not cheat or permit subversive activities on the premises, else she was out of business — permanently.

Business methods of modern structure and efficiency developed under Hammurabi. The civilization of the Sumerians when fused with the mercantile tendencies of the conquering Semites produced capable and methodical entrepreneurs, merchants and traders. Their activities gave rapid rise to commercial laws suitable to the expanding economy. For the first time the negotiable promissory note evolved. The document possessed all the modern requirements of transferability, as exemplified by the following written promise to pay:

> 5 shekels of silver, at the usual rate of interest, loaned by the Temple of Shamash and by I. Company, to Idin and his wife, are payable with interest on sight of the payors at the marketplace to the bearer of this instrument.[2]

This note states the exact amount due (a shekel being a known measure of weight), a definite interest rate (the usual rate also being known), the payees, the payors, the time of payment, the place of payment, and that the note is payable to the bearer. Payment to bearer, or transferability, was not to be found in European business instruments until the end of the Middle Ages, three millennia after Hammurabi. It should also be noted that Idin's wife was included in the note, which again reflects the economic partnership of marriage.

The groundwork laid during this era produced the greatest banking and business house of all time, the House of Yegibi. This Babylonian concern for four centuries, from about 700 to 300 B. C., shared in, and assisted in the financing of, the far flung enterprises of the Babylonian merchants.

One practice which evidences the high level of business development was that most transactions were in writing; written instruments were required by law to a much greater extent than anywhere in the world today. Contracts, partnership agreements, brokerage agreements, sales, receipts, and the like were all put on clay. The requirement for written instruments extended beyond the commercial practices and permeated the entire social structure. Marriage of the high, formal type had to be pursuant to a written contract. Because of the requirement that records be in writing, there developed a profession of qualified scribes who understood bookkeeping, business, commerce and law. Among them were many women; the professional and secretarial woman did not originate in the modern age. Literally thousands of clay tablets or biscuits reflecting all types of transactions have been unearthed from Hammurabi's and later eras; the volume and variety has earned the facetious remark that "if there was anything Mesopotamia had plenty of it was mud."

The keeping of good records and proper legal documents was lacking in the rest of the civilized world, but as the Babylonian merchant traded in foreign lands, these practices followed him, and businessmen everywhere were quick to recognize their value and to adopt them. Babylon's paramount contribution to the then civilized world was sound business procedure.

The Babylonians were also the great mathematicians and astronomers of the ancient world, and they made prime contributions in those fields. They distinguished the "roving stars" (the sun's planets) from the "fixed" stars, and knew much of the heavens, though mystic speculation rather than telescope was the lantern with which they scanned the night. It is from the Sumerians and Babylonians that we get the twelve signs of the Zodiac which confound the superstitious woman of our own day. We divide our circle into degrees and our hour into minutes in accordance with the sexagesimal system of the Babylonians, and our day into two awkward parts of twelve hours each because their day consisted of twelve hours. Much of the religious lore of Babylonia found its way into the Old Testament and was thus passed to us. Such is the tenacity of ancient beliefs, practices and superstitions.

CONCLUSION

The Mesopotamian civilization, one of the greatest in all history, lasted over 1100 years after Hammurabi, with its laws based on his Code. This work was not even approached in excellence and quality until the Roman law of almost two millennia later. Still Hammurabic law was to disappear when in 538 B. C. Babylon fell to Cyrus, an Arian. For two centuries thereafter the land of the Semites remained a part of the vast empire of Persia.

Then to the Near East came a boy, Alexander The Great, inculcated from childhood by his mother, Olympias, the mythologizing princess of Epirus, that he was destined to greatness; schooled in the art of war by the old master, his father, Philip II of Macedonia; and taught to love culture and science by the philosopher Aristotle of Athens. Alexander conquered all before him as he invaded the mainland of Asia Minor. When he stood before the gates of Babylon they were opened to him as a deliverer from the yoke of Persia. In the spring of 323 B. C. he went into the delta of the Euphrates to plan the location of harbors and canals, and there contracted a fever, the "ague" of Hammurabi's Code, from which, along with fatigue, he died at the age of thirty-two in the renowned palace of Nebuchadrezzar at Babylon. Alexander The Great did not live to fulfill his vision of taking Greek culture to the East, but his soldiers helped to bring the culture of Babylonia to Greece, and from Greece it spread to Rome, and from Rome to all Europe, and from Europe to the Americas.

---

[1] Hammurabi, the more popular spelling, is used rather than "Hammurapi" or other spellings.

[2] Wigmore, John H., *Panorama of the World's Legal Systems,* p. 69, one-volume Library edition. Washington Law Book Company, Washington, D. C. (1936).

EGYPT

The Civilization — Monotheism — The Egyptian Woman — Social Equality Between the Sexes — The Period of Decadence

EGYPT AND HER WOMEN WILL BE CONSIDERED ONLY briefly. The civilization of the Nile was parallel in time with that of the Tigris and Euphrates, and woman's rights and social position in each land was more comparable than contrasting. To detail her progress in both would be a duplication in a book of this nature. Mesopotamia was chosen for the principal discussion for two reasons. First, her laws were better developed — Egypt did not have a Hammurabi — and better records were kept of legal documents from which to obtain reliable information. Second, Mesopotamian heritage, through the Hebrews and Greeks to Rome, is more in the direct line of succession into modern Western civilization than is the somewhat collateral culture of Egypt. However, the Hebrews, Greeks and Romans learned much from Egypt, and there were differences in the legal rights of her women and those of Mesopotamia, so a few words must be said of the Egyptian woman and her society. Besides, she was much more interesting than the wives of the humorless Babylonians; and all are fascinated with the great Queen Hatshepsut,[1] Nefertiti, Tiy and Egypt's other famous women.

As early as 4000 B. C. the settlements along the northern 700 miles of the Nile River had a definite form of local self-government and were initiating a social structure which over the millennia developed into one of the most remarkable civilizations of history. By the middle of the third millennium B. C., Egypt had attained a great culture. Architecture and sculpture were highly developed. In practical engineering the Egyptians have been excelled only in modern times and were never rivalled by the Greeks or Romans. In the allied science of mathematics they were far advanced, and in some respects ahead of the Babylonians. Plane geometry was an original contribution of the Egyptians, made necessary in order to relocate their tracts of land after the periodic overflowings of the Nile which destroyed the landmarks and changed the appearance of the valley. Noticeable is that the Egyptians had a much better calendar than did the renowned astronomers of Babylonia and Chaldea. Actually the only fields in which Egypt to a considerable extent trailed Mesopotamia were in law and business practices; in most other aspects the Egyptian civilization was more advanced.

Medicine early took a scientific turn in Egypt. During the first half of the second millennium B. C. their physicians recognized that the brain controlled at least some of the limbs — a new concept in physiology. The medical specialists in many fields knew much about their respective subjects. Gynecologists did a thriving business, and early in the second millennium suppositories were in use as contraceptives. General practitioners, treating the common cold with magic incantation and baldness with animal grease, obtained the same result for each as does modern science. (Magic and concoctions were always rivals of science with the peoples of the ancient world, being more popular with them than with us.)

MONOTHEISM

Moral literature and philosophy had its inception in

Egypt as long before the Golden Age of Greece as it has been since that Age. In the fourteenth century B. C. in this land which always had its many gods, we find the monotheism of the heretic Pharoah Akhenaten (Amenhotep IV): one god not only for Egypt but for all races — an amazing innovation in religion.

Monotheism may at first appear unrelated to woman, but later we shall see its effect, through the Hebrew religion, on Western woman's life. The Hebrew one God was not accredited with the attributes of fertility and love as those qualities are associated with woman; and the concept of masculinity was to dominate Judaism and Christianity to the present day, not the concepts of both masculinity and femininity as in other religions. The early Hebrew language did not even contain a word for "goddess." The Hebrews' low regard for the feminine essence in nature was the exception in the Near East, an exception not altered by contact with other cultures which deified this essence, and not modified by the morals and religion of Egypt where the Hebrews prospered for generations. But Moses was to learn from the ill-fated attempt to impose monotheism on the Egyptian people, the better to establish it among his own.

Akhenaten's "sole god" was Aten whose visual emblem was the sun which gave life, light, heat and growth to all living things. However, the sun was merely Aten's reflection, not the god himself, which was unseen and could not be portrayed in human form. Aten was an all-powerful, beneficent force, eternal and universal; a god of love, not a fearful deity demanding sacrifices to appease him or to gain his favor; a god of peace, not of war. His works were manifold and his designs excellent; he was a distributor of good to all mankind; and "there is a Nile in the sky for the strangers," not alone for the Egyptians. He was the "Creator of the germ in woman, Maker of seed in man, . . . Nurse even in the womb, Giver of breath to animate everyone that he maketh!" So wrote Akhenaten, the youthful poet-philosopher-pharaoh, two thousand years before the West was converted to monotheism.

Worship of this beautiful god Akhenaten ordered throughout the land by his authority as pharaoh, but the people could not fathom the concept of one universal god and the priests of the many gods opposed it with all the power of their class. Akhenaten not only disapproved of the multitude of gods but of the magic and animal sacrifices deeply rooted in religion. He went so far as to deprive the priests of the many gods of much of their wealth and many of their privileges. He emptied their temples of the concubines of the gods (actually of the priests) and was so opposed to concubinage that he refused to have children by a secondary wife, though the Queen bore him no son. He was happy with the lovely Nefertiti (Beauty Forever and Ever) and the seven daughters she gave him. He believed the priests too should be satisfied with their wives; and to this they might have submitted, but not to the loss of power and worldly possessions. History teaches one thing about the ancient priest class: it was always willing to share the hereafter with the people but it definitely preferred to possess the best of this earth for itself. (No such class exists in Western civilization today; present-day clergymen, sincerely devoted to spirit, morals and good, are not comparable to their prototype.)

The failure of the Egyptians, a highly intelligent people, to adopt the sublime monotheism of Akhenaten may to us appear irremissible, but throughout history the people and the powerful classes (priests, warriors, landowners, or whoever they may be) have leagued against reform in order to maintain the status quo in ideas and beliefs. This is especially true where the society is prosperous and stable and the people are secure. The powerful see no point in risking the loss of their advantage which change could eventuate, and the people hesitate to risk the security of tried, and to them, proven beliefs and habits. Changes therein often make vices of former virtues and virtues of former vices, thus completely undermining established thinking. Also, experience has made the people suspicious, has taught them that "reforms" proposed in their name are not always for their benefit.

The Egyptians were a people with a multitude of gods, and religion entered seriously into everything they did, even into that which they said. Each constantly planned for his soul's survival (which did not necessarily live forever) and for its happiness in the after-life. Akhenaten's sudden and drastic proposal of one god, and at that a god for all mankind, brought concern to the people, fear for their future in this life and beyond. Their ancient superstition of being protected by their own many powerful gods was constantly fanned by the priests behind the back of the pharaoh.

During most of his reign of seventeen years, Akhenaten idealistically thought he could force the establishment of the new religion. In theory the power of the pharaoh was unlimited, and in practice it virtually was. Yet before Akhenaten's death or exile at the age of about thirty he realized his universal sole god was not for his people, lovers of power and wealth. All factions were relieved with the ending of the reign of history's most enlightened heretic. No longer was Egypt ruled by a pharaoh who refused to send his troops to control foreign tribute-paying provinces because of a fantastic religion which questioned the right and morality of one nation to hold another in subjection. No longer sat on the throne a pharaoh who permitted little daughters to play about it and who shared all with his wife.[2] Egypt again became military-controlled and priest-ridden, and a land of many gods.

It would not be long, perhaps less than a century, until Egypt would produce a second monotheist, the Hebrew Moses. Moses would teach his people that the Invisible God of Abraham was the only true God; and this God would prevail over the Golden Calf of the Wilderness, the Astartes of the River Jordan area, the Baals of the Promised Land, and centuries later, even over the gods of Rome. Moses would become the great monotheist of history.

The extent to which he was influenced by Akhenaten's monotheism, especially by a pharaoh's failure to establish it, cannot be known with certainty; but Moses was well informed and well educated, was reared by the Egyptians, probably in the family of the pharaoh, and Akhenaten's rocking of the empire by an idealistic sole god concept unsuited to the people was a lesson not overlooked by one of Moses' learning and insight. He taught the concept of a practical God which the Hebrew people could accept. Unto this God they could sacrifice the firstlings of their flocks whereas Akhenaten had proscribed these time-revered practices. To him the blood of animals on the altars of Aten was heathenish. Also, unlike Aten, Moses' God was a God of war as well as of peace, of vengeance as well as of love, a Lord of Hosts, and a God who damned as well as saved. The day was distant when this God would be obeyed more out of love than fear, when worshippers would ascribe to him only the attributes of love and goodness, as Akhenaten had ascribed to Aten.

Monotheism was not to be given to the world by a philosopher, even one with a pharaoh's power, but by a practical statesman close to his people. It was not to come to us through a society of culture but through a society escaped from bondage. Not even Greece during its Golden Age would forsake its many gods. Her great thinkers were to wonder if there were not one universal and everlasting God, and at Athens there would be serious speculations on this probability, but such impious discussions would be merely philosophical, and held in private only, as when the intelligentsia gathered at the home of Pericles presided over by the intellectual courtesan, Aspasia.

THE EGYPTIAN WOMAN

How did Egyptian woman fare in her advanced society of culture, science and ideas? She fared exceedingly well, from childhood when her white skin turned dark as she played without clothes under the African sun, until death when she passed on to her daughters all property of the family estate. As an adult she was healthy, slim, clean and groomed. She was happier and gayer than any woman of her time. Her dress was as attractive, her ornaments as decorative, and her cosmetics as beautifying as those of modern woman. When she appeared in mixed company her face was artfully enhanced with cosmetics, her eyelids shaded, and her fingernails and toenails painted.

In polite society the Egyptian lady, refined and discriminating, looked down her nose at her Babylonian sister, but basically this sister was a rival, not an inferior except in surface polish and elegance. Yet no Egyptian princess or concubine of the pharaoh ever whiled away the sultry hours in coolness and exotic luxury comparable to that of the Hanging Gardens in the palace at Babylon. Regardless of any differences in the fortunate and wealthy women of the two lands, the poorer wives in both were on a substantially equal level. They spent all their time looking after a houseful of children, spinning and weaving to clothe them, carrying water and grinding grain to feed them; and pregnant all the while.

As in Babylonia, monogamy was the rule, divorces were few, women enjoyed full freedom in public, sexual relations were likely prior to marriage but fidelity was expected afterward, and generally morals were good. (I am not speaking of the later first millennium B. C. period of decadence in Egypt, which was also one of decadence in Babylonia.) There was one outstanding difference in woman's legal rights in Egypt and in other civilizations. In Egypt, inheritance passed through the female line, from mother to daughter, not from father to son. This gave woman an unusual advantage in the society. Also, it caused many families, especially those of wealth, to follow the pharaohs' custom of marrying their sisters, which enabled the men to protect for themselves the family properties. This practice continued in some parts of Egypt even after Christ. In any other land, marriage within the immediate family would have been unlawful incest punishable by severe penalties, as it is with us today.

SOCIAL EQUALITY BETWEEN THE SEXES

Another outstanding feature of the Egyptian society, unique in advanced civilizations, was woman's social sex equality. I do not mean the Tolstoyan concept of sex equality nor the loose conduct of decaying societies in which women obtain equal moral freedom with men, but refer to equality in the stable social relations between the sexes, such as in the many aspects of marriage and in the seeking and selecting of a spouse. No woman of a major civilization other than the Egyptian woman has possessed this personal equality with man.

The Egyptian girl was prepared for it by her rearing and training. The subject of sex was not taboo in the society nor in her presence; there was nothing secretive about it, nothing to warp her outlook. At an early age she understood the natural and practical purposes of sex relations, and thought of them as good. When she reached marriageable age she was not encumbered with a multitude of inhibitions based on the impropriety of the act. Neither had she been taught to suppress her bodily charms. As girls of all ages she relied heavily upon them, but she did so openly and without social disapproval. She encountered no censure if she boldly pursued the male of her choice. Love letters written by Egyptian young ladies reflect an attitude which would today be considered forward and calculating. A girl desiring marriage was at liberty openly to work at obtaining a proposal or herself to propose. Furthermore, while acquiring a husband she was permitted such sexual relations as she considered discreet and advantageous for her purpose. She distinguished virtue and vice "by instinct," a gift from Isis, the goddess of love and fertility, the Earth Mother.

This girl was by no means without morals or religion; actually both were strong influences with her. Neither was she lacking in modesty and restraint, and at all times she was responsive to the advice and influence of her parents. Society simply granted her equality with man in courtship and marriage. She was free, within her training and discretion, in all relations with her lover. She did not have to marry against her will. At the altar she did not meet a stranger as literally thousands of girls have done, often in abject spirit and bitter disappointment. She had associated with her husband prior to marriage as well as with other available men, and in order to do so she had not been forced to the modern method of invitations, functions, and arrangements by others. If the marriage did not last, even though the couple had entered into it voluntarily and had known one another beforehand, the wife could get a divorce. While legally the grounds were not as broad for her as for the husband, as a practical matter, freedom, if deserved, was available to her.

It is certainly plausible to consider that equality for woman in the various relations between the sexes, including the privilege openly to encourage and mutually to further those relations, is an element necessary for her full emancipation. To some, this equality may be thought of as more important than the political rights of voting and holding office, as more beneficial than the legal rights of control of property. Again, others may regard this freedom and openness by the female as unnecessary to equality in results upon the theory that equality may be better obtained by love and subtlety.

At any rate, the freedom permitted Egyptian women in their social relations with men has not been enjoyed, for better or worse, by women of any other age. Today there exists universal social animadversion to such freedom.

THE PERIOD OF DECADENCE

With the decadence of the Egyptian society, generally the first millennium B. C., women began to lose their elevated status. Inheritance through the female line and other tendencies favorable to them rapidly lessened. As so often happens when retrogression sets in, women obtained and cheerfully exercised an increased freedom in divorce. The ease of the marriage dissolution by the fourth century B. C. strikingly appears from the following stipulation made by the Lady Settyr-benne with Teos in their marriage contract:

> Thou makest me thy wife, thou givest me two and a half silver staters as wedding-gift. If I divorce thee as husband, hating thee and loving another more than thee, I shall restore to thee one-half of this wedding gift. I grant unto thee one-third of all my property acquired during our marriage.[3]

The mere fact that this stipulation reflects the contingency of the Lady's wanting and getting a divorce indicates a good chance thereof. The draftsman of a legal agreement does not set forth remote contingencies but only those which can reasonably be anticipated. Also of significance is that the contract spells out that if there should be a divorce, it could be because the wife had found another man whom she loved more than her husband. This reflects a broad liberty for women, actually a disintegration, in the marriage relationship. By comparison with our own society, certainly liberal in divorce, few wives leave their husbands because they are in love with another man, and none flagrantly would violate the presumption that she and her groom will live happily ever after by contracting prior to marriage as to a subsequent change in heart.

It should be said for our Lady that if she did divorce Teos, she would return to him half his wedding gift – a consideration which a modern divorced husband can expect neither from his wife's generosity nor at law.

Not too long after the date of this marriage contract women lost completely their right of divorce, also most other legal rights, as is typical of retrogressing societies. Egypt centuries before had run its course as a great civilization and world power, and was so weak by the time of Cleopatra (69-30 B. C.) that in order for her to maintain the throne of the Ptolemies she was forced to rely alone on her charms as a woman, to become Caesar's royal mistress, and after his death, to play the same role with Antony. Cleopatra was not beautiful in face or body, but her native intelligence, timing, and understanding of men's moods and ambitions were her powerful controls. She is history's outstanding example of the artful use of love and lure for political gain.

Perhaps her meeting with Antony at Tarsus best shows her skill. Certainly her arrival in its harbor was the most dramatic "entrance" ever made by a woman. After Antony defeated Cassius near Philippi (42 B. C.), bringing victory to him and Octavius over Brutus and Cassius in the contest for the Roman Empire, Antony moved about the East. Upon arriving in Cilicia he summoned Cleopatra to Tarsus to account to him for having taken the side of his opponents. She saw in the summons an opportunity for a command performance before the victor. On schedule, the purple sails of her gilded barge were seen approaching the harbor which she entered to the music of flutes and with her banners floating on the breeze. Antony was invited on board, came, and beheld not the expected royal deck of a queen of Egypt, but the temple of a goddess of love. Cleopatra was dressed as Venus in flowing flimsy robes, the surroundings were more than suggestive, and Antony assented with spirit to the young queen's request that he play the part of Bacchus during her visit of state. Their revelry befitted the gods whose roles they adopted, and Antony yielded to the "Serpent of the Nile."

History does not record that he ever took her to task; instead, he followed her to the Land of the Pharaohs. Later she did not hesitate to overture his betrayal to Octavius in the hope of saving her throne. When her offer was refused, neither did she hesitate to die at her own hands rather than that a Queen of Egypt should be the main attraction, fettered in chains which were to be forged of gold, in Octavius' triumph along the streets of Rome. The new conqueror exhibited her lifeless wax image in his parade for the populace.

Egypt was now a second-rate province of the Roman Empire. Long ago had passed into history her elevated and attractive woman who had approached full equality with man. Egypt of the centuries of decadence is history's assertive lesson that a retrogressing civilization reduces woman's sociolegal status to a low level. As Babylonia retrogressed woman's relative status with man also suffered, but not to the same extent as in Egypt. In Babylonia the great Code of Hammurabi bolstered woman's legal rights to the very end of the civilization, yet it could only lessen, not prevent, the devolution of her position. As in Babylonia, the great gains woman had made in Egypt were not transmitted in specific form to the West, although much of Egyptian culture was. This contributed to Western progress, and progress in turn supported woman's advance towards equality with man.

---

[1] Breasted, the Egyptologist, had designated Queen Hatshepsut as "The first great woman in history." She is often referred to as the Queen Elizabeth of Egypt.

[2] Not all Egyptologists share these views of Akhenaten's sublimity in his religion and devotion to Nefertiti, nor that he had no sons. See Immanuel Velikovsky's *Oedipus and Akhnaton: Myth and History*. Doubleday & Company, Inc., Garden City, New York (1960).

[3] Wigmore, John H., *Panorama of the World's Legal Systems,* p. 26, one-volume Library edition. Washington Law Book Company, Washington, D. C. (1936).

THE HEBREWS

Origin-Egypt-Exodus — Sinai and Monotheism — Within Sight of the Promised Land — Astarte's Snare — Phoenicia-Nature Worship — Conquest of Canaan — Settlement in Canaan-Agricultural Baalism — Jehu and Jezebel-The Extinction of Baalism — Woman's Secondary Status — Laws Affecting Women

WE TURN FROM THE LOCATED CIVILIZATION OF MESOpotamia and Egypt to the nomadic Hebrews, poor relatives of the Amorites of Hammurabi and disparagingly called "sand-ramblers" by the Egyptians. The Hebrews came from the Arabian peninsula, the mother of all Semites. Their invisible God — at first nameless, then called Yahweh, later Jehovah — was wholly masculine, and woman was marked for inferiority in their society.

Her status among the early Hebrews is of prime importance because their social views, as well as their religion, were to accompany the spread of Christianity throughout the Roman Empire including Mediterranean Asia and Africa, then throughout all Europe, and later throughout the Western Hemisphere. That the mores of these early nomads — at first a small group of nineteenth century B. C. Asiatic shepherds under Abraham—would become so widespread was impossible to contemplate; but Christ was to be born to their religion, their recorded Old Testament was to become an integrant of Christianity, and as Christianity imbued the West so would the early Hebrew beliefs as to woman's proper place in life.

These beliefs are a preponderant part of the background of woman's rights in present day Christian countries. A knowledge of this background is necessary for an understanding of her sociolegal status in these countries, and to know this background we must follow the wanderings, settlement, statehood and religion of the Hebrews.

Originally they were typical nomads of the arid peninsula of Arabia, constantly on the move for more water and pasture for their flocks of sheep and goats, their principal means of subsistence. About the seventeenth century B. C. they settled with the permission of Egypt in the Nile Delta, probably compelled to do so by prolonged drouth and reduction in the flocks. In this abundant land they lived approximately four centuries and prospered and increased, eating well of meat, fish, fowl, melons, vegetables, and "bread to the full." The "fleshpots" were never empty.

The Egyptians became concerned with the Hebrews' constantly increasing strength, put their several tribes under close watch, and assigned them burdensome tasks and production quotas, particularly during the reign of Rameses II (1301-1234 B. C.). This pharaoh was determined to leave his mark on the ages by the erection of imposing buildings and cities, and the Hebrews were forced to perform most of the menial labor. "And the Egyptians made the children of Israel to serve with rigor: and they made their lives bitter with hard bondage, in mortar, and in brick, and in all manner of service in the field: all their service, wherein they made them serve, was with rigor." (Exodus 1: 13, 14) Construction work was not like watching the herds. It was considered oppressive by the Israelites, and resulted in such general dissatisfaction that they quit Egypt in one mass exodus, *c.* 1290 B. C.[1] under the leadership of their great religious statesman, Moses.

SINAI AND MONOTHEISM

On departing Egypt, the Hebrews wandered within the desert "wilderness" lying to the west of the Red Sea. They were headed north to a land their God had promised to the seed of Abraham, but first they turned south, no doubt to avoid Egyptian forces or allies which they considered advisable to by-pass. The going was rough and slow, the water sources far between, and many longed for the Delta and the full fleshpots; yet Moses was equal to the task he had undertaken of leading the tribes towards a better land to the north.

It was on this circuitous southern route that Moses at Mount Sinai (named after the Babylonian moon god, Sin) received from God the Ten Commandments, one of the great sets of principles for the regulation of man's life. The Commandments were not laws in the same sense as are modern-day statutes or as were the sections of Hammurabi's Code; they were rules of conduct and living. They contained no penalties for their breach (although Hebrew custom did), and were general enough not to become outmoded by changing conditions — the fate of laws. Written for early times, their broad precepts are applicable to modern complicated society and will enhance the lives and advance the morals of all who abide by them. It is because of the Ten Commandments more than anything else that Moses is still distinguished in Judaism, Christianity, and Islam as one of the great moral lawgivers of all time.

It was also at Sinai that Moses laid down the law of one God only for the Hebrews. We recall the biblical account that he, in fury because the people were worshipping the Golden Calf, broke into pieces the first two tablets of stone on which were carved the Commandments as originally given him by God. What they contained is not known, but on the second set of two tablets the very first command, with its preface of credit for the exodus, was:

> I am the Lord thy God, which have brought thee out of the land of Egypt, out of the house of bondage. Thou shalt have no other gods before me. (Exodus 20: 2-3)

This is monotheism stated simply and firmly. And Moses enforced it; the cult of the Golden Calf was rendered impotent.

Moses was now the recognized leader of the Hebrews in all things: religion, conduct, government and law. Through him Yahweh spoke; he was lawgiver, judge, jury, and commander-in-chief; none saw fit to challenge his resolute rule. He sanctioned and restated as law by divine revelation the customs or common law of the Hebrews including the many taboos degrading to woman. An example of the latter is that childbirth rendered the mother unclean and required her purification. The period of purification was twice as long for the birth of a girl as for a boy.

> And the Lord spake unto Moses, saying, Speak unto the children of Israel, saying, If a woman have conceived seed, and borne a man child: then she shall be unclean seven days; according to the days of the separation for her infirmity shall she be unclean. . . . And she shall then continue in the blood of her purifying three and thirty days; she shall touch no hallowed thing, nor come into the sanctuary, until the days of her purifying be fulfilled. But if she bear a maid child, then she shall be unclean two weeks, as in her separation: and she shall continue in the blood of her purifying threescore and six days. And when the days of her purifying are fulfilled, for a son, or for a daughter, she shall bring a lamb of the first year for a burnt offering, and a young pigeon, or a turtledove, for a sin offering, unto the door of the tabernacle of the congregation, unto the priest: Who shall offer it before the Lord, and make an atonement for her; and she shall be cleansed from the issue of her blood. This is the law for her that hath borne a male or a female. (Leviticus 12: 1-2, 4-7)

This concept of uncleanliness and sin in connection with birth existed among various early races as a religious belief, and is thought to have descended from pre-record man's fears and superstitions as to the spilling or loss of blood.

WITHIN SIGHT OF THE PROMISED LAND

From Sinai Moses led the Hebrews to southern Palestine where they maintained a central headquarters for the tribes at Kadesh Barnea. To the north was Canaan, the Promised Land. It was no longer under the control of Egypt but was an area of independent federated cities. It still had strong ties with Egypt, having been for years a part of her trade route with Asia, but even so, Egypt was now too weak to defend Canaan against the contemplated invasion by the Hebrews. Neither could the Canaanites expect aid from Babylon or any other source. Moses no doubt concluded any war would be solely between the Hebrews and the Canaanites.

His first move was to determine the strength of Canaan through scouts. They reported fortifications against which the arrows and javelins of Moses' soldiers would be futile, walled cities which his captains did not have the military know-how to take. Also, the Hebrews lacked organization in the military sense. The journey from the Delta had done much to unite them; yet their thinking was more as individual tribes than as one people. Just as harmful to total warfare – which would be required for the invasion – was the dissatisfaction and grumbling of many over having left Egypt in the first place. Their nostalgic yearning for the Delta's food and settled life now outweighed their dread of the Egyptian task master. Moses felt compelled to delay the invasion. It was after his death when the next generation under Joshua would enter the Promised Land.

For a time the Israelites grazed their herds in the area of Kadesh and to the south, then moved into Shittim and east of the Jordan where it empties into the Dead Sea (north of Moab and the River Aron). Directly across the Jordan was the Promised Land and the ancient city of Jericho which commanded the western plains of the river. The walls of Jericho presented an awesome obstacle, and the nomads stopped at the Jordan.

ASTARTE'S SNARE

At Shittim the Hebrews ran afoul of the sexual practices which were a part of the religion of that land, also of Canaan, Moab, Midian and other neighboring areas. This religion, which we will observe later, was the worship of the Phoenician Baals (gods) and Astartes (goddesses). When the Moabites and Midianites learned the Hebrews had overrun Shittim, they feared for their own countries, which they realized they could not defend against the hostile nomads. They sent to Babylonia for the great magician, Balaam. For a substantial fee he came and cast his curse over the Hebrews, but these provincial shepherds did not appreciate his international reputation and the tension increased. The Moabites and Midianites then decided on a course which the hardy men of the desert could appreciate: their enticement to Baalism by the sexual rites of that religion. According to Exodus, one of the five Books of Moses, Yahweh had warned Moses at Sinai to watch out for this very "snare":

> Take heed to thyself, lest thou make a covenant with the inhabitants of the land whither thou goest, lest it be for a snare in the midst of thee: . . . and they go a whoring after their gods, and do sacrifice unto their gods, and one call thee, and thou eat of his sacrifice; and thou take of their daughters unto thy sons, and their daughters go a whoring after their gods, and make thy sons go a whoring after their gods. (Exodus 34: 12, 15-16)

In spite of this prophetic warning the "snare" worked.

> And Israel abode in Shittim, and the people began to commit whoredom with the daughters of Moab. And they called the people unto the sacrifices of their gods; and the people did eat, and bowed down to their gods. And Israel joined himself unto Baal-peor: and the anger of the Lord was kindled against Israel. (Numbers 25:1-3)

The "whoredom" was not with professionals as we think of that class today; it was with the devotees of Astarte who were the wives, daughters, and consorts of the Moabite and Midianite men. It was not a casual indulgence but a rite and a well developed art. A ritualist spirit "elevated" the sensual practices above ordinary sex routine; wine, temple and appropriate atmosphere were the aphrodisiacs. Many a healthy Israelite took to this ancient religion of the land which he had so recently entered, and for years to come this and subsequent exposures to Baalism were to have a profound effect on Israel.

To the devout among the Hebrews the sexual practices connected with the worship of Astarte were pure licentiousness and an insult to Yahweh. They did what they could to keep uncontaminated their own camps and to punish offenders. An example of their determination is furnished by the killing of Cozbi, "the daughter of a prince of Midian," and of the Israelite man who brought her to his brethren.

> And, behold, one of the children of Israel came and brought unto his brethren a Midianitish woman in the sight of Moses, and in the sight of all the congregation of the children of Israel . . . And when Phinehas, the son of Eleazar, the son of Aaron the priest, saw it, he rose up from among the congregation, and took a javelin in his hand, and he went after the man of Israel into the tent, and thrust both of them through, the man of Israel, and the woman through her belly . . . And the name of the Midianitish woman that was slain was Cozbi, the daughter of Zur; he was head over a people, and of a chief house in Midian. And the Lord spake unto Moses, saying, Vex the Midianites, and smite them: For they vex you with their wiles. (Numbers 25: 6-8a, 15-18a)

While some did not waver in their faith to Yahweh, large numbers continued to fall under the influence of Astarte. It was a trying period for the Israelite nomad. He had a lifetime of hardship behind him and a major invasion ahead; the well-arranged and readily available temptation was of arousing appeal; and he indulged himself in the embrace of this exotic goddess of love. Finally, Moses had enough, and Astarte, as the Golden Calf, was no match for him. The Moabites he decided to spare as they were cousins of the Hebrews and believed to be descended from Lot, Abraham's nephew; but the punishment he decreed for the Midianites was extermination, except for their virgins; and there was sought out and slain every male and "every woman that hath known man by lying with him." Yet the Hebrew warrior did not forget the votaries of Astarte.

What is the explanation for the plan of the Moabites and the Midianites to have their women consort with the Hebrew men? It is not found alone in a desire to save their own lives or their countries as husbands and fathers will sacrifice both to spare their wives and daughters from dishonor. Furthermore, what is the explanation for the willingness of the women, even a princess, as was Cozbi, to give themselves so readily and so shamelessly to the nomadic strangers? The accounting for the plan and its furtherance is found in the early Phoenician religious concepts of the holiness and goodness of sex in all nature — human, animal, and plant. To understand these concepts we must examine this religion and the land from which it came.

PHOENICIA — NATURE WORSHIP

Phoenicia was the approximately 150-mile long and 15-mile wide coastal strip lying along the middle of the eastern Mediterranean shore. With mountains at her back, her outlet was by the sea and the Phoenicians became the great seafaring people of the ancient world. They were Semites, originating in the mother peninsula, Arabia, and were closely related to the Babylonians and distantly to the Hebrews. The Phoenicians were worshippers of nature: of the rivers, rocks, trees and high places, for in them the gods abode. They also worshipped, as did most Semites, the sun which gave them light and life. Each attribute of the sun — its life-giving quality, its fierce heat — had its own name and was regarded as a separate Baal (lord). Also, each Baal had a female consort or Baalath (lady) with the same attribute as her Baal. This identity between a Baal and a Baalath, this complementary relationship of male and female in nature, was the essence of early Phoenician religion. Although Baal was the popular title given to any male deity, Baalath was seldom used for the goddess; instead, the title Ashtoreth was used.

The Ashtoreth of fertility was fervently worshipped and this goddess became the favorite of the Canaanites to the south and of the Jordan area. (Canaan was the original name of Phoenicia and the entire Mediterranean area to the south and west. Later the 150-mile coastal strip was called Phoenicia.) Ashtoreth was not a moon goddess as is often thought, although she was identified with that enchantress of the Mediterranean night to which the Phoenician maiden made her vows of love and directed her prayers of desire. Ashtoreth was the Greek Astarte, and I will use that more familiar name.

The earliest nature or fertility worship of the Phoenicians sanctioned freedom in sex among humans as found in nature among animals. The giving of herself by a woman to man was nature, and therefore won her favor in the eyes of the gods. Many of the goddesses were thought of as both mother and harlot, and both roles in woman were considered as sanctioned by the gods. The Phoenician girl at a young age went to a temple of Astarte where any man who came to worship could have her. Sexual acts and rites were performed before the images of the gods; to witness them gave the gods pleasure, as it does man. The goddess of fertility was often depicted as a naked goddess and exhibitionist displays by her followers were permitted; the pleasurable element of pain in sex was known; and relations with animals were indulged in. Thus these nature worshippers became subjects of dedicated sexual lust.

Yet all was not sex in early Phoenician religion. Women were not permitted to enter the temples of Baal Melkarth, the patron Baal of Tyre—neither were dogs and swine. In time the Phoenicians abandoned their early sexual religious practices (probably during the second half of the second millennium). Nevertheless, the belief in them remained among the less cultured Canaanites of the area of the Jordan. Thus the women of Moab and Midian could entice the men of Israel without violating their standards of religion, virtue or conventionality; freedom in sex was sanctioned by their ancient gods. Furthermore, the admission of the Israelite men to the sexual rites of Astarte was patriotic under the circumstances; patriotism and religion were related concepts in the minds of the ancients. By enticing and converting the Hebrew to Baalism, the women of Moab and Midian were rendering service both to their country and to their gods.

CONQUEST OF CANAAN

The invasion of Canaan finally began around 1230 B. C., approximately thirty years after the Israelites arrived on the east banks of the Jordan, under the able soldier, Joshua. Its timing was prompted by the report of two spies whom he had sent into Canaan to "view the land even Jericho." On arriving in Jericho the spies had gone to "an harlot's house, named Rahab, and lodged there." No doubt this house was similar to the Babylonian taverns of the "ale-wife" who, under the Code, was required to report any suspicious characters upon penalty of death since at these houses spies could pick up information with the least risk of discovery and, even if discovered, with a chance of not being reported. Rahab's house or inn turned out to be such a place for the two Israelites. She knew the obvious purpose of their visit, yet she gave them information and did not report them.

Nevertheless, the king of Jericho learned they were at Rahab's, but assumed she did not know they were spies. He sent his representatives to her to say, "Bring forth the men . . . which are entered into thine house: for they be come to search out the country." Rahab had made up her mind to betray king and city; she, as everyone else, had known for some time that the Israelites would one day invade Canaan, and the Canaanites realized the weakness of their country. The Israelites had overestimated all along the strength of Canaan's walled cities, fearful in appearance to the dwellers in tents of skin. Rahab, knowing the fatal day was near, took advantage of her opportunity to side with the victors. She hid the spies on her roof among some stalks of flax and told the king's men that two strangers had come to her house but had just left, and to "pursue after them quickly; for ye shall overtake them." The king's men left in haste to track down the spies.

Rahab's price for her lack of patriotism was the protection of herself and family, to which the two Israelites committed. It was understood that she, before the city was taken, would bring all her family to her house and display a red sign in the window, and that none of them would be molested so long as they remained inside. Rahab revealed to Joshua's spies that the Canaanites were well aware that the Israelites had conquered the land east of the Jordan and of their numerous victories "and as soon as we had heard these things, our hearts did melt, neither did there remain any more courage in any man, because of you."

The spies reported to Joshua that he could take Canaan, that "all the inhabitants of the country do faint because of us." Joshua ordered an immediate mobilization on the bank of the Jordan and in a few days the long-awaited invasion began. Jericho fell, then one city after another. Canaan had become weak under earlier years of control by Egypt; the walls of some of the cities were not even in good repair. All Canaan was overrun by the herdsmen, and the tillers of the soil were slain by the thousands in the name of the God of war and of the flocks. Joshua was a warrior; kill or be killed he understood, but not mercy or statesmanship.

What of Rahab? She was not only spared but lived and was welcomed among the conquerors. Evidently she was young as she was not married; and obviously she was clever as she misled the king's police in a matter of vital security. There are two traditions as to her later life. One, that she became Joshua's wife; and if so, she was an ancestor of eight of the Prophets. The other, that she married one of the spies, Salmon, and that Boaz was born to them; if this be the case, she was an ancestor of David and Jesus. She was made a saint by the Roman Catholic church and her day is September 1. A few translators of the Bible say the old Hebrew word used to denote her occupation meant "innkeeper" rather than "harlot," but the point is probably academic since the two occupations were as a rule combined in the Near East of this era. We must remember however that prostitution, even without benefit of the rites of Astarte, was not then considered as too immoral;

and Rahab, as all of us, must be judged only by her time and place.

SETTLEMENT IN CANAAN – AGRICULTURAL BAALISM

In Canaan the Israelites stopped their migrating. To these desert wanderers the country they had conquered, although large parts of it were rocky and hard to cultivate, satisfied the prophecy of a land of milk and honey. A settled agricultural life was a drastic change for the Hebrew, and he had to learn from the Canaanite. The routine, as in all early agricultural societies, was to sow, till, reap, and sacrifice to particular gods of agricultural fertility, not indiscriminately to any god. The novice Israelite would not have hazarded any deviation in this cycle, least of all the omission of offerings to the gods whose favor was vital to the success of the crops. He was as superstitious as his era, and besides, sacrifice to an agricultural Baal was not in competition to the God of the flocks, not a Golden Calf worship nor an indulgence in the rites of Astarte. It was merely the procedure for the extraction of a living from the earth. Thus rationalized the Israelite as he turned to the gods of the grain.

Also encouraging Baalism was the intermarriage between many Israelite men and Canaanite women (most of the Canaanite males were slain in the conquest) which brought the conquerors closer to the customs of the land. During this period the Hebrew man married freely outside his family tribe. He had learned while in Shittim that there were women other than his own faithful toiling suppliants – and the women to the west of the Jordan were as adept in Astarte's art as those to the east.

The Hebrew girl would have her day. Also to have their day were those who considered the agricultural rites as an affront to Yahweh, and when Jehu became king they would rise up and rid the land of Baalism forever.

JEHU AND JEZEBEL – THE EXTINCTION OF BAALISM

During the reign of David (*c.* 1010 – *c.* 974 B. C.) Israel was united, and under Solomon (*c.* 974 – *c.* 926 B. C.) developed culturally, but the influences of Baalism continued. Solomon built "high places" of worship near Jerusalem for Astarte and other deities of neighboring peoples (II Kings 23:13) in order to maintain friendly public relations throughout the Near East. This religious freedom continued during the reign of Omri (*c.* 884 – 872 B. C.).

After Solomon, Israel gradually declined, but was still of such standing half a century later that Omri was able to marry his son Ahab to Jezebel, daughter of Ethbaal, king of Tyre. Ethbaal was of influence throughout all Phoenicia. He had been a high priest of Astarte before becoming king upon bringing about the murder of the legitimate ruler. It had been a long road from the sand-rambler to the marriage of an Israelite to a Phoenician princess. The people were pleased and flattered with the alliance. Ahab, a believer in Yahweh, caused a temple to be built to Baal as a respect to his wife. He had the mentioned precedents by Solomon. The great majority of the Israelites saw no objections in this deference to Jezebel's religion, but Elijah breathed fire. He vehemently denounced the worship of Baal in the land of Yahweh.

Ahab was killed in battle against the Syrians and Elijah also died, but Elisha took up the cause against Baalism and the house of Omri. When Jehoram, Ahab's son who succeeded his brother to the throne, was wounded in battle and left Jehu in command of the forces, Elisha saw his opportunity. He had Jehu anointed king and the soldiers immediately acclaimed their popular general and great charioteer. (It is from him we get the word "jehu" meaning any fast and furious driver.) Jehoram, still the legitimate king, died with an arrow in his back; Jezebel was tossed out of her palace window and expired under the feet of Jehu's horses; and all remaining members of the house of Omri were hunted down and their heads chopped off. Jehu, being the candidate of the devout believers in Yahweh, forthwith wiped out the worship of Baal so throughly that it never again influenced the lives or religion of the Israelites.

The accomplishment of the exclusive worship of the God of Abraham brings us to the end of our tracing of Hebrew history. The monotheism of Moses had prevailed. This one God was still a masculine God without feminine attributes; and infixed in this religion, with roots as deep as those of monotheism, was the early nomadic belief in woman's inferiority to man, a belief destined to be impressed on the Western world.

WOMAN'S SECONDARY STATUS

Childbearing was woman's primary function in society according to the Old Testament. There is notably absent in that work any emphasis on the second major function assigned to woman in most early religions: the giving of pleasure to man. The cause of this absence is found in the conflict which began at Shittim between the worship of Yahweh and of Astarte. It was the sexual rites of Astarte which had snared the sons and soldiers of Israel; it was the furnishing by woman of pleasure to man which had brought about the desertion of many followers of Yahweh. Therefore, sex was evil. The impact on the Hebrew warrior fresh from the desert of an entire land of willing and encouraging women was not forgotten when the Old Testament was recorded. The devout chroniclers could not ascribe to woman a function the misuse of which almost had wrecked their own religion; they could not attribute good to this weapon of a competitive religion which Israel had fought from Moses to Jehu with supremacy often in the balance.

The adverse attitude of the Old Testament towards sex in time supported contorted religious concepts, such as the belief that virginity and celibacy were holier than marriage, and has biassed the thinking of the West on sex ever since the ultimate conversion to Christianity of the Roman Empire about the turn of the fourth and fifth centuries A. D. So we see the historical singularity of an Asiatic nature worship, which existed during the second millennium before Christ, still prejudicing modern woman two millennia after Christ.

As previously indicated, the Hebrew woman's status was improved and her life eased after settlement in Canaan and particularly after David drove out the Philistines and initiated peace and prosperity. She continued to be inferior to man but her lot was no longer lowly. Woman was treated with respect, was content, and accepted without concern the laws allowing her father and husband to handle all affairs of business and property. We will not dwell on woman's elevation during this era since it was neither incorporated in the Old Testament nor given consideration as that work spread after Christ. Even during the enlightened time when woman's status was improving, the prophets objected to her enlarged freedom. They especially ranted about cosmetics which augmented the sexual attraction of women.

Cosmetics were in widespread use which itself indicates that the Hebrew woman was not having too hard a time. She had scented oils for the care of her skin; henna from the leaves of the Lawsonia (referred to as "camphire" in the Bible) with which to dye her hair red and to paint her fingernails and toenails an orange-reddish color; galena or lead sulphide of lead-gray color for her eyebrows and eyelashes; lapis lazuli blue to shade her eyelids; carmine, a rich red pigment for her lips derived from the dried bodies of certain insects (still the base of many lipsticks today); perfumes, myrrh and aromatic resins. Many of these ingredients were native and those which were not were imported in ample quantities.

The lady also had mirrors of highly polished metal, pins for curling her hair, and other devices to perfect her appearance. Perhaps property rights were trivial when compared to this array of aids to beauty. The prophesies of doom for Israel unless cosmetics were discontinued did not curtail their use. Typical of her sex, Jezebel, on hearing of Jehu's arrival at her palace and knowing his purpose, fixed her hair, painted her face and eyes, and put on ornaments – for her last appearance.

Also indicating woman's happier lot was better and brighter dress. She had always had color in her clothes, the sign of the Asiatic woman, but now she had an abundance of gay designs, including the latest styles from Tyre, Babylon and other fashion centers. To this the prophets did not object because color was traditional; but we will see later clerical aversion to this wile for attracting the male's attention. The woman of means also took daily baths: this woman once covered with the dust of trails who had thirsted under the Arabian sun. Neither did the prophets object to baths, but again we will see opposition to that.

These personal practices of the Hebrew woman, supports to her self-confidence and happiness, show her good life and increased freedom once her race settled and she could exert her influence on the society. Also, the Hebrew girl of this era was the most beautiful of all Near Eastern women, and her attractions soon became known far and wide. The cultural advancement of Israel was reflected in her spirit and demeanor. The Hebrew man now married within his own society and tribe, often his own cousin. Other Semitic women, including the devotees of Astarte, no longer lured him.

LAWS AFFECTING WOMEN

Adultery by the wife was punishable by death by stoning, but there were few who were accused or at whom the first stone was cast. (A man could not be guilty of adultery as mentioned under Mesopotamia.) The bondsmaid of a husband, found with another man, was scourged; she was not put to death "because she was not free." The wife probably could not obtain a divorce although the husband could at will:

> When a man hath taken a wife and married her, and it come to pass that she find no favor in his eyes, because he hath found some uncleanness in her, then let him write her a bill of divorcement and give it in her hand, and send her out of his house. (Deut. 24:1)

There has been much discussion over what was meant by "some uncleanness in her," but whatever it meant, the husband was the one who said whether or not it existed. Therefore this proviso was a nullity insofar as giving the wife any legal protection. Had a judge rather than the husband been designated to determine if the wife had an "uncleanness" — as a judge under the Code of Hammurabi determined if a Babylonian wife had failed to "keep herself chaste but is given to going about out" — the proviso would have been of legal import. Nevertheless, divorces were few. The purpose of the bill of divorcement was primarily for the wife's benefit so she could establish to others that she was divorced.

The wife did not inherit from the husband; inheritance was through the male line. An exception was where there were no sons, in which case the wife inherited on the theory she would marry her husband's brother or within his family so as not to divert his estate. The bride as a rule received no dowry, but every man was expected to marry and himself provide for his wife and children. The belief of looking after his own family was strong in the Hebrew man. Abandonment of wife and children was virtually unheard of. There were no religious rites connected with marriage; the principal ceremony was the "home-bringing" of the bride. This trip from her father's house to the groom's house was a festive affair with much singing and excitement. After marriage the wife was treated with respect by husband, children, and all. In religion, men took the lead, and at worship the women were segregated. There was little education for girls although they thoroughly learned the domestic arts.

The Mosaic laws were inartfully drawn and ill-arranged with their exact meaning and application often in doubt, yet they patently reflect woman's humble status. Specific laws will not be pursued further. Actually, they did not affect woman of later Western civilizations to the same drastic extent as did the Old Testament's general attitude of her inferiority, and the blame it imputed to her for the sins of the world. Upon these two concepts churchmen after Christ primarily relied to hold woman in subjection. Repeated for centuries was the Garden of Eden story that Eve caused the downfall of the human race and brought sorrow into the world, that all women after her are tainted with her original sin, that woman is man's inferior because she came from his rib, and that the husband is ordained by God to "rule over" the wife. These and other pronouncements of the Old

Testament will be discussed in connection with the misinterpretations put thereon by Western man, but what was to come can be anticipated by reading the following fertility legend:

> Now the serpent was more subtil than any beast of the field . . . And he said unto the woman, Yea, hath God said, Ye shall not eat of every tree of the garden? And the woman said unto the serpent, We may eat of the fruit of the trees of the garden: but of the fruit of the tree which is in the midst of the garden, God hath said, Ye shall not eat of it, neither shall ye touch it, lest ye die. And the serpent said unto the woman, Ye shall not surely die: for God doth know that in the day ye eat thereof, then your eyes shall be opened, and ye shall be as gods, knowing good and evil. And . . . she took of the fruit thereof, and did eat, and gave also unto her husband with her; and he did eat. And the eyes of them both were opened, and they knew they were naked . . . And they heard the voice of the Lord God . . . Unto the woman he said, I will greatly multiply thy sorrow and thy conception; in sorrow thou shalt bring forth children; and thy desire shall be to thy husband, and he shall rule over thee. And unto Adam he said . . . cursed is the ground for thy sake; in sorrow shalt thou eat of it all the days of thy life; thorns also and thistles shall it bring forth to thee; and thou shalt eat the herb of the field; in the sweat of thy face shalt thou eat bread, till thou return unto the ground; for out of it wast thou taken: for dust thou art, and unto dust shalt thou return . . . So he drove out the man. (Genesis 3)

For this woman would be blamed and made to suffer. Thus the belief that she violated God's command, and therefore must multiply in sorrow, for centuries put Western woman under an evil spell, a spell cast in a distant desert in the long ago.

---

[1] The dates and sequences of this chapter generally follow the lucid work of Dr. Werner Keller, *The Bible As History*. William Morrow & Company, New York (1956).

GREECE

Importance to Woman's Rights — The Wife and the Courtesan — Aspasia — Plato — Phryne — Conclusion

THE GOLDEN AGE OF GREECE — THE GLORIOUS FIFTH and fourth centuries B. C. — when art, philosophy and statesmanship reached the highest pinnacle of substance and beauty. Yet the age was golden only for Greek men; her women lived in frustration. And while the glory was everlasting, the Age itself was early doomed. The reason, as put by an authority, Emil Reich:

> In no period of the world's history has man reached so high a state of development: as a consequence, the women suffered by comparison, and it was the failure of the Greeks to develop their women which proved their ruin in the end. Had they developed their women as they developed their men, it is impossible to say where they would have stopped.[1]

Regardless of the treatment accorded women, this period of Greek history is important in the advancement of woman's rights for two reasons. It was the first time when a class of women, the courtesans, had full intellectual freedom with men. It was also the first time when broad equal rights and opportunities for women — social, educational, legal, political — were advocated by an intellectual giant, Plato, with extensive influence in his own day and profound effect on centuries to come. Since Athens was the center of the cultural development of the Golden Age, I use her to exemplify Greece's social pattern which reduced woman to her lowest sociolegal position in all history.

THE WIFE AND THE COURTESAN

There were two classes of women in Athens, as separate, distinct and far removed as segregation permits: the family woman and the courtesan. Each class had within it a wide range in standing. Well-to-do Athenian matrons had numerous slaves and servants; other matrons did their own chores. The courtesans ranged from those of talent and high social standing who associated with the rulers and the cultured to those who furnished only physical pleasure for the common men with whom they consorted.

All courtesans, or "companions" as they were called, moved freely throughout the city, took part in the public life and fraternized at will with the men. Making a living was the primary concern for most of them. The wives were economically secure. They looked after their homes, husbands, sons and daughters, devoting all their activities, their very life, to this end. They were strictly confined within narrow domestic limits and seldom allowed in public except to attend religious festivities. Having children for the imperialistic state was their great duty; guarded virtue, their arid attribute. Demosthenes succinctly expressed the society's attitude as to the respective purposes of the two classes: "We have companions for the sake of pleasure, and wives to bear us lawful offspring and be faithful guardians of our houses."

The sharp distinction between family women and companions was well developed by the time of Pericles (*c.* 490-429 B. C.) and during his administration was incorporated in and fostered by the Law of 451 which prevented an Athenian from marrying anyone not a citizen of Athens. The many Greek men and women who flocked to the city, being born elsewhere, could not become Athenian citizens; yet they were welcomed and readily admitted to the daily life of Athens as they were an asset to the state. They were legally classified as and were called "outlanders."

The men, who cared little about the prohibition against marriage to a citizen, engaged in any trade, occupation or profession for which they were already qualified; some joined the army or navy; they did what they wished. It was different with the large influx of women. Numerous occupations were open to them but the great majority of Grecian women were not sufficiently trained or educated to earn a living by work. Hence most women outlanders became companions from necessity or by choice. Those who did work were domestics, "wool-workers" who spun and wove in their homes, "market-women" who sold merchandise at retail in the city markets, and laborers engaged in other menial tasks. There is a record of one woman cobbler.

These working women were a third category of women in the city from one point of view, and many historians classify them separately; but from the standpoint of legal rights their position was the same as the companion's – all were outlanders. Also, the spread was such in the courtesan class, between those who associated with the intelligentsia and those who were little more than harlots, that the class is often subdivided accordingly. When "Greek courtesan" is mentioned today, it is the high type, the famous ones, to whom reference is made. Mainly because of them the era is often referred to as the Age of Courtesans.

Every courtesan had unrestrained intellectual freedom with her Athenian male associates. She could discuss philosophy, politics, art, morals, religion, sex, or any subject in any group. She could contribute such ideas as she entertained and was listened to and recognized as being of sound judgment if such was the case. In short, she was not discriminated against intellectually because she was a woman. This was a new attitude in society: intellectual equality between men and an entire class of women. Naturally all courtesans could not take full advantage of their opportunity, and in the competition of making a living each had to seek her own level and catch as catch can. Still, most became adept with the ready wit, small talk, repartee and social graces which brighten any woman's life; many displayed superb qualities of thought and action. Virtually all dyed their hair a light color, and blond hair became the badge of their class.

We must discard any idea that the courtesan's mode of life was considered improper. We know that many early cultures thought of women as having the dual purposes in life of child-bearing and giving men pleasure; both were considered natural, worthy and respectable, often of divine fiat. The Greeks followed this thinking but carried it to an extreme by allocating one of these functions to the family woman and the other to the companion.

This division into two classes, one for each function only, suited neither class. Both functions are innate to every woman; for her to fulfill both is life itself. There was never any objection to these two purposes being assigned to woman; the fault lay in limiting her outlets to them when her capabilities and desires were far more extensive. To deprive a woman of one of these two basic functions, thus denying her either marriage and lawful children or companionship with her husband, perplexes her, makes her situation untenable. This is especially true when the woman denied one function sees other women enjoying its beneficial pleasures.

The Athenian wife was well aware of the intimate freedom between her husband and his companion and considered the courtesans as getting the best of the bargain in their contact with the rulers, the cultured and the famous, in their attendance at the popular theatre and other forms of public entertainment, and in their full participation in the public life. The family woman's virtue became not something in which she could rejoice, but a reminder of the liberties she was denied.

At the same time, the courtesan longed for that which the wife had: a husband, a home, children of wedlock, and a lawful respectability. Her new-found intellectual freedom was not something she could regard as a true advance for herself and her sex because accompanying it was the unwholesome shadow of illicit relations.

This meant illegitimate children, which was particularly repugnant to the many courtesans of refinement. While these children were protected and not dishonored, they were still bastards at law. The courtesan did not have the legal position of even a concubine or a slave girl of other societies. Greece of the Golden Age was strictly monogamous and there was no legal tie whatsoever between the courtesan and her male consort. She was free and could revel in her freedom, but not be proud of it because of that which was withheld.

ASPASIA

The life of Aspasia illustrates the highest position which the woman outlander could obtain and also emphasizes the courtesan's intellectual freedom and equality with men. Aspasia was born at Miletus, Ionia, a city of culture where Greek philosophy had originated with Thales; she was the daughter of Axiochus, a man of culture. Nature had blessed her; she overflowed with wit, talent, intelligence and inspirational beauty. At Athens she opened a school in rhetoric and philosophy which she had studied at Miletus under Thargelia. She was a perfectionist in discourse and many learned this art from her. Among those attending her classes was Socrates, the man about town, who enjoyed good company as much as philosophy. He and Aspasia became close friends. Also in attendance was Athens' greatest statesman, Pericles, chief administrator and strategus of the Athenian Empire. Soon Aspasia was his mistress and confidante. Pericles asked his wife for a divorce, to which she readily agreed — she was interested in another man. Aspasia moved into Pericles' home, but not as his wife which was prohibited by his own Law of 451.

Her fame rests largely on her relationship with this great Athenian. She is better known than any of the Ionian courtesans, more remembered than any woman of Greece or of her general era except Sappho, the poetess of Lesbos, who wrote and sang her enchanting lyrics a century before the Age of Pericles.

Aspasia's ability in rhetoric enabled her to aid Pericles with his great orations. He was the outstanding orator of his day and only spoke on momentous occasions so as not to dilute his effect by frequent appearances. His greatest speech was the famous funeral oration, and Aspasia is credited with having composed it although it no doubt contained both her and Pericles' ideas. The speech was delivered at the funeral celebration held at the end of the first year of the Peloponnesian War to honor those who had met death before the walls of Potidaea and in the minor engagements of that year. No major battle had been fought and no great leader had fallen, hence the subject of the speech was not such as to give it fame. However, Pericles, or Aspasia, in addition to honoring the dead, reviewed the political and social life of Athens. That excellent part of the speech causes it to be rated as one of the world's foremost orations. This most eloquent of Pericles' speeches was not sentimental nor written to bring tears to the eyes of the listeners because of the loss of the departed; it had a masculine quality. Aspasia has the distinction of being the only woman credited with composing the greatest speech of a great orator or any speech ranked among the great of all ages.

Aspasia's capabilities, her brilliance and beauty, gave her another claim unique in history. No other woman has had such an intimate association with an array of men whose artistic, cultural and literary attainments were unequalled in all time. Their very names are well known to this day, twenty-four centuries later. Most of Aspasia's contemporaries who helped produce the Golden Age frequented her drawing room; these prominent contacts plus her close relation with the powerful and admired Pericles gave her much influence in Athens and throughout the Empire. This she exerted for good. The emancipation and the education of women was strongly advocated by her at all opportunities.

Aspasia's exceptional position is dramatically demonstrated by the politically motivated indictment against her in 432 B. C. for impiety and evil living. It was then obvious that war was to come with the Peloponnesian League which was headed by Sparta. Many laid the blame for this directly to the policies of Pericles; feeling against him was strong enough that his enemies believed the time had arrived to take the offensive. Unable to discredit him personally with the people, they attacked the influential and well known personages closest to him – a recognized political maneuver of any age.

They brought an indictment against Pheidias, considered by many the greatest of the Greek sculptors, merely because he was a friend of Pericles and associated with the administration. The charge was embezzlement of a part of the gold and ivory entrusted to him for the statue of Athena Parthenos. He conclusively established his innocence yet was retained in custody on another charge, sacrilege, because he had inserted likenesses of himself and Pericles in the Parthenon. An old man, he died in prison before he could be tried on the second indictment. Impiety, always a plausible accusation in the public mind against philosophers, was leveled at Anaxagoras, adviser and intimate of Pericles. He had to quit Athens. Damon, the popular musician and boyhood friend of Pericles, was ostracized.

Of utmost significance is the fact that Aspasia was among those indicted – that a woman was considered of such importance that her personal discredit would reflect on the strategus. No woman had ever before been politically bracketed with a Pheidias, an Anaxagoras, or a Damon. Pericles was able to obtain the acquittal of Aspasia by appearing in person before the Dicastery and delivering an oration so emotional and sincere that tears came to his eyes. The prosecution of his male friends by his enemies was one thing – prosecuting his mistress another. It has always been hard to convict a woman of womanly activities.

It is interesting to note that Pericles was also able to convince the Assembly, in a great oration, that the war was not due to any particular action taken on his advice but was inevitable because of Sparta's jealousy of the Athenian empire. Further, just before Pericles died from the plague during its second outbreak, three years after the war had started with the end nowhere in sight, the Ecclesia legitimized his son by Aspasia. He had lost his two legitimate sons in the plague's first outbreak. These occurrences demonstrate the personal regard the Athenians held in their hearts for their leader. Today he is recognized as one of the world's most enlightened statesmen.

After Pericles' death, Aspasia married a cattle dealer, an outlander like herself. The former gaiety of her drawing room was replaced by the security of a home, her brilliant company by a husband, and her moral freedom by a lawful union. The lovely courtesan, the greatest of them all, now had what all courtesans yearned for.

The character of Aspasia has long been debated. She was mercilessly criticized by the conservatives opposing Pericles. They spread the gossip that she had been the companion of Socrates before becoming Pericles' regal mistress. More damaging was the report that she, Socrates and the likes of them, frequently speculated, behind closed doors, that the gods of Greece might not be actual gods, that perhaps there was one God for the universe of an order different from celestial bodies.

There is one fact, however, which establishes that Aspasia could not have been other than good: Pericles loved her dearly. He was a man of discriminating tastes and associates, of great reserve and strength, head of the democratic party of Athens yet with few intimates, a man of honor. It is not possible that such a man could have been ardently devoted and loyal over a long period to a woman who was basically bad. Also, Aspasia after her death was highly regarded by the refined and arch-conservative Plato. In his *Menexenux* wherein the dialogue is between Menexenux and Socrates, Plato has them marvel at the profound funeral oration composed by Aspasia. He refers to her as a "rare" woman and an "excellent mistress in the art of rhetoric." This reflects her reputation after death in the city where she lived. The evidence supports those who say Aspasia was of good character and of good influence on Pericles and the Empire.

PLATO

What did Plato think of woman and her proper position in society, how did he rate her with man in intelligence and ability; and who was he that his thoughts should influence the world to this day?

Plato was born about a year after the death of Pericles and

lived past eighty (*c.* 428 B. C.-*c.* 348 B. C.). He spent his long years observing, analyzing, correlating, and studying many subjects, especially government. He gave to the world its greatest political treatise, *The Republic,* and ever since the world has honored him as its greatest political philosopher. He came from a highly prominent Athenian family. His father traced his ancestry to Codrus of the eleventh century B. C., in legend the last king of Athens and a descendant of Poseidon, god of the sea and of all water. Many early seafaring peoples considered their entire lineage as having descended from this god, regarding him somewhat as the Hebrews and Christians once did Adam and Eve. Plato's mother's family was related to Solon, the great legal reformer of two centuries earlier and considered the founder of democracy. (From him we get the word "solon" meaning wise lawmaker and in common usage today.)

Plato was well educated pursuant to the orthodox methods of his time. More subtly influencing his thinking was his close association during his formative years with Socrates, and he was one of a small group who could be considered as disciples of that eminent philosopher. As a result new ideas and a searching curiosity were early instilled in Plato. Socrates and tutors were not his only early teachers. In his youth he witnessed the closing years of the long and disastrous Peloponnesian War, the collapse of the Athenian Empire, and the year of anarchy in Athens; and what Plato witnessed, even as a young man, he learned from. He knew the bad as well as the good in life and considered himself a realist, not a philosopher, yet he had the qualities of both. Some thought his views practical, others idealistic.

His background of family, tutelage, Socrates, the glory of Greece, loss of power by Athens, civil strife within the city between democrats and reactionaries, travels, and understanding of government and its processes, were to route his superb mental talents into the realm of philosophy. He was to chart the courses in many fields of thought for others to follow.

On government and politics he taught the moral and rational development of man and woman through long range training and education, and of personal virtue extended throughout the state.

Egyptian sculpture,
14th century, B. C.
Berlin Museum

NEFERTITI

(Beauty Forever
and Ever)

Queen of the Pharaoh
Akhenaten.

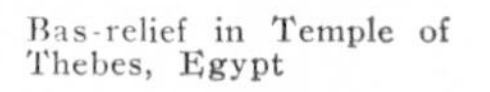

Bas-relief in Temple of Thebes, Egypt

CLEOPATRA VII

(Queen of Egypt 47-30 B. C.)

Royal mistress of Julius Caesar and of Mark Antony.

MOSES (The great monotheist of history)
Restated by divine revelation the Hebrew common law,
including the rules of woman's inferiority.

Sculpture in Vatican Museum, Rome

ASPASIA (c. 470-410 B. C.)

Marble copy of bronze statue by Kresilas, Cretan sculptor of 5th century B. C.
In British Museum, London

From a photograph by Giraudon of painting by J. L. David, in Musee Dobree, at Nantes

TRIAL OF PHRYNE (c. 340 B. C.)

Defended by her lover, the great advocate, Hyperides.

Marble statue by Praxiteles

CNIDIAN APHRODITE

Marble statue in Palace of Justice, Rome

GAIUS (2nd century)

Foremost among the great Roman jurists in giving woman equality in the law.

Engraving after a lost original by Rembrandt

ST. PAUL (First great Christian theologian)
Taught the subjugation of woman to man.

Marble sculpture, 4th century, A. D.

CONSTANTINE THE GREAT (c. 288-337 A. D.)
Emperor of Rome from 324 to 337.

From painting by Ary Scheffer (1795-1858). In Louvre, Paris

ST. AUGUSTINE AND MONNICA

St. Augustine became the Early Church's leading authority on predestination, irresistible grace, final perseverance — and the wife's subjection to the husband.

Woodcut after a contemporary manuscript illustration

INNOCENT III (*c.* 1160-1216)

Pope from 1198 to 1216.

SIR WILLIAM BLACKSTONE (1723-1780)
English jurist and author of the *Commentaries,* the most popular textbook on law in the Colonies during the 18th century.

LUCRETIA COFFIN MOTT

A Quaker and one of the organizers of the first women's rights conventions.

A SUFFRAGETTE TRIO FROM ILLINOIS
Julia Lathrop, Jane Addams, and Cary MacDowell.

Still taken from a contemporary newsreel

SYLVIA PANKHURST

One of the early suffragettes in England, being led away by London policemen.

Mrs. Oliver H. P. Belmont of New York (left) and Mrs. J. B. Battelli of Ohio (center) being greeted by Miss Elsie Hill (with banner) at dedication in 1922 of the headquarters of the National Women's Party in Washington, D. C.

He conceived a utopian society wherein truly just administrators would have sufficient authority and power to enable them to prevail against all improper influences. The state was to be ruled by its selectively bred and morally schooled thinkers and not by the military, commercial, oı other classes. Democracy was found wanting because under it true qualification was not the requisite for those entrusted with political office — an indictment too often true today. Tyranny or dictatorship was the most harmful of all forms of government as it did not cure the fault of democracy yet permitted authority in a ruler with selfish interests — even in one with criminal inclinations.

Plato envisioned an ideal society in which woman would serve side by side with man and in which each person would perform those functions for which he was best suited regardless of sex. Women should have equal training and education with men in all fields so as to permit any particular woman, the same as any particular man, to qualify herself for that which she was best able to perform. He saw only physical and emotional differences in the sexes, which were not grounds, in his sound reasoning, for social, moral and legal distinctions. For his own words as to the equal role women were to play as guardians of the state, consider this passage from Book V of *The Republic* (written in the awkward dialogue form of the times) wherein the discussion is between Socrates as the narrator and Glaucon:

> Let us further suppose the birth and education of our women to be subject to similar or nearly similar regulations; then we shall see whether the result accords with our design.
>
> What do you mean?
>
> What I mean may be put into the form of a question. I said: Are dogs divided into hes and shes, do they both share equally in hunting and in keeping watch and in the other duties of dogs? or do we entrust to the males the entire and exclusive care of the flocks, while we leave the females at home, under the idea that the bearing and suckling their puppies is labour enough for them?
>
> No, he said, they share alike; the only difference between them is that the males are stronger and the females weaker.

But can you use different animals for the same purpose, unless they are bred and fed in the same way?

You cannot.

Then, if women are to have the same duties as men, they must have the same nurture and education?

Yes.

. . .

And, if, I said, the male and female sex appear to differ in their fitness for any art or pursuit, we should say that such pursuit or art ought to be assigned to one or the other of them; but if the difference consists only in women bearing and men begetting children, this does not amount to a proof that a woman differs from a man in respect to the sort of education she should receive; and we shall therefore continue to maintain that our guardians and their wives ought to have the same pursuits.

. . .

Many women are in many things superior to many men.

. . .

There is no special faculty of administration in a state which a woman has because she is a woman, or which a man has by virtue of his sex, but the gifts of nature are alike diffused in both.

. . .

And the proper officers, whether male or female or both, for offices are to be held by women as well as by men.

. . .

You agree then, I said, that men and women (the guardians of society) are to have a common way of life such as we have described — common education, common children; and they are to watch over the citizens in common whether abiding in the city or going out to war; they are to keep watch together; . . . and always and in all things, as far as they are able, women are to share with the men? And in so doing they will do what is best, and will not violate, but preserve the natural relation of the sexes.

I agree with you, he replied.

It is hard to realize how revolutionary was Plato's advocacy of equality for women. Athens had long before determined that its mothers and daughters must be kept virtuous at all costs for the benefit of the state. If that meant seclusion and vegetation for women, such was of little concern. Their purpose was to breed. The pleasure, relaxation and entertainment which men needed from women could be found elsewhere – outlanders were plentiful. Furthermore, male attention and association with the Athenian woman would only distract her from the duty of caring for the family, could even cause her to become less virtuous.

Never has any attitude or policy so degraded woman, both citizen and outlander. It is the one great blot on the civilization of Greece – in the end it undermined her social structure. No society can function long with its women divided into breeders and courtesans. Soon the Athenian male was not marrying until his late twenties and often after thirty. The courtesan suited him, and compared to her and to what he had become accustomed with her, any girl he could marry would be unbearably dull, both socially and sexually. This girl, ably trained in domestic duties, would know how to run the household, supervise the servants and rear the children; but there her talents as a wife would end. She had not seen much of boys or men since she was very young, and no goddess had given her the instinct to understand the male. As a mate she would not be loved and as a wife she would not be respected. All Aristotle could say of the family woman's lot was that she was not a slave.

It is a paradox of history that the most enlightened of all ages for art and philosophy should be the period of most utter abjection for women, their rights and feelings. Even Plato's theories did not actually improve woman's position during his time, though he did influence the progressive-minded. The average man continued with his habitual attitude toward the opposite sex: woman was meant to bear children or to give man pleasure. This is forcefully illustrated by the trial of the famous courtesan Phryne.

PHRYNE

Phryne became a celebrity toward the end of Plato's life. She was born at Thespiae in Boeotia, and her real name was Mnesarete but she was always called Phryne, meaning toad, though not in a derogatory sense. One of her beauty and ambition soon found her way to Athens. There she became the well beloved of the influential advocate, Hypereides. In oratory he was ranked second only to Demosthenes, and by many as his equal. Hypereides, like most Athenians during the Golden Age, made a worship of beauty. At no other period has beauty for beauty's sake alone been so highly regarded: in women, architecture, sculpture, everything. "The Beautiful" was regarded as having an essence of its own, something divine; in Phryne the most ardent admirer of this essence could find all he desired of human face and form.

Phryne was aware of her good fortune; she was also smart, resourceful, and adept in showmanship. Beauty was her asset and she protected it against becoming commonplace by wearing a veil when on the streets. The minimum charge for her affection was one mina, approximately a hundred dollars. Phryne became wealthy. She offered to pay the total cost of rebuilding the walls of Thebes provided the following inscription would be placed thereon: "Destroyed by Alexander, restored by Phryne the courtesan." The Thebans refused the offer, but Phryne's purpose was served: widespread publicity attended the gesture.

Her most dramatic performance was at a mass religious festival of Poseidon held in mystic Eleusis on the coast near Athens. At the very height of the celebration Phryne walked to the edge of the water, let down her light-colored hair, removed her girdle, garment and remaining clothing, then waded into the sea, turned, and stood facing the holiday worshippers as the foam from the waves broke about her body. She slowly returned to the rocky beach. At first the many onlookers were somewhat surprised, but the unexpected scene soon so captivated their imagination that they considered it to exemplify the birth of Aphrodite who sprang from the foam of the sea. Apelles was sufficiently inspired to paint, with Phryne as the model, his famous Aphrodite Anadyomene (Anadyomene was one of the goddess' many titles and means "rising from the sea").

The renowned Praxiteles fell in love with Phryne and immortalized her in marble. One of his statues of her was placed by the side of his statue of Aphrodite in a temple at Thespiae, Phryne's home town. She was also the model for his nude Aphrodite at Cnidus which tourists from the entire Mediterranean area came to view. Men were stirred as their gaze lingered. The town refused a fabulous offer for this attraction and was said to love the statue as the sculptor did its model. It was no doubt this Aphrodite which was copied on the town's coins.

Praxiteles is considered by many to be the greatest of the Greek sculptors, while Pheidias is so considered by others; and certainly each was ascendent in his particular style. Praxiteles gave to marble an emotionalism, a softness, a naturalism. He was the one to reflect in marble the love and passion of Aphrodite. When he looked on Phryne he knew she was his mortal inspiration. Because of him, when the goddess was thought of, Phryne was the image which came to mind. Her fame spread far and wide. Whereever men traveled, along the great caravan routes of Asia and Africa or the distant sea lanes of the Mediterranean, Phryne was known. Wherever men talked of women, from the temples of Athens to the docks of Carthage, she was the favorite topic.

However, Phryne was thought by many Athenians to be a bad girl, and Euthias charged her with impiety in profaning the ancient Eleusinian mysteries and in corrupting the Greeks generally. The trial, *c.* 340 B. C., was before the tribunal of the Heliasts. The death penalty was suggested and possible, but not probable, although banishment was likely if she were found guilty. Hypereides of course came to the rescue of his well beloved and ably defended her, not with tears, Pericles-style as in the trial of Aspasia, but in a fashion as startling as his client's parade into the sea.

To counteract the positive oral testimony against Phryne, Hypereides suddenly stood her in front of the tribunal and, pulling her loose garment from her shoulders, bared her full, round breasts and much of her body. Docilely she maintained her signal pose while Hypereides argued that a woman of the beauty and shapeliness of Phryne had been created by the gods to give man pleasure, that she was a true priestess of Aphrodite, that she should not be condemned for doing that which was ordained for her. The tribunal, after hearing the eloquence of Hypereides — and after viewing the exhibit — agreed with the great advocate and acquitted Phryne. Hence she was allowed to continue her divine pursuits in Athens. Rumor had it that the judges believed they had actually beheld before them the goddess of love and beauty herself; but regardless, it was felt by the legislative authorities that the judges had been overreached, so a law was passed that in the future the accused could not be seen by the judges in certain situations.

Phryne's trial exemplified the attitude of the times toward woman. While it can be doubted that the judges thought they had looked upon the goddess of love, history records they did acquit Phryne because Hypereides "invoked their religious scruples to have pity on this priestess of Aphrodite."[2] They believed Phryne was fulfilling one of the two ordained purposes of woman; they could not condemn that which the gods sanctioned. Also, one member of the tribunal had more than a classical understanding of this divine theory — he was a customer of the accused. It is hard to convict a woman of womanly activities.

To give Phryne her due, she is the most poetic personification of sex which ever stimulated a prosaic world. Mesdames de Montespan, de Pompadour, du Barry and the other clever French courtesans of the Versailles court, and the modern Clara Bows, Marilyn Monroes and Brigitte Bardots, are amateurish parvenus when compared to Phryne, the mortal reflection of Aphrodite, the flesh of love and passion.

CONCLUSION

The lesson of Greece is that woman to her husband must be both wife and courtesan; yet woman knows this without Greece to draw on. Hence that of which Greece actually warns her is to guard against the inclination in society to classify women to fit men's needs. It is good that the male looks upon the female with both esteem and lust, but he must know that every woman has the potential and the desire ably to satisfy both attitudes.

While Greece has been the only culture to carry to an extreme the classification of women to meet the needs of men, the tendency is in all cultures. When we observe a social exaggeration among one people, we can know that its roots exist in all. As said in the opening chapter, the basic nature, thinking, and environment of man has remained constant during the record era. This does not mean that one society may not take a distinct, even unique, turn, but it does mean that whatever the turn, the underlying cause is common to all societies. While the tendency to classify women may presently be suppressed in the United States, it has existed here and still exists in other parts of the world. Women should never be grouped upon a social, moral or other basis. There is little tendency to group men. Let each person stand as an individual and not be judged as a member of some class based on the outlook of others.

---

[1] Reich, Emil, *Women Through The Ages,* Methuen & Co., London (1908).

[2] Wigmore, John H., *Panorama of the World's Legal Systems,* p. 326, one-volume Library edition. Washington Law Book Company, Washington, D. C. (1936).

ROME

The Empire — The Evolution of Women's Rights — Conquest of the Mediterranean World — Period of the Great Jurists: Conditions During First Four Centuries A. D. *- Education - Individual Jurists and Their Thinking - Women's Occupations - Marriage and Divorce. Stoicism — Summary*

WE TURN TO THE WEST WHERE THERE WAS RISING Rome's majestic constellation of empire, which was to glow greater than Greece's glory, to burn brighter than Babylon's brilliance. A constellation of many stars, some bright, others dark: those of war and peace, of order and justice, of power and opulence, of corruption and destruction. A constellation with one lasting star — that of scientific law, which was to be bequeathed to posterity.

When we think of empire in the Roman sense, we must think of all things as being subject to the imperialistic state. There has never been another Western empire which approaches Rome's, nor another people who sacrificed as did hers in order to gain the mastership of the Western World. The imperialism of Athens, except for the restrictions on its women citizens, was lax compared to Rome's daily hardships and relentless requirements. Art, literature, wealth, comfort, and leisure were sacrificed to conquest. Law — the "instinct" of the Roman — flourished. And so sound were Rome's legal foundations laid that with them she governed a world, and upon them nations still build.

Roman law, or the Civil Law as it was later called, is today the basis of the legal systems of most of the countries of continental Europe, as well as of Scotland, Quebec, Louisiana, Mexico, and all Central and South America. Also, Northern Africa and Western Asia are substantially influenced by Civil Law. (The other great legal system of Western civilization is, of course, the Common Law of England followed by most English speaking nations.)

The various stages of Roman law will not be outlined as that would be too tedious for our purpose, but reviewed are two interesting periods in Rome's history of primary importance in the development of woman's rights. The first is Rome's conquest of the Mediterranean world during the last two-thirds of the third century and the first two-thirds of the second century before Christ. The second period reviewed is that of the great jurists, roughly the second and third centuries after Christ, when these giants of the law produced a system of jurisprudence which was logical, equitable and practical to a degree of excellence; a system of justice theretofore unknown and never excelled: "the justice of the Caesars."

THE EVOLUTION OF WOMEN'S RIGHTS

In order that the two eras of the conquest of the Mediterranean area and of the great jurists will not appear as isolated in the continual advancement of woman's rights in Rome, and better to perceive both eras as oriented stages, their discussion is prefaced by a look at the general evolution of woman's rights within the Empire.

In the early years of Roman imperialism woman possessed few

legal privileges, her life was rigorous, and she was under the complete dominance of her father or husband. He was the ruler, in law and in fact, of the family and of the household. In spite of this background, during the second and third centuries A. D. woman gained substantial equality with man — the first time in history when she enjoyed this status and the last time until the modern era. To show the evolution of the Roman woman's rights from subjugation to equality, I take one example: the husband's power to punish the wife.

The husband's legal authority to punish extended to all members of his household, but we will follow this law only as between husband and wife. During the seventh and sixth centuries B. C. the punishment could take the form of death. (The origin of the concept of the husband's power of life and death over the family is unknown, but it existed among many ancient races in their initial stage of development.) Actually, such punishment within the domestic sphere was infrequent in Rome, but the point is that this drastic power existed in the husband and was exercised by him on occasions. The act of putting to death his wife, performed by his own hands, and why he did so, was his business, not that of the state.

The first restriction on this power was the removal of the husband's discretion as to the grounds for death, after which he could inflict the penalty only for those reasons considered sufficient by the collective society. Gradually specific grounds disappeared one by one until only adultery was left, but that remained for centuries in the law, even into the second century B. C., an enlightened era in Rome. However, by then death for adultery was considered too barbaric to contemplate. Still, if in rare instances an enraged husband meted out this severity, he acted within his legal right. The ground of adultery was later restricted to cases where the husband caught the wife in the act, but death was sanctioned more as an excuse for the irrational deed of an infuriated husband than as a just punishment for an unfaithful wife. Eventually death under this agitating circumstance was abolished.

In early Rome the husband also possessed the legal right of chastisement as a means of punishment, and this right continued long after death had been abolished. Originally he could whip his wife for misconduct or disrespect as frequently and as cruelly as he deemed necessary. This right of male mastership was also gradually eliminated; and as the power of death diminished, a husband could not lawfully beat his wife so severely that she might die, even though death was unintentional, nor inflict on her serious bodily harm. In time any corporal chastisement had to be mild and the wife could obtain relief in court from brutal treatment. By the second century A. D. all right of corporal punishment disappeared, as well as the husband's monitorial authority to restrict the person of the wife or to supervise her in any way. However, he was still referred to as head of the house.

The evolution over almost a thousand years of this legal concept permitting a husband to punish his wife, from its original power-of-death stage to its curtain era of dubious flattery, shows how an unsound law disintegrates in a progressing society: one restriction after another limits it until even its mildest application is discarded. Before leaving this example it should be made plain that the Roman husband's power of punishment was not as bad as it reads, because he seldom exercised it in severe form or to the extent allowed by law. Rome was harsh, but civilized. Also, during this entire period there were many compensations for the wife: the husband had definite legal obligations to protect her (even from insults), to provide for her, and to share with her; and there were no legal concubines. Neither were women regarded as chattels. Rome was of the West, not of the East.

CONQUEST OF THE MEDITERRANEAN WORLD

The 131 years between 264 and 133 B. C., during which Rome conquered the Mediterranean World, was a period of transition and of accelerated rights for women in the Empire or Republic. Laws spring from customs and customs from conditions, so to understand the changes in women's rights during this age we must know the changes in conditions. Previously Rome had become a world power by uniting Italy, but the harsh way of life for both men and women continued well into the transition period, though with some moderation. Especially were sacrifices required by the Punic Wars — the three wars with Rome's older African rival, Carthage — the first during the middle of the third century B. C., the second during the latter part of that century, and the third during the middle of the following century. The outcome, of course, was the utter destruction of Carthage and Rome's acquisition of most of her world trade and commerce.

Success in the numerous wars of the period, particularly those after the fall of Carthage, resulted in profound changes in Rome. The loot of one rich area after another brought spoils, slaves, and a taste for luxury which drastically influenced woman's life. A virtual nobility was created among many Roman patrician families who ruled the Mediterranean World by occupying high official positions in Rome and in the provinces. A wealthy equestrian class in Rome controlled vast banking, commercial, and trade interests. Greek culture spread throughout the Republic and a Latin culture began to develop. The world was changing for the Roman woman.

An occurrence toward the end of the second century B. C. (about the middle of the transition period) which was somewhat startling to the male rulers of an empire reflects the expected conflict between the old belief that women should continue to be restrained and the new attitude that they should share in Rome's prosperity and advancement. Some years earlier as a Punic War economy measure, the tribune Oppius had introduced and the Senate had passed a law providing that "no woman should possess more than half an ounce of gold, or wear a garment of various colors, or ride in a carriage drawn by horses in a city, or in a town, or any place nearer thereto than one mile, except on occasions of some public religious solemnity."

Regardless of women's legal status during any particular era, they have always considered it their personal privilege and sacred right to adorn themselves with such dress and ornaments as were available, as they deemed flattering to their appearance, and as they or their husbands could afford. Any laws or regulations limiting this privilege, of which there have been many, have been highly unpopular with the sex, impractical to enforce, and generally disobeyed. This is true whether the restriction has been imposed by Roman Senate legislation, imperial decree, church edict, or present-day city ordinance regulating beach wear.

The Oppian Law was no exception and the dissatisfaction reached such a stage that the Senate decided to deliberate its repeal. On the days just prior to, during, and immediately after the debate, there occurred the biggest demonstration by women in history—they overran the streets of Rome by the thousands. The spectacle is best described by Livy:

> The Capitol was filled with crowds who favored or opposed the law; nor could the matrons be kept at home either by advice or shame, nor even by the commands of their husbands; but they beset every street and pass in the city, beseeching the men as they went down to the Forum, that, in the present flourishing state of the commonwealth, when the private fortune of all was daily increasing, they would suffer the women to have their former ornaments restored. This throng of women increased daily, for they arrived even from the country towns and villages, and they had at length the boldness to come up to the consuls, preters and magistrates, to urge their request. One of the consuls, however, they found especially inexorable—Marcus Porcius Cato.

Marcus Porcius Cato (234-149 B. C.), better known as Cato The Censor or The Elder, was a power in Rome and one of her great orators. His speech on this occasion against the repeal of the Oppian Law was particularly mordant. His opening remarks and other excerpts quoted below reflected the belief of many as to woman's proper place in society and proper relation to her husband, also the effect Greek culture was having on the Empire:

> If, Romans, every individual among us had made it a rule to maintain the prerogative and authority of a husband with

respect to his own wife, we should have less trouble with the whole sex. But now our privileges, overpowered at home by female contumacy, are, even here in the Forum, spurned and trodden under foot; and because we are unable to withstand each separately we now dread their collective body. . . .

Had I not been restrained by the respect for the modesty and dignity of some individuals among them, rather than of the whole number, and been unwilling that they should be seen rebuked by a consul, I should not have refrained from saying to them, 'What sort of practise is this, of running out into public, besetting the streets and addressing other women's husbands? Could not each have made the same request to your husband at home? Are your blandishments more seducing in public than in private, and with other women's husbands than with your own? . . .'

Often have you heard me complain of the profuse expenses of the women – often of those of the men; and that not only of men in private stations, but of the magistrates; and that the state was endangered by two opposite vices, luxury and avarice – those pests which have ever been the ruin of every state. These I dread the more, as the circumstances of the commonwealth grow daily more prosperous and happy; as the empire increases; as we have passed over into Greece and Asia, places abounding with every kind of temptation that can inflame the passions; and as we have begun to handle even royal treasures: for I greatly fear that these matters will rather bring us into captivity than we them . . .

Of all kinds of shame, the worst, surely, is the being ashamed of frugality . . .

Be assured that when a woman once begins to be ashamed of what she ought not to be ashamed of, she will not be ashamed of what she ought. . . .

If the law ceases to limit the expenses of your wife, you yourself will never be able to limit them.

After the debate, Livy says, "The women next day poured out into public in much greater numbers, and in a body beset the doors of the tribunes who had protested against the measure of their colleagues; nor did they return until their intervention was withdrawn." The force and volume of the women's demands for the restoration of their rights (their finery) proved more effective than the essence and quality of Cato's speech. The law was repealed. A triumphant, tumultuous celebration ensued; expensive and variegated dress and fine jewelry appeared as if from nowhere, and with noisy rejoicing the women marched "in procession through the streets and the Forum, bedizened with their now legitimate finery."

As noted from his speech, Cato resented the spread of Hellenic culture within the Empire. During his time Greece was fast becoming a Roman province (her last year of any semblance of independence was 147 B. C.) and the Empire was fast becoming Hellenized in its customs and tastes. Cato's fear that Eastern ways "will rather bring us into captivity than we them" was prophetic. It later became a saying that *Greece captured Rome*. Cato and those like him could not stem the tide, yet they were able to retard it and to deprive women of valuable rights. Many Romans strongly felt Rome's success during the past centuries had been due to her strict way of life, and they continued to live by that standard. Cato's life in public and in private was severe, frugal, and exemplary; his treatment of his wife as one of his slaves was a virtue from his point of view. He and those of similar attitude sincerely regarded every limitation which they could place on women as wholesome for the Empire.

They were able to obtain the passage of the Lex Voconia in 169 B. C., which prohibited women from acquiring property by will, and a second law limiting women's acquisition of property by succession. These restrictions on the transmission of property by both will and succession struck at the core of woman's rights; yet they were enacted, submitted to, and continued in force for years without serious female protest. They were not an Oppian Law.

Since women had the legal privilege of dressing in a manner suitable to them – and Rome never again after the repeal of the Oppian Law made any serious attempt to regulate their dress — we must see the new styles which the transition period inaugurated for the coming eras. Especially popular was the suggestive stola, a flowing garment draped over the shoulders with folds in front which emphasized the breasts and often considerably revealed them, sometimes one more than the other. From the folds the gament reached gracefully to the ankles, with sleeves to the elbows. When out of doors or not among their intimates, all women wore a palla or shawl over their shoulders, wrapped to cover their bosom. In time the stola became more modest or was replaced by the dalmatica somewhat in the nature of a cloak — not by legislation, by women's own accord. The extremely styled stola lingered among those of bad repute. At select social affairs women wore the cyclas, a transparently thin robe trimmed in gold, provocative and, as the wearer moved about, disclosing. In time it became more modest. "All fashions end in excess," said Paul Poiret, the leading Parisian couturier of the 1920s. Although there were cyclic changes in styles, as today, the basic Greek dress remained for over four centuries. The materials were imported cotton, linen, and silk, and the Roman woman was as well and as stylishly dressed as any woman.

Cosmetics were in general use and, of course, continued throughout the Empire as long as it lasted. It was said that a husband never saw his wife's face. The coiffure became woman's crowning glory and startling effects were produced by its elaborateness. Ivory, gold and silver combs and pins augmented the display. Woman's naturally colored hair, blending evenly with her natural skin coloring, was too ordinary for her discriminating tastes — but black, auburn and chestnut dyes relieved her feeling of averageness. Wigs were freely used. At one period yellow hair was the rage; the Italian brunette preferred the blond look. The Roman woman did not have hose — an economy for the Empire which Cato was never to realize — but fancy footwear blossomed. Jewels of all descriptions adorned the wealthy matron from head to foot; long strings of pearls were in high favor, golden chains plentiful, and exotic stones commonplace.

While Greek dress and ornaments became popular faster than her culture, many Roman women, especially during the latter part of the transition period, diligently pursued the study of Greek literature, poetry and art.

In 186 B. C. another Senate decree dealing primarily with women was passed outlawing the Bacchanalia or festivals of Bacchus, except in a few special instances. The Bacchanalian mysteries were initiated in southern Italy by women who met in secret three times annually, but as the movement spread, men were admitted and the meetings were increased to five times monthly. In Rome women were converted by the hundreds and the original mysticism became lost in designed licentiousness. Food and wine were standard aids to the rites, the better to attract more and more men. Says Livy, "When wine, lascivious discourse, night, and the mingling of the sexes had extinguished every sentiment of modesty, then debaucheries of every kind began to be practised, as every person found at hand that sort of enjoyment to which he was disposed by the passion most prevalent in his nature."

The women were not of the prostitute type as we use that term; they were women loosed from centuries of restraint, modest by day, wanton periodically by night when in orgiastic mood they offered willing bodies in a simulated mysticism. This sudden sexual boldness of women was a definite sign of the times, something they would not have dared to display prior to this transition period. By *sign* of the times is not meant *typical* of the times. The average Roman woman was still on her good behavior, and this diversion from the strict life was short-lived in Rome, though considerable difficulty attended its suppression in southern Italy. Freedom with clothing woman had obtained, but her unbounded license in sex was not for Rome of this era.

Nevertheless, the Bacchanalia foreshadowed what lay ahead for the Empire.

PERIOD OF THE GREAT JURISTS

Conditions During First Four Centuries A. D.

The second and third centuries, when the Roman jurists reached their height, are characterized by four factors directly affecting women: laws, corruption, Stoicism, and the growing religion of Christianity. Each factor reacted on the others. I emphasize these two centuries because, as mentioned, it was during them that woman gained equality for all practical purposes. However, the factors influencing woman during the second and third centuries also existed in the first and fourth, with any differences being only in degree. Rome was mistress of the world throughout all four centuries — Alaric and his Goths were not to sack her until 410 — but during the first century she was strong, during the fourth, weak.

As early as the second century, Emperor Marcus Aurelius realized the Empire was declining due to its corruption and also that he could do nothing about it. He did hold in check the hostile German tribes, but their increasing strength and the Empire's decreasing vitality foretold to him the future. From a military standpoint, Rome was to be on the defensive against the restless hordes to the North.

We have seen that the corruption and the decreasing vitality which concerned Marcus Aurelius began during the latter part of the era of conquest; but mild were the indications of decadence in the adoption of Greek habits, in the spread of Oriental luxury, and in the sexual boldness of the Bacchanalian rites. During the four centuries after Christ, the Roman woman became corrupt, immoral, and profligate; and while this was, of course, true for the man, in sexual indiscretions and divorce the female set the pace. In the first century the corruption was the vacillation of strong men and women, by the end of the fourth it was the waywardness of degenerates.

Throughout this period Christianity was slowly spreading within the Empire. In the beginning its converts were of the meek and downtrodden, but during the first part of the fourth century it was strong enough to gain the protection of the Emperor himself, Constantine The Great. During his reign paganism and Christianity were equally protected, with Christianity gaining the ascendance, more of which we will soon hear. After the sack of Rome by Alaric, paganism was never again a real factor. In the peoples' minds the gods of Rome had grown too weak to succor them from their misfortunes, and the Christian God offered a sedative for mortal woes in the promise of a hereafter.

It was a sorry lot of Romans and Greeks who, in the fifth century, became Christian converts in droves, understanding not its true principles but following its surface ceremonies with images, lights, incense, and parades which resembled the older pagan rituals. About all that can be said of these degraded converts is that they furnished a fodder in the later conversion of the conquering Germans which at least enabled Christianity to present a united front while hastily absorbing by the thousands these progressive semi-barbarians.

The influences of Christianity and corruption as a rule were antagonistic, but both worked against the structure of the Roman state, one replacing its ancient gods and the other sapping its moral strength. Christianity and Stoicism (discussed later) worked for the betterment of individual man, but they were antagonistic as to woman's rights. The views of the jurist dominated the law, and they gave legal equality to woman.

Education

No element influenced the great jurists in giving woman equality more than did woman's own capabilities, and a paramount factor in making her capable was education.

This started in earliest childhood with no distinction between the small boy and girl. Also of importance, each received equal care and tenderness, which was by no means the case in many societies. Young parents were taken to task by their elders for any shortcomings in the rearing of children. The Greek philosopher Favorinus of Athens and Rome was incensed at the young mothers of the second century who, mindful of the shape of their breasts, refused to nurse their children. As to this "outrage against nature" he asked, "Is it consistent to nourish with one's blood, in one's body, some unknown thing, and then to refuse to nourish it with one's milk, when one sees it alive, and when it is a human being?" Quintilian, the great educator and professor of the preceding century, advocated education from the cradle and in the home prior to the school years, and to this end urged a better home life. He decried that children grew up in luxury, heard improper language, saw mistresses and "male objects of affection," and learned things shameful to be told. "From such practices springs habit, and afterwards nature. The unfortunate children learn their vices before they know they are vices."

It can be assumed that young parents of the period were not quite as bad as their elders thought and, as parents today, concealed their shortcomings from their children as long as they could. Certainly there was real home education, toys in the shape of letters and numerals, spelling, reading aloud, grammar and arithmetic. Next came school with boys and girls attending the same classes and no difference in their training except for those things considered natural to one sex only, as girls learning to spin and boys to box. After the school years the education of the well-to-do young man and young lady continued, and the well-to-do included thousands of families. As brother and sister pursued their education at home under capable tutors, and as differences in sex influenced them, naturally their training followed their respective interests. Still the home in which the young man could learn of art and literature presented his sister with the same opportunity, and while he was being taught to speak in public she was learning what to discuss in the drawing room — from small talk to Greek philosophy.

The young woman was also schooled in many practical subjects, as politics, knew who was who in Rome and throughout the Empire, and understood that whom one knew is as important as what one knew. She was artfully trained to use her feminine charms to advantage, and also taught to run a household and look after a husband and children even before she married. As a woman, she would think as straight and reason as soundly as her brother, husband, and male associates; and she would take her place among other women who as a class would be the cultural and intellectual equal of men.

Yet there was one aspect of life for which this girl was not prepared, nor even sufficiently appraised. This was the moral freedom which she must soon encounter in the society. Before marriage she was sheltered and her activities cautiously guarded. Unlike Babylonian and Egyptian girls, she was permitted no intimacies of love or sex before or while in the process of obtaining a husband. When she married she was not only a virgin but had experienced no association nor courtship with her future husband, a preliminary considered needless and ill-advised. The Roman language had no word meaning "to court" or "to woo." This girl would have a formal engagement arranged by the respective parents, but she would see little of her fiancé. Naturally she heard talk of scandals and marital misconduct, but she was without practical understanding of their significance. After marriage and upon the ebbing of its initial ties, she would be vaulted into a different moral world with the strict parental restrictions of her girlhood replaced by unconcealed opportunities for indulgences condoned by an indifferent society. She would "enjoy" equal moral freedom with man as well as equal intellectual freedom and equal legal rights.

Individual Jurists and Their Thinking

Who were the great jurists to give this free, educated, and capable woman equal standing with man before the law and in the society? By what reasoning did they break with the tradition of her secondary status imbedded in Rome's social structure since its very beginning; by what process did they elevate her to legal equality, a position for woman without precedent in the laws of any land or time?

There was Julian, the judge, author of the *Perpetual Edict,* the first true code of practice, *c.* 130; Gaius, the jurist, author of the *Institutes* and other profound works between 130 and 180; Papinian, the counsellor, close personal friend of the Emperor Severus and influential during the early part of the third century; Ulpian, the counsellor, of the same period; Paulus, the practical jurist; and Modestinus, pupil of Ulpian, of about 250. Forerunners of these professional lawgivers were earlier clear legal thinkers, including Quintilian, whom we have mentioned;

Hortensius, the noted trial lawyer of the first century B. C.; and Cicero, the effective advocate of the first century B. C., known today to every educated boy and girl of the West because of the classic style of his orations.

It was Ulpian who said, "Justice is the constant and perpetual will to allot to every man his due," thus designating for all time the mental process by which the judge was to render justice — justice on an individual basis, to every man according to his particular due without consideration of outside influences. It was Papinian, "the illustrious," who forfeited his life because he bluntly declined to render a legal opinion demanded of him by the Emperor Caracalla *justifying* that Emperor's assassination of his brother who occupied the throne with him. It was Gaius who nullified for all practical purposes the male guardianship of woman's property, holding this legal theory no longer applicable since it had "no valid reason as foundation" and "seems rather specious than true," pointing out "as a matter of fact, women of mature age do manage their own affairs." It was the capability of woman to look after her affairs, the fact that she could and did look after them, which was material to Gaius; sex was not relevant to the issue.

These great jurists not only rendered realistic justice in individual cases but sought to advance the general welfare by sound legal principles. They were strongly influenced by the morality of the Stoic philosophy and from it came their modern-sounding pronouncements that a defendant is innocent until proven guilty, and that a defendant is entitled to the benefit of any reasonable doubt. This philosophy also held that by the natural law all men are equal, a revolutionary belief in an age when the society and the law recognized stations in life from emperor to slave, yet a belief which was to grow to legal fruition in later centuries. Stoicism also taught the elevation of woman and encouraged her full equality with man. Its concepts of fairness and justice to all combined with the practical and scientific reasoning of the professional jurists to advance Roman jurisprudence to its greatness.

To have a scientific legal system, the judges of the law must be allowed to determine what as a matter of fact is relevant and material to the conclusions they reach. "As a matter of fact" does not include as a matter of tradition, of religion, of public opinion, of anything except existing factual situations. It follows that god-given laws have no place in such a system. It may be true that, if a people are caused to believe the laws to which they are subject are of divine origin, they will more readily obey them, but the difficulty with such a theory is that laws emanating from above are not subject to alteration when conditions change. If the gods have decreed certain rules of conduct as proper and to be followed, that gives a sanction to those rules which continues after their value has ended.

Should women be inexperienced and incapable businesswise when the gods pronounce a set of laws, the wise ruler or priest through whom the laws are transmitted will see that the gods prohibit women from conducting business without proper safeguards to compensate for their lack of ability; yet when women do become able to "manage their own affairs" the then ruler or lawmaker cannot abrogate the old restraints against them, since the people have believed, perhaps for centuries, that the restraints have divine sanction. Thus the laws of a present period are determined by woman's position in an earlier period. Material facts existing in the present period, as woman's capability to handle her own property, are sidetracked on the theory that obeying the gods is required.

Divine law was foreign to the Roman mind. The Roman jurist especially recognized that laws are not static and cannot be allowed to come to rest in a progressing society, but must always conform to conditions as fast and as often as there are substantial changes. Gaius would have derided a view that the gods had made woman inferior to man and, therefore, his decrees should perpetuate this status. The question he determined was not how she was made or what she was meant to be, but what she actually was in his time and place. If the gods intended her to be inferior, she had no doubt gotten out of hand, but that was the concern of the gods, not something which a judge of existing facts could consider.

In addition to the power of the judge to determine what facts are material, a second essential element, in fact a *sine qua non,* of a scientific legal system is a judiciary distinct from the administration. The executive and legislative powers may be combined in one authority, be it emperor, oligarchy, representatives of the people, or otherwise, and still, if the judiciary is left to itself to decide cases, a legal system of a scientific nature will develop. There will be decisions to which litigants can look for precedents, a known procedure to follow, and a standardized application of rules to actual cases. There is no substitute for independent jurists in a legal system if science in law is desired.

Also, the jurists must be professionals and of limited numbers; they cannot be untrained large groups of citizens as in democratic Greece. The trial of Aspasia had fifteen hundred judges or jurors, and a hundred was not uncommon in a trial of average importance. When a person is exercising one-hundredth of the responsibility only, he is not especially motivated by his duty, and responsibility divided to that extent takes on a political complexion rather than a judicial one. Furthermore, the decision of a group of untrained judges in one trial is not precedent for what another group, or even the same group, will do in a later trial involving the same issues. No rule of law will have been laid down; everybody will have voted as he thought just (at best) and gone his way without concern over legal principles for future application. Justice may be done, but science will not be added to the law.

In Rome the policy of a limited number of highly trained professional jurists was strictly adhered to. They occupied a foremost position in the legal system long before Christ, and for centuries sponsored the scientific development of the law. This sponsorship was given a magnanimous blessing when Augustus (63 B. C. — A. D. 14) decreed that judges in civil cases should follow the written opinions of the jurisconsults and that these opinions carried his imperial authority. This gave the highest of earthly sanctions to the decisions of the jurists.

Later emperors wisely followed Augustus in this respect. Some designated particular jurists whose opinions would be law or on whom this *ius respondendi* would be conferred. Naturally such authority was sought by many, but it was reserved for the great and never bestowed as personal or political favor, not even by the worst of the emperors. There was something in the Roman, a faculty instilled from childhood, which gave him a respect for the law, a sense of its value to the individual and of its necessity to the state, a resoluteness that it should not be tainted by the corruption of man nor era.

The quality of those jurists whose opinions and works became law is shown by an imperial decree as late as 426, called the Law of Citations, which provided that only the works of Papinian, Paulus, Gaius, Ulpian, and Modestinus, and authors quoted by them should be followed. Thus Rome, which could hardly defend herself in the fifth century, clung to the justice of the Caesars: scientific and just law laid down by great professional lawgivers.

Gaius' *Institutes* was still the leading textbook for lawyers and law students. In truth he must be given more credit than any of the other second and third century jurists for the science in Roman law, because it was he who first took specific legal rules and generalized them into broad legal principles to form a system of laws for society. An example is his classification of legal rights in the *Institutes,* Book I, Section 8: "Every right which we exercise relates either to persons, or to things, or to actions." After observing literally thousands of man's legal rights, in his mind they fell first into these three main categories, then into various sub-classifications; and in this manner he classified virtually the whole body of rights into a coordinated framework. His approach and method brought to the law a scientific relationship between individual rules.

Gaius must also be given high credit for many of the specific rights gained by women. Two of the realms in which she made major gains were the economy and marriage and divorce.

Women's Occupations

Women have the most difficulty in obtaining full equality with men in the fields of gainful occupation and economic enterprise. Equal rights in marriage, divorce, education, citizenship, and other spheres of a personal nature have not been opposed with the concern and selfishness as have woman's rights which challenge man's economic control and security. Until recently in the West, including the United States, women endeavoring to earn money in the competitive fields (even to make a living for themselves and children) were thoroughly resented, not only by men but by other women who recognized the competition with their husbands. Also, these other women sensed another competition — that of the alert working woman being more attractive to men. Religion, motherhood, family, ostracism, snobbery, and social slights repeatedly were invoked to discourage the woman's desire to enter the business world.

During the second and third centuries Roman women overcame this attitude and engaged freely in all forms of work, occupations and businesses. They competed in the hundreds of retail trades and were admitted to membership in the guilds of those trades; they engaged in agriculture and owned estates and slaves; they participated in the professions and acquired standing in their work. Many were wealthy in their own right, their holdings extensive, and their enterprises required able agents and representatives. Other women were shopkeepers, innkeepers, vendors, barbers, hairdressers, and even charioteers. A few fought in the arena in mild or mock battle — precursors of the modern female wrestlers and matadors who display their skills in our own culture. Women practiced medicine, and tried their own cases in the courts. Wives assisted their husbands in all types of businesses, even in the administration of provinces and some held consular rank.

The only women looked down on for engaging in occupation were actresses, not because that field or any field *per se* was denied women, but because acting, if it could be called that, consisted primarily of lewd dancing and exhibitionism, accompanied by crude jokes typical of a modern master of ceremonies for a sideshow stripper. Immoral Rome found vulgarity extremely distasteful. At one period acting was so disreputable that laws were passed and enforced which prohibited senators and their children from marrying any woman who, or whose father or mother, was or had been in the theatre. This was not to discriminate against women but to guard the dignity of the senatorial station. In time the dancing improved, the laws were relaxed, then discarded – the senator regained equality with the plebeian in matters of the heart.

Marriage and Divorce

Marriage and divorce are always of prime importance and interest to woman, particularly in her role as mother. To the Roman jurist marriage was a civil contract between equal contracting parties. A ceremony was of no legal import. The relationship of husband and wife arose because a man and a woman agreed between themselves to become husband and wife, not because the state or the gods made them such. Both the contractual and the equality elements of marriage, as well as its romantic aspect, are found in Modestinus' concise definition: "Marriage is the union of a man and a woman and a partnership of all life; a mutual sharing of laws human and divine."

Since marriage was a contractual relationship, each party to the contract had to give his or her consent. This meant marriage could not lawfully be forced on anyone. Actually, this safeguard was of little practical advantage to the Roman girl because of her marriage at an early age. The legal age therefor was twelve, a customary age fourteen, and at nineteen the girl had about lost her opportunity to be carried across the threshold, the ceremony symbolizing the tradition that the husband possessed the wife. Courts were reluctant to dissolve a young girl's consummated marriage on her plea that she had not consented to it. They held that if she had been silent she had indicated her consent, and found other ways to validate the marriages of the society in which was imbedded the belief that parents could better select a spouse than could a child. Still, if the young bride established her protest to the marriage and the judge concluded she had actually been forced into it, he released her under the law, an escape denied to girls of earlier and later periods.

At all periods the Roman husband enjoyed the privilege of divorce, exercisable either at will or for certain causes broad enough to give him adequate practical latitude. Without examining the various grounds of divorce available to the husband for any particular period during the second and third centuries, whatever they were, the wife also possessed them. This followed as a matter of course in the reasoning of the jurists from the predicate that marriage was a contract between equal parties. If one could dissolve the contract for no reason or for a specific reason, so could the other. It was not that the jurists necessarily approved of divorce; it was the concept of contractual equality which caused them to permit the husband no advantage.

Not even adultery, that exclusive prerogative of the husband for ages, was treated any differently for the two equal parties. It was denied to both alike under the law and, therefore, a good cause for divorce by either. The equality was carried to the extent that if a husband had committed adultery, he was not heard to complain that his wife was also guilty, and vice versa. (This is the rule in most English-speaking jurisdictions today.) Adultery was always grave under Roman law as worded, and severe penalties were prescribed therefor. From a practical standpoint these penalties were unimportant during the period under discussion, adultery being too common to enforce them or to prosecute the guilty. It was a part of the times, routine more than Bacchanalian. There were affairs galore and wives as well as husbands had paramours and "slave-pets." In spite of its commonness, adultery was a lesser social evil than was divorce.

Women exercised their equal divorce rights merrily and apace, without restraint or embarrassment. Adultery may have been illegal and indiscreet, but divorce was not. Many a matron of the upper bracket would have half a dozen husbands within the period of her attractive years. The wife who had only one husband during her lifetime was considered so worthy that she was often put to rest with an inscription on her tombstone which recorded that she was the "woman of one man."

Generations of power, luxury and wealth had so undermined the morals of the Roman woman that there were no excesses nor immoralities in which she declined to indulge. She freely exercised her equal legal rights, but without concern that rights carry concomitant responsibilities. No excuse is made for the Roman man. He may have restrained himself in divorce more than the woman, but he was just as depraved. Thus Rome, still at the height of her power, had within her framework the cancer of destruction, a cancer eating at the basis of her society, the family and the home. Even the virginity of the sacred Vestals was for public consumption only, not for the Vestals.

Many marriages were without children because of the sterility of the husband or the wife, and often the husband was impotent from excesses in sex and drink. Barren marriages were a major problem of the Empire, and caused a constantly decreasing birth rate. The emperors and others were concerned but none could remedy the problem or lessen its causes. Augustus endeavored to reduce divorces by various laws, such as his decree requiring a more formal document of marriage dissolution, executed in the presence of seven adult citizens – which alone reflects how easy it was to terminate marriage.

In divorce Augustus set a poor example for the Empire. His first marriage, politically motivated, was to Antony's stepdaughter, but after a short time he divorced her and married Scribonia, herself twice divorced, who bore him Julia, his only child. Next Augustus, at twenty-five, decided he wanted the married Livia Drusilla, so he divorced Scribonia and forced Livia's husband, although Livia was pregnant, to divorce her, then married her (38 B. C.) after the birth of the child. The union was most fortunate. Livia was of the prominent Claudian family and gave Augustus powerful connections which he needed; and more important, she made him a good wife, a wise counsellor, and an empress in whom the public had great confidence. She gave him no heir, but one of her own sons, Tiberius, succeeded him to the throne. Augustus was one of Rome's strong emperors, and Livia, his equal, one of her strong empresses. As they matured they practiced the household virtues of their forefathers, led exemplary lives, set an example of domestic virtue, and did what they could to lessen the vices of the times.

Julia became the Empire's most sex-savored play girl, and so flagrant were her moral breaches that Augustus banished her. Her daughter, Julia Minor, followed in her mother's ways and was also banished. Next ordered into exile was Ovid,[1] the author of *Ars Amatoria (The Art of Love)*, a textbook in poetical form on the techniques of sex with advice as to the best methods for acquiring lovers and for seducing wives and husbands. But banishments served no moral purpose. Ovidian love had already spread to a receptive reading public and the boldness of the royal Julias continued to excite the pleasure-craving society. Augustus, always supported by Livia, issued numerous decrees designed to improve the morals of the Empire, but they also failed in their purpose. Even the strongest of Roman emperors could not legislate morals.

STOICISM

During the first four centuries after Christ the philosophy of Stoicism permeated the Empire's entire structure: social, legal, political, and religious. This philosophy, founded by Zeno of Citium and Athens near the end of the fourth century B. C., taught a materialistic reason. The soul existed in the body and was itself corporal, otherwise it could not have existence. This corporal soul was reason, mind, knowledge, ruling principle; and these qualities were the same as virtue. Therefore, virtue was corporal, and being corporal, could be obtained by effort, by practice and action; and worthy conduct and overt devotion to duty developed man's virtue or soul. The philosophy addressed itself to the individual; any man by effort could improve himself regardless of worldly rank or circumstances. Among its great disciples were the slave Epictetus and the emperor Marcus Aurelius, and both lived by its teachings. It was a philosophy of moral strength within the individual, and gave an equality to all mankind in the paramount realm of morals in that each person could develop his corporal virtue in disregard of conditions and environment.

Stoicism drew no distinction of sex. Worthy occupations and

good works would improve women as well as men. The Stoic Musonius Rufus of the first century concluded that "human tasks are open to all, and common both to men and women, and nothing is necessarily appointed exclusively for either." As to "virtue" — the mind or reason — he concluded that there is no difference in the nature of the sexes: "But whatever things have reference to virtue, these one may rightly affirm to be equally appropriate to both natures, since we say that virtues do not belong more to the one than to the other."

Though a different approach, this is of the same essence as Plato's equality for man and woman, yet he was not a Stoic and objected to the materialism of their philosophy which caused them to "drag everything down to the corporeal." Nevertheless, Plato and most of the Roman Stoics placed woman on a moral and mental plane with man.

This philosophy of elevation for the individual, regardless of sex or other classification, helped destroy the public attitude of woman's inferiority, even of the slave's deprivation of all rights. It taught morality in law and emphasized the intent and responsibility of the individual, whoever or whatever he was. While the philosophy elevated the thinking of the Roman world, it found few believers who were willing to practice its granite morality. The development of virtue within the individual by constant effort and daily practice was not easy for the Roman man or woman subject to the influences of power, intrigue, wealth, and passion.

Yet some were able to resist these influences by the application of Stoicism. One was Marcus Aurelius (121-180), who became Emperor in 161 after being trained from boyhood in this philosophy. He was the last of the great pagan Stoic philosophers and his fame rests more on the love and regard he held for his fellow man than on his being an Emperor of Rome. He was imbued with the dream of Plato's perfect society and endeavored to be the philosopher-prince of *The Republic,* to establish the truth of Plato's hypothesis that the state would prosper if her princes were philosophers or her philosophers were princes. He believed with the other Stoics that there was a spirit in man, and counselled: "Look within." In his age of many evils he wrote, "The reason which governs (the universe) has in itself no cause for doing evil, for it has no malice, nor does it do evil to anything, nor is anything harmed by it. But all things are made and perfected according to this reason." There was no vengence in this reason – no eye for an eye: "The best way of avenging thyself is not to become like (the wrongdoer)." Marcus Aurelius emphasized in his writing and exemplified by his life the virtue of doing one's duty and of not being concerned or troubled with other things, "for they are either things without life, or things without reason, or things that have rambled and know not the way."

To his mother he gave credit for the godliness in him. He set up an endowment for young girls, prohibited the bathing together of the sexes, disdained to give credence to the rumors about his wife, and did what he could to improve the morality of woman. But this noblest of all Roman emperors was helpless to check by law and decrees the corruption which had spread through the life blood of the Empire. He could only set an example for the people. Not even the most worthy of Roman emperors could legislate morals.

SUMMARY

To correlate the four factors affecting women during the four centuries after Christ:

Stoicism, Christianity and the law allied against corruption, but their opposition was of theory, and corruption prevailed. The laws against offenses involving moral turpitude continued on the books as strong as ever, but they were not enforced. The Stoic morality of self-discipline and self-reliance was too lofty, cold and exacting for the average person. Christianity's appeal of divine aid for all was not thought to be needed until near the end of the age – not so long as the gods of Rome were strong.

Stoicism and the law supported woman's legal equality, which also prevailed. On the other hand, Stoicism offered a corporal soul which made shallow the morality of the pagan religion of the state. This cleared the way for Christianity's spiritual soul and the Old Testament theory of woman's inferiority, which would prevail in later centuries.

Corruption dealt the death blow to woman's equality. Genesis and the views of the Hebrew nomads *per se* were not alone sufficient to take from her the legal position she had gained by sound juristic reasoning predicated upon her own capabilities, but Christian and pagan alike blamed her for the lessening of the family ties, the low birth rate, the sexual freedom, the constant divorces, and the ills of the times. Swept with corruption's current she had misused her legal privileges, even in the eyes of the man who joined in her moral breaches. All that was needed to drag her from her pedestal was a religious belief confirming that she, this Eve of Eden, was responsible for the sins of mankind.

---

[1] The middle-aged Ovid and Julia Minor were lovers, and this may have entered into his banishment. He was sent to Tomis (modern Constanta) on the Black Sea, and she to the small island of Trimerus in the Adriatic, both in 8 A. D.

EARLY CHRISTIANITY

Distant Desert Drums — Jesus, Paul, and Peter — The Early Church: Tertullian - Saint Augustine. The Political Ascendency of Christianity

On leaving the worldly empires of Babylonia, Egypt, Israel, Athens and Rome for the spiritual empire of Christianity, and before following the Old Testament theories of woman's inferiority as they permeated the West after Christ, we will recall: In the Mesopotamian (Sumerian and Babylonian) and in the Egyptian civilizations during the first part of the second millennium B. C., woman occupied an elevated station, though not an equal station with man. The background of her station in each land was two millennia of social progress. The Hebrew woman, once her tribes settled in Canaan, was rapidly uplifted as the society advanced for three centuries. With one millennium of progress by Rome — the first great truly Western empire — woman gained full equality. Clearly, a society's habitancy within a defined area over an extended period is essential to progress, and in turn progress is the paramount influence in woman's advancement.

An exception to this rule, so positively stated in the first chapter, is Greece of the Golden Age. I will not say the exception proves the rule since that cliché does not indicate the extent to which the rule is impaired by the exception or the value of what is left. Hence Greece is not invoked to support my theory that society's forward momentum is woman's great advocate. However, I do say that the theory was appurtenant to the Golden Age; there were simply other overriding forces which smothered the gains woman should have made in Greece as its flame of knowledge lighted the Mediterranean world. Her expected progress could not prevail against those forces — forces so potent that they separated women into two classes: the confined caretakers of citizen children and the pliable peddlers of pleasure.

Still the theory manifested itself as was evidenced by the intellectual freedom of the courtesan and the social and political philosophy of Plato, and by such incidences as Aspasia's public urging of the emancipation of all women, courtesan and wife alike. Though the advancement of the society was not without effect in woman's improvement, plaintive in a way were the products: the dream of a man who knew his utopia could be achieved if only there were a people with the fortitude to tread the long and arduous route of moral training which he coursed; the forfeit of the courtesan's body for her free association during her appealing years with the exalted male. Yet the dream has stirred the imagination of all ages which have followed, and woman ever since has known she was man's intellectual equal.

We must also recall, before proceeding with Christianity, that this religion was not born in a land and era of beliefs in woman's elevation, nor in a civilization as it was intellectually advancing — in that of neither Mesopotamia, nor Egypt, nor Israel, nor Greece, nor Rome. It did not arise from the plentiful plains of the Tigris and the Euphrates, nor of the Nile, nor from the Promised Land, nor from the shores of the Mediterranean; but from the desolate desert of Abraham and Moses. There the ancient goddesses of fertility of other lands had succored not nature, nor civilization, nor woman, nor homelife. There, instead, the bleached bones of beast and man along the arid trails marked the harshness of existence. These omens of death and desolation — not temples to fertility — symbolized the life of weary woman as she served her man and bore his children and followed him to the next waterhole.

This desert's laws for society as recorded in the Old Testament, of divine revelation, were bedrocks of Christianity. Yet Jesus taught social precepts of a different order. It was not he but his disciples and followers who for centuries beat the distant desert drums of woman's inferiority.

JESUS, PAUL, AND PETER

Jesus is significant in the development of woman's status in the West. Yet he did not specifically preach either her equal rights and immediate elevation or her unequal rights and traditional subjugation. It has been argued that his failure affirmatively to advocate removal of woman's disabilities was a tacit acceptance of her existing inferiority, and on the other hand, that his failure overtly to sanction her lower position was a purposeful avoidance so as not to hinder her advancement when the time therefor arrived. Both arguments assume — since Jesus never said in so many words that he did or did not favor woman's equality — that his record is negative on the subject, and various authorities positively take this position.

They overlook the full significance of numerous instances recorded in the New Testament which plainly reflect Jesus' firm belief in woman's broad equality. His consistent attitude towards individual women was of fairness, understanding, and sympathy; and perhaps no occurrence illustrates this better than the following:

> And the scribes and Pharisees brought unto him a woman taken in adultery; and when they had set her in the midst, they said unto him, Master, this woman was taken in adultery, in the very act. Now Moses in the law commanded us, that such should be stoned: but what sayest thou? . . . He . . . said unto them, He that is without sin among you, let him first cast a stone at her . . . And they which heard it, being convicted by

their own conscience, went out one by one, beginning at the eldest, even unto the last . . . When Jesus . . . saw none but the woman, he said unto her, Woman, where are thine accusers? hath no man condemned thee? She said, No man, Lord. And Jesus said unto her, Neither do I condemn thee: go, and sin no more. (John 8:3-11)

This is certainly not a condoning of man's ancient privilege of adultery which was denied to woman, but an attitude of tolerance and fairness to a particular woman in the application of the law: if the man is himself guilty he must not cast a stone at the guilty woman. And what stronger evidence can there be of a belief in equality in marriage than the following pronouncements that husband and wife are "but one flesh" and that the husband should be denied the prerogative — again an ancient one — to put aside his wife at will?

And the Pharisees came to him, and asked him, Is it lawful for a man to put away his wife? tempting him. And he answered and said unto them, What did Moses command you? And they said, Moses suffered to write a bill of divorcement, and to put her away. And Jesus answered and said unto them, For the hardness of your heart he wrote you this precept. But from the beginning of creation God made them male and female. For this cause shall a man leave his father and mother, and cleave to his wife; and they twain shall be one flesh: so then they are no more twain, but one flesh. What therefore God hath joined together, let not man put asunder. (Mark 10:2-9)

For Jesus to go contrary to a law which God had revealed to Moses, especially a social law embosomed in Hebrew custom as was the husband's right of divorce, and also for him to take the side of woman, was a drastic step requiring resolute moral courage — something Jesus possessed and unfalteringly exercised in matters of belief, though it brought him death.

Jesus' pronouncements on women did not better her social and legal position while Christianity grew for four centuries within the Roman Empire and thereafter until modern times dominated Western laws relating to woman. The pronouncements which were to prevail were those of Jesus' contemporary apostles; they were the link between the Old Testament and the Early Church. They thought of woman not as man's equal, particularly in marriage, but as his lowly inferior and subject to his command and complete control. Their views were of the East. This was to be expected as most of the apostles were uneducated and provincial – but not the influential Saul, the Pharisee, later called Paul. Nevertheless, he believed with the others in woman's inferiority. In view of his lasting control over Christian beliefs of all ages, including the indelible effect of his views on woman, an understanding of Paul is essential.

He was born, reared, and educated a Jew and was strictly taught in Jewish law, though in later years he considered the revered Torah as secondary to faith in Christ. Regardless of his orthodox training, many of Paul's ideas came from Greek literature with which he was fairly familiar. He was not particularly versed in religious philosophy, yet was the first great Christian theologian. He grew up at Tarsus at a time when it was one of the most cosmopolitan cities of the world. On its wharves and in its public places there mingled Occidental and Oriental, Jew and Gentile, Greek, Roman and Egyptian. Its "amalgamated society" led to "a higher plane of thought and action," and it was a foremost center of Stoicism. While there is little evidence in Paul's writings to indicate he was influenced by this philosophy – and certainly he was not by its attitude of equality for women – it does appear that he absorbed much of the broader thinking of Tarsus.

Paul was of an independent nature. He was "free born," the son of a Roman citizen, and a Roman citizen himself. His character and ideals were positive and none had a neutral reaction towards him. To the Christians he was second only to Jesus; to his enemies "a pestilent fellow, and a mover of sedition among all the Jews throughout the world, and a ringleader of the sect of the Nazarenes." (Acts 24:6)

Inherent in him was the rare ability to realize when he was in error and, thereupon, to change his course. He expressed himself positively as he saw things at the time, and if he later reversed his thinking, he spoke his new opinions just as positively. Emerson could have had Paul in mind when he said: "Else if you would be a man, speak what you think to-day in words as hard as cannon balls, and to-morrow speak what to-morrow thinks in hard words again, though it contradict everything you said to-day." Paul's very nature was such that he was courageous and energetic in spreading Christianity. It is little wonder that this man became, exclusive of the Master, the foremost Christian, and that Christians of all ages took to heart the beliefs he espoused, both religious and social, and gave them literal application.

His views on woman were dogmatic, and never were they tempered by the growing attitude of her equality within the Roman Empire. He has been quoted on woman's place in life from thousands of pulpits and in thousands of writings, as to be expected from his standing in Christianity. He said that she should be subject to her father or husband in all things, and that the subjection should be complete. She was permitted to learn, but her instructions were to come from the male members of her family. She was not to teach nor to have authority over man. She was to leave all business and public affairs to her husband, if married; if not, to her father or other male relatives. She was not to express opinions and was to keep quiet except in her home or with other women. To Timothy, Paul wrote:

> Let the woman learn in silence with all subjection. But I suffer not a woman to teach, nor to usurp authority over man, but to be in silence. (I Timothy 2:11-12)

A father who decreed his daughter should not marry "doeth better" than one who permitted her to marry. (I Corinthians 7:37-38). To the Corinthians, Paul wrote:

> There is a difference also between a wife and a virgin. The unmarried woman careth for the things of the Lord, that she may be holy both in body and in spirit: but she that is married careth for the things of the world, how she may please her husband. (I Corinthians 7:34)

To all women he denied their cherished desire for attractive dress and ornament:

> I will therefore . . . that women adorn themselves in modest apparel, with shamefacedness and sobriety; not with broided hair, or gold, or pearls, or costly array; but (which becometh women professing godliness) with good works. (I Timothy 2:8-10)

In Paul's thinking there were at least two good reasons supporting woman's inferiority, both based on Genesis. God had created man first, woman second; therefore woman was second to man – it was as simple as that. Also the serpent had deceived Eve, but not Adam; therefore, Eve was to blame for the Original Sin. Paul put it thus:

> For Adam was first formed, then Eve. And Adam was not deceived, but the woman being deceived was in the transgression. Notwithstanding she shall be saved in childbearing, if they continue in faith and charity and holiness with sobriety. (I Timothy 2:13-15)

These same reasons, that Adam came first and that Eve was to blame for the fall of mankind, plus Eve's being made from Adam's rib, were eagerly invoked by churchmen after Paul to relegate woman to inferiority. The rib theory made an especially strong case against her. How could something created from one of man's ribs be his equal? It was actually taken for granted by both theologians and medical practitioners that men had one less rib than women, until some layman had the wit to count the ribs of both a male and a female skeleton. At any rate, the Christian man had little difficulty in concluding that he occupied a higher level than woman, both on earth and in the eyes of God; and as to the husband's being over the wife, this was settled by the specific pronouncements of God himself that Adam should rule over Eve (quoted in the Garden of Eden episode).

The views of Paul were also the views of Peter. Peter was strong, and was the outstanding disciple of Jesus during the period of Jesus' ministry. Though he did not affect later generations as Paul affected them, his influence was great and his statements on women were freely quoted. He taught that wives should "be in subjection" to their husbands, pointed out that "Sara obeyed Abraham calling him lord," referred to woman as the "weaker vessel," and generally urged her inferiority.

Paul, Peter, and other contemporaries of Jesus, by sanctioning the traditionally lower status of woman among the Jews of their time, furnished support for woman's secondary position to man even into our own century.

THE EARLY CHURCH

The Early Church wholeheartedly adopted the apostolic theory of woman's inferiority and expounded and enlarged it with the zeal of a growing religion.

> The naked back of woman felt the sting in the Christian Church, even more so than before, of five lashes, and their names were Genesis, Exodus, Leviticus, Numbers and Deuteronomy.[1]

In its beginning the church could only preach the social rules laid down in the five books of Moses and trust that its converts would follow them — Rome made the laws. In time the church would be the lawmaker in the realms most affecting women, and when that day arrived the Old Testament would dominate woman's life to an extent never anticipated, not even by Paul, and never intended, not even by Moses.

(In this and the following chapter we shall see the conversion of the Roman Empire to Christianity, and it should here be said that the Christian background of the Old Testament was no worse from the standpoint of woman's status than would have been any other religion which the Roman world might have adopted. That world was soon to require a replacement of its outmoded gods, and any culture to which it could turn for a new religion would have held woman in low esteem. Gone were the civilizations of Babylon and Egypt when women were fast approaching equality; Greece had nothing to offer, and there existed nowhere another belief which spiritually could compare with Christianity or which would have been acceptable to the sensitivity and intellectuality of Rome.)

The attitude of the Early Church on woman is exemplified by two of its most powerful writers, Tertullian, of the second and third centuries, and St. Augustine, of the fourth and fifth. They are chosen since Augustine is ranked first, Tertullian second, among the early great fathers.

Tertullian (*c.* 155 – *c.* 222)

Tertullian was the first of the profound writers of the Early Church and is considered the founder of Christian Latin literature. He was born at Carthage, North Africa, of good family, and received an excellent education. He quickly became an authority on history and was also versed in the works of the Greek philosophers. Plato was his favorite. In his late thirties he went to Rome where he became a Christian and seven years later he was an established authority on the Bible. His memory is said to have been prodigious, especially for historical and biblical dates and incidents. He returned to Carthage in 197, and wrote extensively on Christian theology. He strongly opposed the Catholic Church's becoming a political organization, and finally broke with it on that account.

As to woman's place in life, he wholeheartedly accepted the views of the apostles and of the Old Testament. He advocated the unquestioned authority of the husband over the wife, denounced the entering by women into any fields considered as belonging to men, objected to divorce, and called second marriages a species of prostitution, on the fallacious premise that this was no different than having two wives at the same time. He hammered continually on woman's inferiority to man. Not satisfied with strongly expressing his views on the broader controversies of his time as to woman's proper status, he busied himself with such things as her clothing, and dictated that unmarried girls, wives, and widows alike should dress simply and uncolorfully so as not to arouse the desires of men. As to the lack of color, he drew an analogy to the Creator of nature, and claimed that since God had not made red or green sheep or other animals, women should not affect these colors. Also, the "natural grace" of women must be concealed as it is dangerous to the beholder's eyes.

In a writing addressed to his wife, he expressed satisfaction that on the day of resurrection there would be "no resumption of voluptuous disgrace" between them. He considered woman as not having the ability to understand religion and of such a make-up that "it brings shame to reflect on what nature she is." He blamed Eve and exonerated man for the sins of the world and considered Eve's iniquity as having been passed on to all women. To those of his day he said:

> Do you not know that each one of you is an Eve? The sentence of God on this sex of yours lives in this age: the guilt must of necessity live too. You are the devil's gateway; you are the unsealer of that forbidden tree; you are the first deserter of the divine law; you are she who persuaded him (Adam) whom the devil was not valiant enough to attack. You destroyed so easily God's image, man. On account of your desert, that is, death, even the Son of God had to die.

To prevent women's attendance at any public event was of particular concern to Tertullian and contemporary church fathers. Even mixed private affairs were regarded with suspicion since men who attended them drank wine, and wine strengthened the evilness of their thoughts on seeing the opposite sex. Women were not to attend marriage feasts because marriage suggested sex and they might hear improper comments or remarks. They could be away from home to attend church or to engage in acts of mercy and charity, but while on the streets they should be veiled and while in church covered as a sign of their subjection. They were never to be on the streets out of curiosity, as that would add idleness to the unbecoming conduct of appearing in public.

Tertullian lent his influence and his abilities as a writer and thinker to any idea for woman's restriction and subjection. Actually, as he grew older, he became abnormal on the subject, often irrational, as is indicated by his quoted views. It must be said in his favor, however, that he was justified in opposing the constantly increasing divorce rate and decreasing birth rate in the Empire, and he succinctly stated the apprehension of many, regardless of their attitude on woman, when he wrote, "Divorce is now looked upon as the sole fruit of marriage."

Tertullian's age was the period of the great jurists, thus while the Christian woman was kept silent and off the streets other women of the Empire enjoyed full freedom in their private and public lives. The views of the church of this age, dominated by Tertullian, had little effect on Roman law, religion and society, as Christianity was not yet that strong. Still it was effective among its converts and was firmly establishing itself within the Empire. As Christianity spread, the malediction against women of its foremost authority swayed more and more converts who relied on his understanding of scriptural intent.

We have in Tertullian the twisted views of a misogynist, and, as we shall see next, in Augustine the confused thinking on sex of a reformed indulger, with both men fated to disserve woman through the medium of religion, though each was of learning and intellect and had within him the touch of greatness.

Saint Augustine (Aurelius Augustinus, 354-430)

St. Augustine was born of Roman descent at Tagaste, a small town in Numidia, North Africa. His mother Monnica was a Christian at the time of his birth; his pleasure-loving father was not, but became one before he died. St. Augustine was not reared or educated a Christian, although he was made a catechuman as a child and his mother acquainted him with the principles of Christianity. He received his higher education at Carthage and was a good student. He was influenced by Plato and referred to him as a demigod. At Carthage he joined the Manichaeans, a sect which held evil to be as original and eternal as good,[2] and which believed its founder, Manes, had given the world higher and better precepts of truth than those of Christ.

After leaving college St. Augustine taught rhetoric at Carthage and Tagaste. By his late twenties he was entertaining serious doubts as to Manichaeism, was uncertain as to his future, and decided to go to Italy. He went to Rome first, then in about a year (384) to Milan. There he was joined by his then widowed mother who proceeded to take her 31-year-old son under her wing. Soon St. Augustine was learning more of Christianity and in about two years (387) was baptized. Monnica, because of her influence in her son's conversion, and because of her own exemplary and good life, is among the venerated women of the church.

On accepting Christianity, St. Augustine quit gainful work and devoted himself to the study of his new religion and to writing, particularly against his former heretic sect of Manichaeism. It was during this period that he began to acquire a reputation in the field of theology. Next he decided to return to his birthplace with his mother and some friends, all of whom desired to retire to a large extent from the ways of the world and devote themselves to religious meditation and learning. Monnica died en route, but happy with her son's conversion and especially with his plans to lead a dedicated Christian life.

After about three years of seclusion at Tagaste, St. Augustine was drafted for the priesthood at Hippo, a nearby seaport of about forty thousand population. Soon he was named Bishop of Hippo. This meant he could not leave as bishops were not transferable in Africa at the time; so he lived there the rest of his life, and became famous for his prolific and creative writings on Christianity, theology, and philosophy. He possessed keen powers of observation, had a scientific approach towards good and evil, and realistically recognized the wholesome and unwholesome influences of his time. He understood the temptations of life and the difficulties of the individual in resisting the many unsavory customs of the age.

> Thou torrent of human custom! Who shall stand against thee? how long shalt thou not be dried up? how long roll the sons of Eve into that huge and hideous ocean, which even they scarcely overpass who climb the cross?

His understanding, moral strength, and fame grew by the day.

The views on woman of this famous man were impressed on the West for centuries, and still linger. He was by far the most influential writer of the Early Church. To understand how he regarded woman after he became the great Bishop of Hippo, we must know more of his earlier restless life and relations with women. In his youth St. Augustine was fond of the opposite sex and joined his classmates at Carthage in the usual indulgences. During his late teens he sincerely loved and lived with a girl who bore him a son. Such occurrences were not uncommon nor regarded as particularly indiscreet; and his young mistress, of good character, exercised a wholesome influence over St. Augustine by reining his former promiscuousness. When he went to Italy he took her and their son. Monnica wanted to go with them but, while she was praying in a seaside chapel, St. Augustine purposefully sailed without her.

When Monnica later arrived at Milan she insisted that marriage to some girl of proper standing was the only course for her son, and soon she had made all necessary arrangements. As a result, St. Augustine's devoted companion of many years was sent back to Africa. Her despondency was such that she immediately entered a religious community. St. Augustine also was emotionally disturbed over the separation. The ten-year-old girl who was to be his wife was considered too young to marry, so while waiting for her to reach a suitable age between twelve and fourteen, he took another mistress to console him for the loss of the former one. His disturbance subsided. He uttered a prayer at this period which revealed his ambivalent attitude toward women and religion: "Give me chastity, but not yet." He was still not ready to follow the advice his mother had given him as a young man "in private with great anxiety . . . not to commit fornication; but especially never to defile another man's wife." This, at the time, he considered "womanish advices" which he would "blush to obey."

Nevertheless, soon after becoming a Christian, St. Augustine endeavored to lead a pious and productive life, and as said, he left Italy to further that purpose. As a result, his prospective marriage never took place. Perhaps Monnica had planned it that way, fearing a wife would be a hindrance to his religious work and intentionally arranging a marriage which might never occur, but it takes some reading between the lines in St. Augustine's later works to conclude this. At any rate, Monnica not only converted her son to Christianity but initiated his future greatness in that religion without distraction from wife or mistress. About a year after St. Augustine's return to Africa his son died, thus he was freed of all family responsibility. The period of celibacy which he and his friends spent at Tagaste was the founding (388) of the Augustinian monastic order, the oldest of its kind in the West.

Monnica and the Bible had created in St. Augustine an attitude that natural sexual desire was contrary to the spiritual element in man. As he grew older he developed a fixation of guilt because of his conduct as a youth, and in his thinking there raged within man a major conflict, nature versus Godliness. Woman exemplified evil nature — she was a constant temptress of the flesh. Besides, a woman — Monnica — had run his life. Not that he admitted his resentment of this, but it is evident in his writings. As bishop he conceded the great worth of Monnica's advice regarding sex given him as a young man, but he attributed this valued lesson as having actually come *from* God, merely *through* his mother.

Also he gave God full credit, with none to Monnica, for his conversion in Italy, writing that in his garden one day when he was wishing for the end of his "uncleanness" he heard a child from a neighboring house chanting, "Take up and read; Take up and read." He interpreted this as a command from God to read from the volume of St. Paul which he had recently acquired, so he went directly into the house, picked up the book, opened it and read the first passage on which his eyes fell:

> Not in rioting and drunkenness, not in chambering and wantonness, not in strife and envying; but put ye on the Lord Jesus Christ, and make not provision for the flesh. (Romans 13:13-14)

As to the reading of this message, St. Augustine later said:

"No further would I read; nor need I: for instantly at the end of this sentence, by a light as it were of serenity infused into my heart, all the darkness of doubt vanished away." This sudden seeing of the light by St. Augustine, rather than his gradual conversion by the methodical efforts of Monnica, is not borne out by later actions on his part. Nevertheless, he always preferred to regard his conversion as a single dramatic event with conflict tearing his soul. The occurrence became known to the faithful as the Garden Scene, and was said by St. Augustine to have been such that thereafter he "sought neither wife, nor any hope of this world." He immediately reported what had happened to his mother, and later wrote that she rejoiced for she perceived God had given her more for her son "than she was wont to beg by her pitiful and most sorrowful groanings."

To St. Augustine concupiscence was the Original Sin with Eve primarily at fault, but salvation was available through the Virgin Mary since she conceived without sin. Most men and women would be lost because this original sexual lust was inherent in every person and only a few could overcome it. St. Augustine was the first to extend the fabrication of Original Sin to celibates, virgins, and babies. He regarded marriage in the nature of a necessary evil and considered celibacy preferable (as did Monnica). He quoted with approval, "It is good for a man not to touch a woman," (I Cor. 7:1) and "He that is unmarried thinketh of the things of the Lord, how he may please the Lord; but he that is married careth for the things of this world, how he may please his wife." (I Cor. 7:32-33)

If marriage was entered into, the wife, as admonished by Paul, must obey the husband and be without authority. Based on this, St. Augustine concluded woman was not made in God's image as was man.

> How can it be said of a woman that she is in the image of God when it is evident that she is subject to the rule of her husband and has no authority.

Because Paul said a wife should be ruled by her husband and be without any authority, St. Augustine considered that way of married life as ordained by God. From this premise and others drawn from the Bible, he reached various absurd conclusions regarding women, one of which was that wives should be in the nature of bond servants to their husbands — or rather to their "lords":

> That from the time they heard the marriage writings read to them, they should account them as indentures, whereby they were made servants; and so, remembering their conditions, ought not to set themselves up against their lords.

He praised the woman, who, scathed by an angry husband, would not at the time "give an account of her actions" but would wait until the husband "was smoothed and tranquil, and in a temper to receive it." He preached that women should not dress so as to display any feminine charms, and as for nuns he provided they should bathe only once a month except in cases of an extreme emergency. Daily baths had been the practice in the Roman Empire for centuries and other than the Egyptians, the Romans were the cleanest of all people until modern times. The restriction on nuns' bathing was to make them less attractive to men. So we see a great intellect engaged in trifles and concurring in, not opposing, the Old Testament customs assigning to woman a lowly position in life.

> Thou torrent of human custom! Who shall stand against thee? . . . how long roll the Sons of Eve into that huge and hideous ocean?

St. Augustine was one man who possessed qualities which should have enabled him to determine woman's proper place in life and society. To an extent he possessed the scientific traits of a Darwin, the analytical observatory powers of an Aristotle, and the perseverance of a Goodrich. He was never a woman hater as Tertullian became, always enjoyed writing of his virile youth, and did not think of woman as something to abhor, only to resist. While in most things he had an instinctive understanding of natural causes and effects, the struggle of flesh versus spirit, always in his mind, prevented him from seeing woman as she is. Though this Augustinean struggle has largely been abandoned in modern thinking, its ugly corpse still casts its shadow over woman in myriad misunderstandings and inhibitions on sex.

St. Augustine's brilliance was devoted primarily to the spiritual — with deliberate restraint of his scientific inclinations — and he became the leading authority on predestination, irresistible grace, final perserverance, and other theological complexities. The theologian, mathematician, and poet in him combined to describe God as a circle whose center is everywhere and circumference nowhere. His practical nature caused him to realize the need of his decadent age for a strong secular moral power — as well as a strong spiritual influence — hence he espoused the theory of Church supremacy over the state, a theory of later potent effect as we shall see under Canon Law. His religious and moral philosophy dominated church thought for a thousand years, and helped to shackle woman to her inferior status throughout the Middle Ages and to retard her advancement well into the Modern Age. St. Augustine is the church's great son.

He died at the age of seventy-six while the Vandals were laying seige to Hippo, declining to flee at their approach and urging that the city — his city — be defended to the last man. St. Augustine had lived to see the fall of Rome and to see Christianity become the dominant religion of her once great Empire, dominant not only in the spiritual realm but in the political as well. To follow Christianity's political ascendency within the Empire we turn back a century.

POLITICAL ASCENDENCY OF CHRISTIANITY

Constantine The Great (*c.* 288-337)

During the fourth century the Roman world was in the process of adopting Christianity. This new force was now more actuating than the belief in the gods of Rome; was stronger than the determination of the influential conservatives to maintain the established order. Christianity's becoming the religion of the Roman Empire was called by Freeman "the miracle of history." From a political standpoint the groundwork for this "miracle" was laid when the capable and diplomatic Constantine became Emperor in 312 and when in the following year he and Licinius, meeting at Milan to coordinate the fruits of their victories, issued their famous *Edict of Milan* granting tolerance to all religions, especially to the Christians. Both wanted their support.

Constantine at this period took no religion seriously, and certainly not the pagan philosophy of the state religion. The Christians had interested him long before he became Emperor and as he was steadily moving toward that highest of worldly goals. He had discerned that the believers in Christ were of a higher moral standard than the average citizen, had observed that many of them would endure persecution for their beliefs, and he assigned a pragmatic value to the quality which made them devoted to their cause. Such men made good allies and loyal soldiers. He treated the Christians with fairness and respect before becoming Emperor, protected them afterwards, and they were on his side. He further endeared himself to them when, after the *Edict of Milan,* he took a solemn oath that, before his victories which made him Emperor, he had witnessed a fiery cross in the noonday sky bearing the inscription "By this conquer."[3]

At Rome, Constantine was installed as Chief Pontiff of Jupiter, the head of the state religion. His statements as to his personal religious views were nebulous and non-committal, but Christian and pagan alike seemed satisfied. Constantine was determined that both should live together at peace within the Empire; and this they did, *with his supervision.* There was continual antagonism between the two religions and in addition the Christians constantly quarreled among themselves. Various sects had already developed; the Christians who had endured persecution were critical of those who had welched; and mushrooming dogmas bred bickering everywhere. Regardless, Constantine was equal to the task of quieting the differences between the Christians themselves, and between them and the worshippers of the deities of Rome. He knew he must support both Christianity and the state religion, that if he took one side to the extent of overtly opposing the other, the Empire would be in an uproar with civil war in the offing.

It is a credit to his sagacity and diplomacy that no serious trouble developed and that he controlled both Christian and pagan during the world's greatest religious transition period. He is unexcelled in history as a religious and political mediator. Later civilizations were to war over spiritual beliefs and later Christians were to torture, mutilate, kill and burn other Christians because of church dogma; but under Constantine all were at peace and secure regardless of creed or fundamental religious differences.

When Constantine's showdown came in 324 with Licinius (now his opponent and the last one who still had an army, and who for some time had considered it politically expedient to persecute the Christians in spite of the *Edict of Milan)*, Christian, pagan, barbarian, and slave fought with like enthusiasm under the banner of the popular Constantine. Most of the captains and officers were pagan, but the watchword was "God our Savior." When his legions swept the superior numbers of Licinius from the field at Adrianople and again defeated him at Chrysopolis, Constantine was the undisputed master of the East as well as of the West; and the Christians had earned a secure place throughout the vast Empire.

Constantine was by now thoroughly impressed with Christianity. Upon his initiation (324) of the extensive layout of his future capital, located in the East and named Constantinople after him, he let it be known he would proceed until the "invisible God" saw proper to stop him, and gave out other statements to obtain the support of the Christians for his great project. This imperial attitude surrounding the birth of the new capital of the Empire presaged the approaching political doom of paganism, although its rites, as well as those of the Christian Church, were a part of the impressive ceremony for the dedication of the magnificent city. Constantine continued as head of the ailing state religion but leaned more and more toward Christianity.

About this time Constantine realized the seriousness of a dispute among the Christians over a belief which Arius, a priest of Baucalis, Egypt, had been preaching for approximately six years. Arius took the position that Christ was not of the same eternity and substance as God. He argued that if Christ was God's son, Christ had to have been created at a period after God and therefore during the existence of time; and further argued that if Christ was created he could not have come from an existing substance as that would not be a creation; therefore Christ was neither coeternal nor consubstantial with God and was of a spiritual order less than God. He further postulated that the Holy Ghost (now called the Holy Spirit which better conveys the concept of this deity) was less than Christ. Bishop Alexander strongly opposed these views, considering them polytheistic and contrary to the interests of the church. He persuaded the Egyptian bishops to remove Arius as priest, but many of them actually believed as Arius did, and his views continued to spread.

Constantine was concerned, not so much with who was right but with the threat to the unity of the church, believing a disruption would be bad for both himself and the Empire. To get the dispute decided and ended, Constantine called a council of all bishops throughout the Empire to meet in 325 at Nicaea, expenses paid for those attending. Present were 318 bishops and many other clergy and interested spectators. Constantine presided, listened patiently to the deliberations and participated only when he thought necessary.

The council decided that God, Christ, and the Holy Ghost were of the same eternity and substance and that this Trinity was one God. Several bishops were unable to understand how there could be three different Gods in one God. The main argument to support this oneness was that reason and logic must not fashion the concept of the Trinity, that it was a matter of faith. Most of the bishops soon became convinced that Alexander was right, but seventeen stayed with Arius until very near the end, when all except one left him and signed a creed that God and Christ were of one essence. Constantine approved the creed, ordered Arius and the dissenting bishop exiled, and gave an elaborate feast for the others. In spite of the council's stand the dispute continued, especially in the East, but its seriousness from a political standpoint was removed and in time the council's action became the belief of all Christians. Perhaps the greatest paradox in religion was the presiding by the Chief Pontiff of Jupiter, the earthly representative of dozens of pagan gods and goddesses, over this first Christian ecumenical or universal conclave which decreed the existence of only one God.

The monotheism of Moses again had prevailed. Never since has it been in question. This one God was still the God of Moses, of the Old Testament, though as a Trinity he now reflected the humanitarian qualities of Jesus. Also, this God was still wholly masculine. He was not thought of as having any of the attributes especially imputable to woman; he had not absorbed the qualities of the Roman goddesses of fertility, beauty, and love. There had been no fusion of Christian and pagan beliefs, so often the case where two religions have existed in the same land.

In addition to removing the threat to the monotheistic character of the Christian God, the council augmented the standing of the church throughout the Empire due to the Emperor's attendance and participation. The church was also gaining influence with the Emperor, and to remove one of its complaints, Constantine revoked the decrees of Augustus encouraging marriage, providing for benefits for women with three or more legitimate children, and penalizing unmarried men. These laws discouraged celibacy.

Constantine died in 337, and just prior to his death was baptized a Christian. By the turn of the century, a relatively short time, most of the Roman world was converted to the new religion. Throughout the Empire the statues of the many gods (except for works of art) found their way to the lime kilns, the pagan emblems were replaced by the Cross, and the Vestal Virgins by the Christian Virgin. Freeman's "miracle of history" had come to pass. Or was it a miracle? There is evolution in religion as in philosophy, morals, science and other ideas, and during the fourth and fifth centuries the West had reached the stage when it could no longer believe that stars, earthen gods, and deified emperors controlled man's life, while the invisible God and the noble teachings of his Son appealed to hope and reason. The millennium-old Roman religion passed into mythology, the fate of most religions. The Western world's conversion from paganism to Christianity — the great transition in religion — had been accomplished without bloodshed, even without upheaval. History testifies that Constantine was a ruler deserving of the title "The Great."

Though the religion of Rome ran its course over fifteen centuries ago, Roman Law lives on. During the Middle or Dark Ages many of its basic precepts became a part of the secular Canon Law, and when Canon Law ran its course, it bequeathed these precepts to the Modern Age. Among them was not the concept of woman's equality as laid down by the great jurists. This concept disappeared early during the retrogressing Dark Ages. Thus the regaining by woman of substantial legal equality within the twentieth century is not traceable to Roman Law, neither is the twentieth century high regard for womanly attributes traceable to Roman paganism. As Canon Law seared on the Dark Ages the Old Testament brand of woman's inferiority, it severed any link between the present and Rome in the evolution of woman's status, and became the link between the present and the Early Church, the apostles, and the Mosaic Law.

---

[1] Langdon-Davies, John, *A Short History of Women* p. 205. The Viking Press, Inc. (1927).

[2] Nesbitt, Rev. Ralph Beryl, Associate Minister of the Fifth Avenue Presbyterian Church, New York. *Augustine — Sinner and Saint.*

[3] The exact wording of the legend on the Cross, as repeated by Constantine, is in dispute; also exactly where and when he claimed to have seen the revelation.

CANON LAW

History and Structure: Before Innocent III — Innocent III — After Innocent III — Combination of Government of Laws and of Men. Women's Rights under Canon Law: Dress and Appearance — Celibacy — Marriage. Conclusion.

CANON LAW WAS THE CHILD OF ROMAN LAW AND Hebrew Law, parents differing in tradition, religion, and circumstances — parents who were virtual strangers though for generations they had lived side by side in the Roman Empire. Their offspring was a curious hybrid with leopard spots of East and West, not a true admixture or blending of the parent laws. The spots did not change, the particular rules coming from one or the other parent remaining unmodified for centuries. From the East came the laws to rule woman's life.

The Canon Law effectively perpetuated the views of the Early Church as to woman's secondary place to man. Nevertheless, it did much to protect her, and in certain instances affirmatively to promote her legal rights, but always within her status of inferiority. It never let her forget her place. After the collapse of the Roman

Empire, the church became the most powerful organization in the Western world, the Universal Church of that world, everywhere dominating all spiritual thinking and regulating all religious activity. In addition, it made widespread encroachment in secular affairs, and in matters affecting women its laws gained complete supremacy over Roman Law. Therefore, the church's position on woman during the Middle Ages is all important. Its secular powers lasted over centuries, unyieldingly increasing through the papacy of Innocent III at the turn of the twelfth and thirteenth centuries, and after him decreasing to its disappearance during the Modern Age.

To understand the Canon or Papal or Church Law, both ecclesiastic and secular, as it affected women, requires a familiarity with the position of the Roman Catholic Church in the Christian world and also with the authority exercised by its popes.

Before Innocent III

Early in the church's history, the bishops of Rome, with the once pagan title of Pontifex Maximus, became the leading bishops of the church. This naturally followed from Rome's dominant influence and exalted place in the world. Her bishops also claimed to be, and were generally regarded as the direct successors to Saint Peter, which further enhanced their prestige. In the fifth century they began seriously to claim papal or supreme authority over the entire church, and in 445 the Emperor Valentinian III formally decreed that the bishop of Rome, then Leo I, had such authority. With the blessings of both Saint Peter and the Roman emperors, these bishops or popes were generally recognized as having plenary power within the church and over its entire membership in the spiritual realm.

Next the popes and church began extending their authority to secular affairs as well, and with remarkable success. Considerable impetus was given to this extension in the ninth century by the Decretals of Isidore, later known as the False Decretals. They contained a letter, forged by an unknown monk, purporting to be over eight hundred years old, from Pope Clement I, addressed to all church clergy, reading in part as follows: "Their (the people's) duty is to obey you as they would God himself . . . All princes, high or low, and other peoples, tribes, and languages, who do not obey shall be infamous, and shall be cast out from the kingdom of God and the company of the faithful."

As of the date claimed for this letter, 91 A. D., the Roman Emperor Domitian was ruler of the Empire, and the Christians, if they had caused any trouble under him, would have had to scamper to save their skins. For Clement to have declared that the people should obey his clergy, and that all princes, high or low, who did not obey would be infamous, would have been so absurd and impolitic that he would have been thought mad. Furthermore, Clement I was probably the freedman of T. Flavius Clemens, cousin of, and at the time on friendly terms with, the Emperor; and if so, he would not have stirred up any difficulty. (He definitely was not the Clement referred to in Paul's *Epistle to the Philippians,* as claimed by Origen.) But whoever he was, he had the welfare of himself and other Christians to think of and would not have issued the farcical pronouncement ascribed to him. The monk dated his letter several centuries too early.

Isidore was an assumed name evidently for the Archbishop of Seville, who is considered responsible for most of the faked letters or decretals contained in the Decretals of Isidore. Many documents in the collection were authentic and they served to allay suspicion of the cleverly prepared false ones. Seventy letters appearing to have been written by the popes of Rome of the first three centuries were established as forgeries, but only after they had served the purposes of the bishop and the church for many generations. Decretals of the popes are of the highest rank in the law of the church being in the nature of legislation or legal opinions or both. The Decretals of Isidore enhanced the authority of the clergy generally, with particular attention to the welfare of the bishops who were given increased protection against removal from office and granted additional privileges.

The next compilation of Canon Law was in 1151 by a little known monk named Gratian at the University of Bologna, Italy, and was private rather than official. It was comprehensive and of good structure, being arranged in systematic order according to subjects. The False Decretals did not purport to cover many important phases of Canon Law, were arranged only in chronological order, and it was difficult to ferret out the pronouncements on any particular issue. Even though Gratian's compilation was private in nature, it served such a useful purpose that in practice it was accepted as authoritative. All looked to it to ascertain the Canon Law, professors taught from it, it became known as the Decretum of Gratian, and in a sense it created Canon Law by making it widespread, uniform, and ascertainable. Something of this concrete nature was necessary if the law was to develop as a true legal system.

The Decretum contained sundry pronouncements by popes of long ago, the very names of whom were unknown to the church membership; and it was largely upon these ancient documents that the church claimed further extensions of power during the twelfth and following centuries. Some of these early documents were spurious, although in the main the Decretum was authentic. Also, Gratian's various comments throughout the work were purposefully made distinguishable from the authoritative law. There is no question but that he made a major contribution to the progress of Canon Law.

Innocent III (*c.* 1160-1216)

We come next to one of the most remarkable men in the church and in all history, Innocent III, Pope from 1198 to 1216. He was no doubt the youngest of all popes, attaining that exalted position at the early age of thirty-seven. On the same day the preceding Pope died, January 8, 1198, the cardinals by unanimous vote elected Innocent to the papacy although he was not a bishop of the church, not even a priest. Those positions were conferred on him the following month. Innocent was of an aristocratic and influential Italian family, had been educated in Paris and Bologna, was versed in both Canon and Civil Law, and was of unquestioned ability and high purpose. He soon wielded the greatest of power, not only within the church but in secular affairs as well, and not only over the people but over the most powerful of rulers.

Marriage had long been under the jurisdiction of the church, it was no longer the civil contract of Roman Law, and Innocent enforced the church's views on that subject against prince (if politic to do so) as well as commoner. He compelled Philip Augustus of France to divorce a present wife and take back his former one; prohibited Peter of Aragon from a marriage he desired; and required Alphonso IX of Leon to divorce his wife because they were related within the degree prohibited by the church, although children had been born to their union. Innocent decreed the children, however, to be legitimate. Incestuous marriage, even though the relationship was distant, was of the gravest concern to the church. These are but examples of the control Innocent exercised over sovereigns, and actually minor examples, being chosen because they relate to marriage. His major conflict with a ruler, the notorious King John of England, is discussed in the chapter on Magna Carta.

Innocent was a supreme autocrat, the most powerful personage in the West, and was not subject to being judged by any man. He was more a ruler than a divine and issued thousands of bulls covering all phases of temporal life. He took the position that the Lord left to Peter the governance and regulation of the world; that Peter as God's vicar on earth was "preeminent over all, . . . the whole wide world and all that dwell therein"; that sovereigns as well as commoners were subject to the authority of this Disciple of Jesus; and that the popes succeeded to this supreme authority. On one occasion the Emperor of Constantinople called Innocent's attention to the failure of Peter to have made such an extensive claim for himself and to Peter's own words in his First Epistle whereby he counseled: "Submit yourselves to every ordinance of man for the Lord's sake: whether it be to the king, as supreme; or unto governors . . ." Innocent's answer was that Peter's advice to submit to "the king as supreme was addressed to lay folk and not to the clergy." But Peter had made no such distinction.

Innocent's readiness with answers to scriptures which did not support his own purposes, and his ability to find biblical premises to substantiate his conclusions of supreme power, were not wholeheartedly accepted by all, particularly in Germany and England; yet few were willing openly to take issue with him. It was said of him, because of the vast political power which he wielded, that he was the successor not to Peter but to Constantine.

This power Innocent exercised for good. By nature he was incorruptible, and in an age when corruption permeated all institutions. Like the ideal Stoic, his strength was within him. He is ranked among the highest intellectuals of the church, and the church still points to him with justified praise. Yet it never canonized him. He inaugurated numerous church reforms, some even though they meant reduction in revenues, as the one which prohibited the sale of bogus relics to the believers. He called and presided over the Fourth Lateran Council (the twelfth ecumenical council), the most important council since Nicaea; but unlike Constantine he did not preside and listen, he dominated the council. It was his dogmas which the council pronounced, his policies which fifteen hundred church prelates from throughout the Christian world adopted without thought of contradicting him. "As if eleven centuries had fallen away," says Durant, "he was a Roman emperor, Stoic rather than Christian, and never doubting his right to rule the world." Through Innocent III, Rome was again Mistress of the West.

After Innocent III

After Innocent III the temporal power of the popes decreased, though gradually, so Canon Law continued its development as a legal system. Innocent had concluded that there should be an official Church Code issued by the pope, but was too busy during his arduous tenure to make any progress in this direction. There were two objections to the Decretum of Gratian: it was without papal sanction, and it contained uncertainties on numerous issues. Since the Decretum, students had made compilations of their own, and over the years five major works, called the Compilationes, had evolved.

To coordinate this supplemental material, Gregory IX, in

1230, caused the five Compilationes to be reduced to one work from which duplications and outmoded rules were eliminated. The only new material added to Gregory's condensation was 196 chapters of his own issuance and nine decretals of Innocent III. As conceived by Innocent, this work was sanctioned by the pope, and thus became the first official code of laws of the church. Gregory issued it as a supplement to the Decretum, thereby giving papal sanction to the Decretum itself. This code, a major step in Canon Law, was not only official but was systemitized into books, titles, and chapters or sections, in the same form as the present day legal codes. It was prepared under the supervision, not of a monk or a layman, but of a professional jurist, Raymond of Pennafort, one of the judges of the powerful Rota, comparable to the Supreme Court of the United States.

To prevent confusion from again arising because of a mass of private works, Gregory prohibited them. He reasoned that the Decretum, plus his official supplement, contained enough legislation and case examples for the development of the necessary abstract principles and general rules of Canon Law. Time, of course, disproved this idea of a static basis for all future laws, and later popes issued other official supplements, and private compilations appeared again. Gregory's prohibition against the latter was forgotten. In addition, church councils, after much debating and labor, ground out hundreds of rules. Confusion again resulted.

Combination of Government of Laws and of Men

As Canon Law developed throughout the Dark Ages into a definite legal system, secular church rule became more a government of laws than a government of men; but never to the same extent as the modern unified democracies or as the older compact societies. At best Church Law was a combination of government of laws and of men. A paramount cause preventing church rule from reaching an advanced government-of-laws stage was the continuing confusion in its multitude of rules, pronouncements, and dogmas. This confusion I purposely accentuate because, to my thinking (although I have not seen the view expressed elsewhere), uncertainty was the strength of Canon Law — paradoxical as this may at first sound.

It was this uncertainty which gave the individual administrator of the law (the bishop and, at the local level, the priest) great latitude by way of interpretation and application, and in Canon Law there always seemed to be the right amount of uncertainties to permit the local ecclesiastical courts and administrators to render justice suitable to their particular locale. The wide divergence in opinions, in economic levels and in social strata throughout the hodge-podge Western world of the Dark Ages made impracticable a strictly government-of-laws system applicable to all.

The local priests and administrators over many centuries were able to give aid and protection to the people because the Canon Law permitted them to exercise their individual views of right and wrong, to do good or evil within its framework. And they did good.

WOMEN'S RIGHTS UNDER CANON LAW

With an understanding of the development, structure, and nature of Canon Law, and of the power of the popes, we can better comprehend its specific laws which affected woman's well-being. The laws discussed will be of the Gratian-Innocent III-Gregory IX era, or of the twelfth and thirteenth centuries, the period of the church's greatest secular power, and, therefore, the period best representing the supremacy of Canon over Civil Law. Canon Law at no time accepted the reasoning of the Civil Law that sex was not a justifiable basis for legal discriminations. Yet in spite of the prejudicial attitude of the medieval church toward woman's legal status, it was able to take over the running of her life, regulating marriage, divorce, and all domestic affairs.

Gratian's Decretum cogently ranked woman inferior to man, reflecting the attitude of the Early Church writers, Paul, the Old Testament authors, and Moses. Gratian relied heavily on

St. Augustine to show that woman must be kept firmly under man's control. We will recall that the theory of woman's secondary status was taking its tenacious hold on the thinking of the Roman Empire by the time of Augustine, but by Gratian's day it was positive law and its strict imposition was of vital concern to the church. Gratian, therefore, made it a point to set forth the many Canon Law personal prohibitions against women, an example of which was that a wife, at her own instance, must not be away from her husband at any time during the marriage relationship except for short periods of worship. Gratian also detailed such Canon Law disabilities for woman as her non-access to the criminal courts (except to prosecute for the death of a close relative or in a case of high treason), the practical effect of which prohibition was to give the husband a virtual immunity from criminal punishment for any fraud or crime which he committed against the wife.

Since Gratian's work became widespread, if there was a clergyman in Christendom so uninformed as not to know of woman's limited position in Church Law, Gratian enlightened him; if there was a tendency in any locale to increase woman's legal rights, Gratian smothered it.

Dress and Appearance

Woman's dress and appearance were regulated by sundry laws as well as by custom. She was to do nothing to alter her appearance as a woman and thereby lessen the outward badges of her inferiority. Excommunication was the penalty for cutting off her hair, which God had given her "as a sign of her subjection." Paul had said woman's hair signified her subjection to man. A woman definitely was not to wear men's clothes. This prohibition was still in full force three centuries after Gratian. One of the accusations against Joan of Arc was that she dressed as a man. Before being removed from her cell for the stake in the market square of Rouen, Joan was redressed in woman's clothes so the good people attending her public burning would not have to gaze on a girl in man's attire.

Celibacy

Under the Canon Law as collected in the Decretum, a woman could be forced into a convent with relative ease. Parents could take vows while their daughter was an infant which would later bind her to a nunnery for life, regardless of her wishes on becoming old enough to know her own mind. Also, a daughter on becoming twelve could take the vows over the objections of her parents, and many a parent's heart was broken by the strict enforcement of this rule. If a single woman or widow took the vows, changed her mind and married, she was excommunicated. Celibacy had become a laudable state for women — almost as much so as for men. The widespread worship of the Virgin Mary planted the desire for unmarried life in the mind of many a young girl. Convents also became asylums for girls disappointed in love, for widows before the normal moderation of their sorrow, and for women otherwise temporarily disturbed — asylums often hastily sought and soon, but too late, regretted.

Christianity is the only religion ever to make a virtue of celibacy. The sole pagan indication in the West of this attitude was the Vestal Virgins of Rome, too minor to be an exception to the seriousness with which the church, over hundreds of years, exalted the unmarried state. Fertility, as the essence of all nature, was the spirit of pagan worship. The virgin birth of Jesus, in the thinking of society in the maladjusted Dark Ages, detracted from the matron who bore her children as the result of a "base" sexual act and elevated the virgin who remained "pure" throughout life. In the tenth century the nun Roswitha, in one of her classic plays, depicts Christianity as the purity of woman and paganism as the "vigor" of man — her genteel label for his sexual passions. In another play she speaks of "the Eternal Father, author of Nature" having given Mary the power to conceive without losing her "purity."[1] Sex, even in marriage, was degrading. Concupiscence was the Original Sin of the Old Testament.

However, the celibate women of the convents did gain an advantage denied the family women. This was their association with men on an intellectual basis: a relationship progessive women of all ages have desired. The nuns' contact with men was limited and periodic only, but they were permitted to discuss religious affairs and dogmas with the men of the church, to engage in literary and educational pursuits in company with men, and to advise, even modestly to argue, on these subjects with the males with whom they came in contact.

Such liberties were unthought of for the wife. A thirteenth century work, *Holy Maidenhood,*[2] decried the "sorrows of wedlock" and proclaimed that if woman marries "she loses freedom and high dignity." Purity was "the only heavenly virtue," wedlock was "lower in grace," and it was the devil who "would cast maidens from their high state." In comparing nun and wife, the nun was described as a free woman, the wife as a slave. It is a twist of history that the nun of the Dark Ages, to an extent, gained intellectual freedom with man by celibacy as had the courtesan of the Golden Age by familiarity, both in periods when the family woman was confined to the home.

Naturally the nuns' contacts with men produced some sex relations, and reams were written on various affairs for the benefit of the public. Scandal, then as now, was news, a favorite topic of conversation and literature, and no doubt many instances of routine sex were dramatized beyond their significance. The wholly abnormal life of the nun was certainly conducive to breaches of the strict moral code, but no excuse was extended by society to those who sought escape from the sexual dry rot of the convent. Yet the same conduct in the male clergy was largely overlooked, even expected.

Marriage

All Canon Laws relating to women were not unfavorable. One, that the bride must consent to the marriage, was a substantial contribution to woman's rights from a legal standpoint, although to a lesser degree in actual practice. After the fall of Rome the Civil Law rule that consent was essential to a valid marriage had given way to the father's complete control of his single daughter's life. While the revival of the rule was publicized by Gratian, it was — as in the case of the young Roman girl — of little practical benefit to the daughters subject to Canon Law; and one refusing to marry the man of her father's choice could find herself incurring severe parental punishment from beatings to confinement in a convent. Nevertheless, the necessity of the prospective bride's consent was a forward step and the very fact that it was the law gave protection in many instances.

This, and other rights granted woman prior to marriage, must not be thought of as mitigating her inferior status after marriage, or as impairing the husband's control over her. Gratian carefully detailed the rules as to the husband's authority; he also carefully repeated the age-old observance that women are veiled during the marriage ceremony so "they may know that they are lowly and in subjection to their husbands." A married woman under Canon Law was more slave than partner of her husband, more servant than mistress of her household.

Another forward step in marriage, and one of more practical value to woman than the requirement of her consent, was the Canon Law prohibition of marriage without clergy or witnesses. For centuries many couples, especially of the lower classes, married privately by simply taking one another as husband and wife and saying the vows customary for their particular age and place. The Canon Law spoke of these marriages as secret or clandestine and modern writers discussing them use these terms, but they were not actually of that nature, as secrecy was not intended and the couple forthwith lived openly as husband and wife. Private, to distinguish these marriages from those which were public in the sense that a clergyman performed the ceremony and third party witnesses attended, is a more nearly accurate designation.

The private ceremony was comparable to any oral transaction or contract where only the two interested parties are present. The evidential difficulties inherent in such a situation are patent. One party can deny the entire occurrence, and the other may find it difficult or impossible to establish the facts with any certainty. And the more important to society the occurrence, the more pernicious its privacy. Many spouses, usually husbands, denied their private marriages and abandoned their families. It was this social evil which the church endeavored to mitigate, and eventually it stamped out the private marriage practice. From its earliest existence the church zealously protected the marriage union.

CONCLUSION

With the coming of the Modern Age (the sixteenth century) secular Canon Law ran its course, though it had served well the Middle Ages in many respects. Nationalism became the spirit of the times. Also, the separation of the Protestant nations from the Catholic Church reduced the area in which the church's and the pope's spiritual influence was supreme.

In England this separation, both secular and spiritual, came with relative rapidity by legislation from 1532 to 1534 which completely eliminated papal jurisdiction throughout the realm and established the king as head of the Church of England. The Statute of 25 Henry VIII transferred all cases to the king's jurisdiction and prohibited "any foreign inhibitions, appeals, sentences, summons, citations, suspensions, interdictions, excommunications . . . from the See of Rome, or any other foreign courts or potentates of the world. . . ."

With the ending of the Canon Law's secular jurisdiction (in Catholic as well as Protestant countries), it made its great contribution to the Modern West: it passed on the rules of the Civil Law which it had adopted and nurtured for over a thousand years.

Canon Law also passed on the rules and theory of woman's secondary place. This law was in the direct line of descent from the Mosaic Laws, the apostles and the Early Church to the common law of England and our own discriminations against women. The fact that Henry VIII and the Pope parted ways did not mean the abrogation of the laws unfavorable to woman or the lessening of the attitude of her inferiority. These laws and attitude had already become a part of the growing English common law.

Thus, in the evolution of woman's rights, we see the Canon

Law as a major link anchored to the mores of nomads of the ancient Arabian desert, as a link based upon church encroachment within the sphere of the law, which encroachment in turn was based upon false documents and autocratic power. Such are the links connecting the early beliefs of woman's inferiority and the modern discriminations against her.

---

[1] *The Plays of Roswitha,* translated by Christopher St. John. Published in English by Chatto and Windus, London (1923).

[2] *Hali Meidenhad,* edited by Oswald Cockayne. Published in English by Trübner and Co., London (1866) as No. 18 of the Original Series of the Early English Text Society Publications.

MAGNA CARTA

Of all of Innocent III's relations with sovereigns, by far the most important to the present-day English Common Law group of nations was his conflict with King John of England and the subsequent close political affinity between the two of them. The outcome of the conflict is usually referred to as Innocent's greatest victory and as the humiliation and vassalage of John.[1] This is correct as far as it goes; but the vassalage was also John's greatest victory over his enemies and was craftily planned by him to obtain that specific result. The extended dealings between the Pope and the King of England directly affected the granting of Magna Carta, the most far-reaching of all documents in the obtaining of our fundamental individual rights and liberties.

That document had no relation to women's rights as such but is considered here because of its basic importance and background of common law rights for all. Thus women and men are equally interested in the Charter and its principles; and it is the same broad principles of liberty and of good and fair laws, first established by the Charter, on which women of today must rely for equal legal rights with men. Yet the Charter is seldom specifically referred to by those advocating the removal of unfair legal restraints against women.

In July, 1205, a vacancy by reason of death existed in the office of Archbishop of Canterbury. According to custom any vacancy was filled by the monks of Christ Church, but the king's views as to who should be or not be selected were given the utmost consideration and were often controlling. This was proper because the Archbishop of Canterbury was also the Primate of England, and in that capacity he exercised high level secular powers in addition to his ecclesiastic authority as Archbishop.

But John had been ruling for six years when the vacancy occurred, and that was long enough for all to have learned thoroughly to distrust him; so a majority of the monks met hastily in secret and named Reginal, one of their own number, as Archbishop. It was principally the younger monks who met and several of the older electors would not participate. Nothing but trouble, regardless of John's past behavior, could result from this surreptitious action. The office was too important politically. In ignoring the King, those monks who made the selection allocated far too much importance to the procedure which permitted them to do the actual voting and they disregarded the spirit and intent of their formal authority which definitely contemplated a selection satisfactory to both king and church.

John immediately acted in as bad faith as had the majority of the monks by, in effect, forcing a minority of them and other church officials to meet and select as Archbishop a weakling King's man, Bishop John de Gray. The king had no authority to make the selection himself since the rights of the church also were to be protected by the long standing custom of choosing an archbishop, so rather than flaunt tradition outright John chose to use duress on those with a semblance of authority to act.

Sponsors of both Gray and Reginal hastened to Rome to submit their respective claims to the Pope. Each group believed they would get his support. Neither got it. Innocent preferred his own friend, Stephen Langton, who was residing in Rome at the time. Innocent, as John, had no authority to name an archbishop but, also as John, he had certain persuasive powers, and the monks who had gone to Rome submissively chose Langton as Archbishop on the untenable theory that, as representatives of the electors back in England, they could do the selecting. Some of those supporting Gray revealed they had taken a solemn oath to support only him, but this posed no difficulty for Innocent; he simply absolved them from their oaths. This third selection, more contrary to custom than either of the other two, was immediately accepted by the clergy, and immediately rejected by John. He refused to allow Langton to set foot in England on threat of imprisonment, although prior to Langton's selection he had committed himself to the proposition that the Pope's decision would control — this, of course, was when he thought Innocent would confirm Gray.

Two factors favored Langton's selection. He was not allied with either the King's or the monks' faction in England, and more important, he was a good man with a compelling desire to do what was best for England, king, and church. The difficulties with his selection, regardless of neutrality and qualification, were that the King had no part in it and he was in effect the Pope's personal appointee. Langton and Innocent had been close friends for years, so John naturally, although erroneously, assumed Langton's primary loyalty would be to the Pope rather than to England, and even if not, John wanted an archbishop loyal to him instead of to England. John's refusal to recognize Langton did not bring any immediate action from Innocent, who patiently tried to negotiate and to arrive at a satisfactory solution. As long, however, as John thought he had the upper hand there was no dealing with him, and temporary upper hand was as far as he could see.

Finally, in 1208, Innocent acted, and by interdict forbade public church services, Christian burial, various sacraments, and other religious practices throughout England. This did not disturb John, so the following year Innocent excommunicated him and later absolved all from their oaths of allegiance to him. Still John did not budge; he was not the type to be concerned over paper decrees and edicts, papal or otherwise. He simply proceeded systematically to pilfer the church of its properties, assets and income — and the crown's financial gain convinced him he was the victor.

Innocent was not to be outdone. He unleashed a thunderbolt against John which, on paper, deposed John as king, transferred all his dominions to Philip Augustus, King of France, and sanctioned Philip's invasion of England. Philip was unscrupulous, but unlike John he acted with deliberation and not in anger. He was a better ruler than he was a man. He realized the opportunity tendered him by Innocent and began preparations for the invasion of England.

Few rallied to John's support; the people of England, particularly the powerful barons, were disgusted with him. In addition to his trouble with the church resulting in the suspension of public worship and sacraments, which cast the shadow of damnation after death over the faithful, John was guilty of many acts of tyranny, unjust taxations, ingratitude toward those who supported him, harshness toward those who opposed him, and shocking personal immoralities. This was too much for his realm to condone. While papal edicts may not have disturbed him, the threatened invasion of England did, especially since it was now obvious that friends in his own country were few. So John made his move.

He started negotiations with Innocent offering to recognize Langton and the church's future right to choose the Archbishop and to govern itself in ecclesiastical matters; to restore all church assets which he had escheated to the crown; to rescind his orders against those of the clergy and others who had obeyed Innocent, and not to punish them; and finally, to turn over England and Ireland to the Pope and receive them back as his vassal. As John anticipated, this flattering and suppliant offer was too appealing to be refused, and after some negotiation, Innocent, in 1213, sent his envoy to England to go through the formality of receiving England and Ireland for the Holy See and turning them back to John to administer as the See's feudal vassal.

Langton arrived in England and assumed the duties of his office in July of that year, eight years after the vacancy had occurred in the See of Canterbury. John's excommunication was withdrawn; he was now the Pope's representative in England and Ireland, and the Pope was God's vicar on earth. It would be sacrilege for Philip to invade a province of the Holy See. Philip was sorely disappointed at the turn of events and felt he had been imposed upon by the Pope, but he did not invade. Also, John's own barons, clergy, and people could not oppose him without doing offense to church and Pope, and they did nothing. Innocent's great victory saved John, and England continued with as sorry a ruler as ever sat on her throne.

John now felt so secure that he decided to invade Poitou, France, to which he had good claim. The Northern barons refused to join him or to support the expedition financially as he considered they were obligated to do. Forgetting his desire to invade Poitou, John rashly headed north to punish the barons. Langton also headed north to reason with John and overtook him at Northampton. Langton insisted that the barons should not be punished prior to a trial in court and a judgment of guilt, that John had no right to prejudge them. Typical of John, he at first paid little attention to Langton, but support grew for Langton's position so rapidly that John considered it expedient to follow his advice. With this out of the way, John again decided to invade Poitou. He embarked in February, 1214, with high hopes and confidence, but the expedition was a complete failure. This ended John's ambitions in France, and he returned to England in disrepute.

When Langton had come to England as Archbishop, John had agreed and sworn not only to honor the church but to restore good laws to England. Langton was determined that John do both. It had been discussed between Langton, some of the more important barons, and others of influence, that the practical way to get John to do what he promised was to obtain from him a charter setting forth in black and white the agreed reforms. It may have been Langton who first suggested a charter, but at any rate he backed the proposal with effect and persistence.

Also, there had turned up the century-old coronation charter of Henry I, great-grandfather of John, granted in 1100, which supported with remarkable fortune the current demands of Langton in that it contained specific and positive stipulations that both the church and the King's subjects would be free of unjust laws and regulations and that good laws would be granted for all. In time doubt arose as to the genuineness of the document, but it served Langton well: he had it as well as John's oath to back his position.

Langton was determined to obtain a charter from John setting out the rights he had promised. Langton could not force this alone but he concluded he and the barons together could. They trusted Langton because of his intervention in their behalf at Northampton and because of his now-known sincerity in wanting what was best for England. A meeting was arranged between King and barons, and a charter was demanded. John asked for time and was given until April 26, 1215, approximately four months. In the meantime both he and the barons prepared for war. They did not trust John to grant a charter, and he did not intend to. Also, both sent envoys to Rome. John's envoys forcefully reminded Innocent of his duty to protect his vassal. Innocent urged all to adjust their differences.

John now made another crafty and completely insincere move to insure the Pope's continued support. He took an oath to raise and to lead personally an army to the Holy Land. Thus he assumed the role of a Christian crusader dedicated to the Pope's pet project. Innocent wanted to believe him and did; the barons laughed at his solemn oath.

As the deadline of April 26 approached the barons advanced toward Oxford, where the King was staying at the time. John sent Langton and the Earl of Pembroke to negotiate with them. The Articles of the Barons were drafted — with Langton playing an influential part — and were sent to the King with an outright demand that he accept them. The barons threatened to take his castle if he did not accept — they knew the language John understood. Also, they immediately infiltrated London and announced that those who failed to work with them could expect armed retaliation. John's supporters again left him, so he sent word to the barons that he would concede the guaranties they requested, and June 15 at Runnymede was the time and place agreed upon for the King to deliver.

Both sides appeared as planned, John with Langton and a

handful of supporters, the barons in more strength, although much of their support was kept in the background so as not to make an overt show of armed resistance to the King. Nevertheless, John understood the situation. Magna Carta was agreed to with little ceremony, engrossed probably four days later, and copies were sealed and sent to various parts of the realm.[2] The Charter reflected the Articles of the Barons and guaranteed specific rights and liberties to barons, landowners and church.[3]

To John the granting of the Charter meant nothing more than a temporary expedient to relieve himself of an untenable position. He immediately took steps to reverse his action, sending envoys to Rome to present a prejudiced picture to Innocent, and also representatives to various cities on the Continent to recruit mercenaries. While waiting for results from these two steps, in sinister mood he laid his plans for the utter destruction of the Northern barons and the revocation of the Charter.

Innocent rallied to his paper vassal, and on July 7, 1215, wrote the Papal Legate in England and others stating his disappointment with the Archbishop and those bishops who had participated in the "wicked conspiracy" against John; charging they were "undoubtedly worse than the Saracens, for they were trying to depose a king who, it was particularly hoped, would succor the Holy Land!" He ordered excommunicated "all such disturbers of the king and kingdom of England together with their accomplices and supporters." Langton would not publish the bull or take any action against the barons and, with the King's permission, left for Rome to talk to the Pope.

On August 24 Innocent issued another bull addressed to all the faithful in Christ who saw the bull. It went into much detail, reviewing that John had turned over England and Ireland to the church and had received them back as fief; that he was splendidly preparing for the relief of the Holy Land; that "the enemy of the human race" (the devil) had stirred up against John the barons of England; and that John was of good intentions and the barons of bad. The bull also made excuses for John's having granted the Charter, stating that when the Archbishop and bishops would not take any action, John, seeing himself bereft of counsel and help, did not dare to refuse that which the barons had dared to demand; and that by such violence and fear as might affect the most courageous of men, he was forced to accept an agreement which was shameful, demeaning, illegal and unjust, thereby lessening unduly and impairing his royal rights and dignity. After this lengthy preface, Innocent proceeded to declare forever void the Great Charter, this greatest of all grants of liberties, in the following language:

> . . . we utterly reject and condemn this settlement, and under the threat of excommunication we order that the king should not dare to observe it and that the barons and their associates should not require it to be observed: this Charter, with all undertakings and guarantees whether confirming it or resulting from it, we declare to be null and void of all validity forever. Wherefore let no man deem it lawful to infringe this document or our annulment and prohibition, or to presume to oppose it.

With Langton en route to Rome there was no one in England to publish the bull according to strict procedure, but as said, it was addressed to all who saw it and its commands became well known to the barons. They were, therefore, confronted with choosing between the Pope and the Charter. They chose the Charter. The Pope's influence, although great, was not as compelling as their class self-interest nor as motivating as their determination to keep deserved liberties so difficultly obtained.

After Langton's refusal to publish the bull of July 7 and to take the action therein required against the barons, the representatives of the Pope in England suspended him as Archbishop. On arriving in Rome, Langton presented to the Pope a full and, as he saw it, a correct report on the grant of the Charter and on the complicated social, ecclesiastical, and governmental factors involved. His words fell on deaf ears. Innocent even confirmed Langton's suspension (which remained in effect for two years), kept him at Rome in virtual custody, and specifically prohibited his return to England.

John rapidly gained the upper hand at home. Without Langton the barons were confused on how to proceed, since it was he who had furnished most of the major planning as well as the spirit in opposing John and in obtaining the Charter. He was the real leader, not so much of the barons, but of the cause. In his absence, the barons took an ill-advised, almost irrational, step in that they sent a delegation to France in the autumn of 1215 and offered the throne of England to Louis, heir to the throne of France, whose wife was a granddaughter of Henry II. Philip, not wanting openly to oppose Innocent and for other reasons, took a stand publicly against his son's acceptance of the barons' offer, but privately told him to accept and, for a second time, set in motion the necessary preparations for the invasion of England. This time it took place. The French troops landed at Stonor on May 22, 1216. They moved directly to London which was opposed to John.

The Papal Legate in France had forbidden the invasion before the embarkation. Being unable to stop it, he came to England, arriving at the same time as the French, and issued a wholesale excommunication of the French troops and of all Englishmen opposing John. John, displaying considerable military ability, deployed his forces so as to prevent the union of the French and the Northern barons. England appeared to be confronted with a long and bitter civil strife with strong religious overtones. The warring sides were evenly divided and it was hard to estimate with which the advantages lay. Then, suddenly John died, October 12, 1216, from dysentery. This should have ended the war, but the throne of England was too great a prize for Louis and Philip to forego merely because the reason for the war was gone.

However, by now the barons were realizing their mistake in seeking the aid of the French. Louis looked upon them somewhat as traitors to their own King and his general attitude was such that it appeared he would be as bad a master as John had been. So the barons suddenly concluded that even though John had forfeited the right to rule and to be succeeded by his lawful heirs, there was another living person who had a much better claim to the throne of England than did Louis.

This person was Eleanor, the Pearl of Brittany, also called

the Fair Maid, a charming beautiful brunette about thirty years of age. Had the laws of primogeniture been followed to the letter, she would have been ruler of England instead of John. Because of this she was being held in strict confinement at formidable Corfe Castle in the Isle of Purbeck. Few knew where she was or even that she was in England. Earlier, when Europe thought her younger brother, Arthur, would be King of England, Eleanor was betrothed to Louis, the same prince who now invaded England, but Philip had called off the engagement when it appeared John, Arthur's uncle, would become king. (This was the Arthur whom John had caused to be put to death after capturing him in Poitou while Arthur was trying to capture his old grandmother, John's mother.)

Events had been most unfortunate for Eleanor, not only as to the throne but as to marriage as well. At one time Richard (The Lion Hearted) while on a crusade in Palestine, had proposed her marriage to Saphadin, brother of Saladin, provided Saladin would make them King and Queen of Jerusalem and Saphadin would become a Christian. Saphadin declined to change his religion and the marriage plans were abandoned. Other considered royal marriages for Eleanor had not worked out and time had passed her by. Actually, there was now little chance of her obtaining the throne of England and the barons were not giving serious consideration thereto. She simply furnished an excuse for them no longer to support Louis, although a weak one since they had known all along of her status.

As a practical matter, everyone realized the throne would go either to Louis or to John's son, a fine lad of nine. Supported by the Royalists and the church, this son was crowned King as Henry III by the Papal Legate at Gloucester on October 28, 1216. The venerable and respected William the Marshal accepted the Regency, and success attended the arms of the Royalists. With the barons now against him, Louis, by the Treaty of Lambeth in September, 1217, withdrew his pretensions to the throne and departed England. Pursuant to a secret stipulation he was paid a small war indemnity.

Things also took an important turn in favor of the Charter.

Many of the influential leaders surrounding the young King were its strong supporters. As a result the Charter was reissued by Henry III with slight modification, the main reason being to let all know that the new government intended to honor its grant of rights.

Innocent had died in 1216, and the new Pope, Honorius III, allowed Langton to return to England in 1218. For the remainder of his life Langton was highly respected and played an important part in the affairs of his country, always using his influence for the Charter. His power was such that Honorius recalled his Papal Legate (who was among those who had suspended Langton in 1215) and agreed not to send another legate to England as long as the Archbishop lived.

The reissuance of the Charter by Henry III — in practical effect by those former adherents of John now connected with the Regency — was of prime importance in that it removed any likelihood of the Charter's becoming a minor document construed to have dealt only with a limited number of rights for certain groups in existence at the time. The reissuance made the Charter's guaranties the policy of the government and during the next century it was reissued thirty-eight times, thus becoming firmly established as the law of the land. Its first reissuance, which set the pattern for the future, was perhaps as significant as its original grant.

Now, to appraise those connected with Magna Carta. John was a rascal. He harassed England one way or another throughout his entire reign and finally brought on the French invasion. Although that was his war to maintain his throne, in a sense he died fighting for his country to repel a foreign foe. And he fought with such determination, ability and force that he disconcerted his enemies and rallied his friends. Just prior to his death he had more honest English supporters who were primarily interested in their country than at any other period during his reign. By holding in check both the French and the barons, John bequeathed success to those who carried on after him. By the final defeat of the French in England and by his own earlier defeat in France, the two countries became separated, which allowed each to go its own way without foreign intrigues, to the untold benefit of both. England, now to herself, could fully develop the Common Law in her own special liberty-loving way. Without John there would have been no Great Charter. Liberty was blessed. John was indeed an ill wind which blew good.

What of Innocent? His life purpose was to increase and maintain the temporal power of the church, which he believed to be best for mankind. It is unfortunate that his policy ran into conflict with the grant of liberties in England. He was not opposed to civil liberties in principle; he simply endeavored to increase his power in England as elsewhere to the end that a better world would exist. He actually thought that through John he was furthering his great purpose and accordingly stood by his vassal. None doubts Innocent's sincerity. None can say to what extent greed, turmoil and chaos would have bridled the world of his era had it not been for a strong church and a resolute Pope.

The barons acted in their own interest; still the lesser nobility, the small landowners and the freemen obtained important rights under the Charter, and the barons cannot be denied an unwavering determination to promote needed rights and to oppose oppression at great hazard to themselves. This landed class risked life, limb, and property, the destruction of their way of life, and the impoverishment and humiliation of their families. Their risk is emphasized by the failure of a few of the barons to be on hand at Runnymede. The absent ones knew that if they attended and John later had the opportunity, he would seek them out and destroy them. So knew the barons who attended: if death was listing their names, they were on hand notwithstanding,[4] and liberty enrolled them.

As to Langton, the highest tribute must be paid him. He unflinchingly stuck to his purpose of doing what was best for England, with a fortitude unexcelled in history. Often his role was to take issue against Pope and King, and this he did in firm manner. In his age for an archbishop to oppose a pope publicly and with determination could bring disgrace; and for a primate to oppose a king openly and ally with his enemies could bring death. Yet Langton repeatedly took both these risks. He was a master mediator between powerful papal and national trends, between monarchial and baronial aspirations, and between factions with extreme self-interests. He was able to conciliate and bring tranquility to troublesome situations, the underlying causes of which seemed hopelessly at conflict, and in the end to achieve his unselfish purpose. The English speaking peoples are forever indebted to this Catholic English prelate who played the dominant role in the conception and birth of the Great Charter.

History appraises the Charter as our great grant of rights and liberties. Yet it contained no general declaration of constitutional rights, no broad assertion of basic liberties. On its face it was more in the nature of an agreement between the participants. Still it specified particular rights of fundamental value such as that "no Freeman shall be taken or imprisoned or disseized or exiled or in any way destroyed . . . except by the lawful judgment of his peers and by the law of the land." These exact guaranties of trial by jury and of due process (or law of the land) are found in the Bill of Rights to the Constitution of the United States and in all state constitutions. Regardless of that which the Charter specified or did not specify, it established two great principles: first, that there is a law above the sovereign, the government, the church, or any other institution which might arise for the regulation of man's life, which law none can legally violate and to which all those possessing authority are subject; and second, that man-made laws must be good, fair, and beneficial, and government must not oppress the individual or the church or other institution dear to man. It is these concepts of Magna Carta which are our great heritage.

With Magna Carta, granted during the latter part of the Middle Ages, we close the historical portion of this book. A familiarity with history is necessary to comprehend woman's rights. Rights do not exist in the abstract. To understand them, one must know the times.

The transition from the Middle Ages to the Modern Age brought no major advancement for woman. However, it did for the common man who gained individual liberties and privileges which, under the existing social order, was perhaps a requisite, and certainly an aid, to the later advancement of woman.

In the chapters on Rome and on the Early Church we saw, as to woman's status, two Romes — the Rome of the jurists and the Rome of the church. The jurists, influenced by the existing fact of woman's capability and the Stoic morality with no distinction as to sex, held that woman was man's equal. The church, influenced by tradition and divine revelation, held that she was his inferior. One of these diametrically opposed theories had to succumb. We know that the Canon Law, which dominated the Middle Ages, abandoned, where woman was concerned, the rules of the jurist and strictly followed those of the church. These rules of woman's secondary status extended well into the Modern Age and long after secular Canon Law had itself succumbed to nationalism.

Even in England — the land of Magna Carta where rights for individual man were rapidly to increase — woman failed to gain except in minor ways.

It would be the early nineteenth century before the inauguration of movements which would culminate in major gains for woman, and these movements would originate in the United States where a new spirit of freedom and independence had permeated the culture.

---

[1] Durant in *The Age of Faith,* p. 763, says: "When King John rejected Langton as archbishop of Canterbury, the Pope drove him by interdict and shrewd diplomacy to add England to the list of papal fiefs."

[2] Four copies are extant, one in Salisbury Cathedral, one in Lincoln Cathedral, and two in the British Museum.

[3] When the American Bar Association was invited to hold its 1957 annual meeting in London, it decided to erect a monument at Runnymede as a tribute by American lawyers to the granting of Magna Carta, "the origin of a way of life in freedom under law." The dedication ceremony was designed by Sir Edward Maufe, R. A. and held July 28, 1957.

[4] The coats of arms of 26 of the barons appear on the Charter; also those of John and Langton and the obverse and converse of John's seal.

United States

NINETEENTH CENTURY

The American Spirit — American Woman as Portrayed by De Tocqueville — Establishment of the Textile Industry: Eli Whitney — Samuel Slater — Francis Cabot Lowell — The Lowell Girls — Female Labor in the National Economy.

IT IS FASCINATING TO THINK ON THE AMERICAN. OUR land was discovered, conquered and settled by adventurers, and their spirit is always with us. We look to the distance and hasten there because of an inner expectancy which promises that something great and exciting lies beyond, and what that is we must know at the risk of life and fortune. This spirit has possessed many men of many ages, but nowhere other than in America has it been a continuing and steadfast way of life. For years our ancestors with fortitude moved westward, regardless of the feared and unknown Wilderness.

Scotch-Irish Rebecca Boone dried her tears after her oldest son was shot to death by an Indian war party near Cumberland Gap in 1773, and calmly said to Daniel that she was willing to continue the journey into Kentucky, the no-man's land of the

Indians, if the other members of the party wished to proceed.

A handful of Texans under Sam Houston attacked the superior trained forces of Santa Anna at San Jacinto in 1836 and, by routing the self-styled "Napoleon of the West," paved the way for the acquisition by the United States of an empire from Texas to California to Washington.

This spirit is not limited to race, class, or creed. Under General Jackson at New Orleans in December 1814-January 1815, there fought side by side aristocratic Creoles and Santo Domingan Negroes, backwoodsmen and Barratarian pirates, Tennessee militiamen and Mississippi Dragoons, colorfully garbed seamen from over the world and 'coon-skin capped frontiersmen, and Protestants and Catholics.

This was an American army, welded from an American medley by the firm will of an American commander, hawk-nosed Old Hickory. When the battle came his orders — passed along the line in drawingroom French, the drawl of the Southerner, the twang of the Westerner, and the oaths of the pirate — were obeyed by every man as if this stranger had always been his commander. In the city the Sisters prayed softly at the chapel altars. The well-disciplined veterans of the British army — Wellington's troops and the famous Ninety-Third Highlanders — were repulsed in crushing defeat.

Such are the manifestations of the American spirit which imbue all who inhabit this land, regardless of race or creed. And it is reflected not alone in battles and in gaining and settling territory, but in our entire life, industry, science, financing, and all progress and accomplishments. This spirit, as we shall see, has markedly affected the family, the social attitude towards woman, and her legal rights and place in the economy.

It was evident in the chapter on Egypt that a secure people hold to their beliefs and habits, are hesitant to gamble what they have for the chance of betterment; that their security tends to restrain rather than to promote innovations in beliefs. This is not true in the United States; innovations come with ease and rapidity and misoneism is unknown, yet once we were established as a nation we have been the most secure people in history. The

American desires the continuance of security in the flow of his thinking, possessions, and living, but he does not move in dread of its loss. The perpetuation without impairment of his liberties, his rights, his social status, he takes for granted, even in this age of precarious coexistence. He is optimistic beyond the bounds of reason, yet his plans develop. The feeling of security, optimism, and adventure has given independence, and that is the greatest of American traits.

The American woman, as the American man, is endowed with the full, bounteous American spirit. This spirit, insofar as woman's status is concerned, was of especial significance during the first part of the nineteenth century, as will appear from the three subjects chosen for discussion for that period.

The first is the character of its women as observed first-hand by De Tocqueville, the most illustrious political philosopher of the nineteenth century. I question if anyone can – and I am sure I cannot – portray these women better than did he, so that chapter in the main iterates the discerning findings on American women of the 1830's by this capable historian of democracy in the United States. Women of that general period are selected because I consider it was they, their independence and capabilities, and their age, which launched the movements culminating a century later, during our own lives, in the almost equal sociolegal status of women. Back of their age were underlying potent forces promoting woman's equality, and De Tocqueville also is heard as to them.

The second subject is the successful establishment of the textile industry in the United States, chosen because female labor accomplished that establishment and because it serves as an indisputable example that women as a class, at a given opportunity, can make to the economy of a society a major contribution not related to the domestic circle.

The third subject is the woman suffrage movement in the United States with roots that also date to the first part of the nineteenth century. This long, arduous and unrelenting fight, of course, lasted well into the present century, and while successfully terminated here, it continues in various countries of the world. Yet the end nears for gaining the universal elective franchise for women.

AMERICAN WOMAN AS PORTRAYED BY DE TOCQUEVILLE

I do not hesitate to avow that, although the women of the United States are confined within the narrow circle of domestic life, and their situation is in some respects one of extreme dependence, I have nowhere seen woman occupying a loftier position; and if I were asked, now that I am drawing to the close of this work, in which I have spoken of so many important things done by the Americans, to what the singular prosperity and growing strength of that people ought mainly to be attributed, I should reply – to the superiority of their women.

So wrote Alexis De Tocqueville (1803-1859) in his *Democracy in America,*[1] published in Paris in January of 1835. De Tocqueville possessed the gift of understanding social and governmental institutions. He applied this talent to democracies and the complicated factors causing Western societies to progress in that direction, and he is considered the first great historian of modern democracy. His comparison of aristocratic and democratic nations and the effect of the two attitudes on the character of women is unexcelled. Anyone disputing his opinion that the singular prosperity and growing strength of the United States was mainly attributable to the superiority of its women should be armed with strong reasons to the contrary.

De Tocqueville believed that for centuries there had been strong forces at work making all men more and more nearly equal, for examples, that "the Crusades and the wars of the English decimated the nobles and divided their possessions; the erection of communities introduced an element of democratic liberty into the bosom of feudal monarchy; the invention of fire-arms equalized the villain and the noble on the field of battle; printing opened the same resources to the minds of all classes; the post was organized so as to bring the same information to the door of the poor man's cottage and to the gate of the palace; and Protestantism proclaimed that all men are alike able to find the road to heaven." He believed equality was ordained and that those who opposed it opposed divine will. Christianity, he reasoned, had done much to create a spirit of equality by teaching that all men are equal in the eyes of God. If in his eyes, why not among men? was natural thinking.

De Tocqueville also advanced "that the social changes which bring nearer to the same level the father and son, the master and servant, the superiors and inferiors, generally speaking, will raise woman and make her more and more the equal of man."

During his middle twenties, he sensed the fundamentalness of this growing concept of equality among Frenchmen. All men were by no means equal in the France of his day, and certainly women did not have equality with men, but the tendencies toward equality for all were apparent to him. The French Revolution was over, Napoleon was dead, and the Bourbons had been restored to the throne of France. "The monarchy of the property class" was firmly established when Louis Philippe I became "King of the French" on August 9, 1830, after he had sworn to support the constitutional charter.

De Tocqueville sensed the time had arrived when a careful study should be made of the then existing social elements which were causing men to approach equality with one another, and women with men. The best place to make such a study, he concluded, was the United States, where these elements had freer play than in Europe. He discussed his idea with friends, two of whom readily decided to go with him to the New World. In order to obtain permission from the French Government to visit the United States, they gave as their reason a desire to study its penitentiary system. The French penal system was in dire need of reorganization and it was understood the American system was better than that of any European nation. The government thought highly of De Tocqueville's project, gave its permission for the visit, and on May 9, 1831, he and his two companions landed in the United States.

He stayed until February of the following year, with the exception of twenty days spent in Canada, and diligently devoted his efforts to study American society and government (with little attention to her penitentiary system). He talked to hundreds of persons, from the President to southern slaves, and gathered information from many officials, industrialists, clergymen, and farmers. Albert Gallatin, who had relinquished position and fortune to come to America and with whom De Tocqueville had much in common, helped him materially in a correct understanding of the society. So did the many women from the coast to the frontier whom he continually consulted. The close observations of democratic, Protestant America by this aristocratic royalist and devout Catholic eventuated in a work which was proclaimed by all as unbiased and profound.

On returning to France he immediately wrote his *Democracy in America*. He had not been actively allied with any particular political party and had no reputation as a writer or statesman, hence he encountered considerable difficulty in finding a publisher, but finally one agreed to print five hundred volumes. The book was an immediate success with many editions to come. In England the Liberal Party received it with enthusiasm, and it was reviewed by no less a personage than John Stuart Mill.[2] In the United States its translation was read extensively and several colleges adopted it as a text book on constitutional law. The author's fame quickly spread throughout Europe and America – the book had become a sensation for political treatise. Its purpose was not to praise democracy; actually De Tocqueville doubted that government by the people could ever work in France and was not sure it would survive indefinitely in the United States, although he was convinced it was the ideal form of government for the Americans of that day. The book simply portrayed the people and the democracy of the United States as they existed.

De Tocqueville's conclusions on the American woman of the first part of the nineteenth century are considered to be the best on the subject. He found her to be the most moral woman of Western civilization and far above her European sister. He gave as reasons for her premarital morality the equality which existed in a democracy, the lack of class distinction, and the privilege of a young man to marry a young lady of his choice without restraint from family or custom. Because of these social characteristics "no girl then believes that she can not become the wife of the man who loves her; and this renders all breaches of morality before marriage very uncommon: for, whatever be the credulity of the passions, a woman will hardly be able to persuade herself that she is beloved when her lover is perfectly free to marry her and does not." Equality and freedom in marriage, according to De Tocqueville, also removed one of the main causes of infidelity after marriage. Since the wife had freely consented to the marriage, had allowed herself to be selected by her husband, and the selection was based on factors which supported the marriage union, she had no excuse for intrigues, and if guilty, the society had no condonation for her actions.

> In aristocratic countries the object of marriage is rather to unite property than persons; hence the husband is sometimes at school and the wife at nurse when they are betrothed. It can not be wondered at if the conjugal tie which holds the fortunes of the pair united allows their hearts to rove; this is a natural result of the nature of the contract. When, on the contrary, a man always chooses a wife for himself, without any external coercion or even guidance, it is generally a conformity of tastes and opinions which brings a man and a woman together, and this same conformity keeps and fixes them in close habits of intimacy.

De Tocqueville also concluded that morality in American women throughout life was strengthened because the young American girl was not unduly sheltered up to the time of her marriage. He observed that the Americans had learned that in a democracy individual independence is great, youth premature, customs fleeting, public opinion unsettled, paternal authority weak, and marital authority contested.

Under these circumstances everyone realized woman could not be repressed in "the most vehement passions of the human heart" and the surer way to protect her was "to teach her the art of combatting those passions for herself. As they could not prevent her virtue from being exposed to frequent danger, they determined that she should know how best to defend it; and more reliance was placed on the free vigour of her will than on safeguards which have been shaken or overthrown. Instead, then, of inculcating mistrust of herself, they constantly seek to enhance their confidence in her own strength of character. As it is neither possible nor desirable to keep a young woman in perpetual or complete ignorance, they hasten to give her a precocious knowledge on all subjects. Far from hiding the corruptions of the world from her, they prefer that she should see them at once and train herself to shun them; and they hold it of more importance to protect her conduct than to be overscrupulous of her innocence."

There is available no better analysis of the morals and character of the nineteenth-century girl and young lady of the United States than the following by De Tocqueville:

> No free communities ever existed without morals; and, as I observed in the former part of this work, morals are the work of woman. Consequently, whatever affects the condition of women, their habits, and their opinions, has great political importance in my eyes. Among almost all Protestant nations young women are far more the mistresses of their own actions than they are in Catholic countries. This independence is still greater in Protestant countries like England, which have retained or acquired the right of self-government; the spirit of freedom is then infused into the domestic circle by political habits and by religious opinions. In the United States the doctrines of Protestantism are combined with great political freedom and a most democratic state of society; and nowhere are young women surrendered so early or so completely to their own guidance. Long before an American girl arrives at the age of marriage, her emancipation from maternal control begins: she has scarcely ceased to be a child when she already thinks for herself, speaks with freedom, and acts on her own impulse. The great scene of the world is constantly open to her view: far from seeking concealment, it is every day disclosed to her more completely, and she is taught to survey it with a firm and calm gaze. Thus the vices and dangers of society are early revealed to her; as she sees them clearly, she views them without illusions, and braves them without fear;

> for she is full of reliance on her own strength, and her reliance seems to be shared by all who are about her. An American girl scarcely ever displays that virginal bloom in the midst of young desires, or that innocent and ingenuous grace which usually attend the European woman in the transition from girlhood to youth. It is rarely that an American woman at any age displays childish timidity or ignorance. Like the young women of Europe, she seeks to please, but she knows precisely the cost of pleasing. If she does not abandon herself to evil, at least she knows that it exists; and she is remarkable rather for purity of manners than for chastity of mind. I have been frequently surprised, and almost frightened, at the singular address and happy boldness with which young women in America contrive to manage their thoughts and their language amid all the difficulties of stimulating conversation; a philosopher would have stumbled at every step along the narrow path which they trod without accidents and without effort. It is easy, indeed, to perceive that, even amid the independence of early youth, an American woman is always mistress of herself: she indulges in all permitted pleasures, without yielding herself up to any of them; and her reason never allows the reins of self-guidance to drop, though it often seems to hold them loosely.

Through the clear eyes of De Tocqueville was presented a new type of woman whose firm morality distinguished her from other women of her day. This morality was not puritanical but pragmatic, not religious but stoic, not from above but within; and her good conduct was a day-by-day practice, did not need to be sustained by a dedicated life or a convent, and required no male moral monitor. This woman could participate in life to the fullest, live in her own time, and retain her balance.

Like the Roman girl she was a virgin when she married, but her virtue was based on self-discipline and parental advice rather than on seclusion and parental restriction. Unlike the Roman girl of the centuries after Christ, she was not transposed by marriage into a different moral environment, but wedlock was a step in a world she understood. She would not fling aside her instilled training upon taking a husband, but would work shoulder-to-shoulder with him and lie only in his bed, and she would marry but once. If she left the security of the established coastal area for the Western frontier, it would be an adventure of courage and toil, not of intrigue and ease as when the Roman matron accompanied her husband to a province.

The United States was still in the stoic phase of the cycle through which great civilizations pass, and adaptable woman was playing her part. There were comforts and wealth in the older sections but self-reliance and strict morality were characteristics of the people wherever located. A prolonged era of prosperity lay ahead for the nation. Perhaps Rome of Cato's day is the best comparison of an older great civilization to the United States of the early nineteenth century. However, the tempo of woman's acquisition of rights was to be much faster in the United States than it had been in Rome. It was four centuries after Cato before the Roman woman was virtually man's legal, social, and intellectual equal; one century after De Tocqueville's visit until women of the United States had acquired that status.

The American woman of the first half of the nineteenth century freely associated with the men of her class somewhat as did the Babylonian and Egyptian woman. Also, no thinking person questioned her native intelligence and powers to reason, and she was rapidly acquiring the intellectual freedom of the courtesan of Greece, yet not at the same price the courtesan paid. She did not have the courtesan's opportunity to associate with a plethora of greatness in art, philosophy and literature but only because it did not exist in America. The cultural advantages which the country offered were fast opening to her, though they were usually of a more practical nature than philosophical theories and beauty in art. This American woman also performed ably the function of the Athenian family woman, actually doing a better job of raising a larger family than her ancient sister of fewer duties and more protection. The Athenian matron, who saw the world only from the porthole of her secluded home and learned of life second-hand from her husband, was not prepared to impart to her children realistic information and to make proper decisions on empirical living.

It is the mother with whom children are in continual daily

contact and who must teach them the multitude of little things which total into habits, manners, attitude, and character. If she is not informed and educated, the children suffer. Fathers who are at work cannot supply this necessary constant training; and neither can the modern housemaid in her infrequent moments between housework, television, and telephone. Rare is an adequate substitute for an educated, informed mother.

ESTABLISHMENT OF THE TEXTILE INDUSTRY

The American Revolution of 1776 brought to the Colonies political independence from Great Britain, but not economic independence. Most manufactured goods and articles continued to come from England, as there was an acute scarcity in this country of machinery, mechanics, skilled workmen and know-how. We still had a frontier economy with continual movement westward and a jack-of-all-trades type of production. The producers were doing well within their limitations: inventing, tinkering, adapting and turning out practical and needed items — they were not modern, do-it-yourself, helpless hopefuls. Nevertheless, they could not do the job of mass production necessary for the expanding economy of the new nation, and industry in the European sense was sorely needed.

This soon came, and to the textile industry because of woman's contribution. To appreciate the full significance of her contribution — illustrated by the Lowell story — it is necessary to understand the establishment in the United States of mass production and of the textile mills. This understanding can best be conveyed in perspective by a review of the cardinal efforts of Eli Whitney, Samuel Slater, and Francis Cabot Lowell.

Eli Whitney (1765-1825)

Eli Whitney was to point the way for mass production and to lay the foundation for the present American system of manufacture. When the southern cotton planters copied his cotton gin, thereby illegally depriving him of most of the financial benefits of his invention, or thereby justifiably resisting his injurious private monopoly of separating by machine the cotton and its seed — however it should be stated — the South did the North its greatest favor. Whitney, born, reared, and educated in New England, returned there and proceeded to initiate the transformation of the North's economy as he had the South's.

In 1798, the tension with France over her treatment of American merchant vessels and shipping was approaching the breaking point, and the United States government wanted arms in a hurry. War, of course, was never declared, but while the tension was growing, Whitney sought a government contract for the manufacture of muskets. He had no capital, plant, material, organization, nor workmen; but he did have a plan to mass produce large numbers of muskets — actually a plan suited to the mass production of any mechanical metal product. He also had the cotton gin as positive proof of his practical inventiveness. The government went along with his proposal and gave him an advance of $5,000 on a $134,000 contract for ten thousand muskets. This was a tremendous order for an American, and several officials doubted if Whitney could ever fill it. An influence resolving the doubt in his favor was the fact that the administration did not know where to place the $600,000 Congress had appropriated for the purchase of arms. Europe could not supply them as it was arming itself, and the established domestic arms producers were not prepared to handle a job of this magnitude. The fact that a federal appropriation was about to go begging indicated the nation's inability to manufacture in quantity. The best the government could do was to trust a man who possessed only the intangible asset of creativeness, a risk rarely taken by public officials.

Whitney's plan was to make the various individual parts of the ten thousand muskets identical so that any set of parts necessary to compose a musket would fit together, or the same parts would be interchangeable, and further, to accomplish this identity or precision factor by the manufacture of the parts with power-driven machines operated by common labor. Theretofore all rifles had been made by the hand cutting, filing and fitting together of the parts for one particular rifle, not for a large number of rifles nor even for any two. The workman took a metal template for each separate part – an ordinary dress pattern is the best known example to convey the idea of a template – and hand chiseled the part by following the template. Still the same parts were not identical or interchangeable, though such a workman had to be skilled regardless of the lack of uniformity.

Whitney proceeded to design and build machines which would cut by templates, a different machine for each template or for each part of the musket. The mechanical principle was a rotating iron wheel with teeth in the rim which cut by the template, and since all teeth hit at the same point, identical parts were cut. An unskilled workman could operate the machines and turn out many more precision parts than a skilled hand workman could turn out unidentical parts. The construction of the power-driven, precision-cutting machines did not come easily. Whitney was opening up a new field and his difficulties and setbacks were many. In the end he overcame all problems and produced the muskets in accordance with his original plan and thinking. Thus was initiated the milling machine and the "uniformity system" which are still the bases of our manufacture of metal products. Division of labor was also a part of Whitney's plan, with each worker operating a particular machine and producing only one component of the musket.

Whitney's ideas were due in the progress of manufacture. In 1776, Adam Smith in his *Inquiry Into the Nature and Causes of Wealth of Nations* had advocated division of labor. A workshop in France had a machine for precision jobs, England had a metal bore which was accurate, and Rhode Island had automatic machines for the manufacture of nails and card teeth although precision was not involved. At Middletown, Connecticut, a manufacturer of pistols was working on the idea of making the individual parts by machines, with division of labor. Other manufacturers in the United States had thought out various labor-saving devices and processes, but each, whether mechanical or division of labor, was for one step in the manufacture of a particular product, to save time or money in one plant, and was installed as the manufacturer picked up an idea in his own operation. It was Whitney who conceived the general abstract plan of the "uniformity system" for machine manufacture of precision parts by division of labor, no matter what the metal product. (To this the cotton gin was relatively minor.)

Whitney's overall plan also included the welfare of his workers. After he established his plant at Mill Rock, Connecticut, he built good stone houses for the married men and their families, and for the single men he operated a boarding house with a housekeeper. This housekeeper and her assistants not only cooked for the boarders but washed and mended their clothes and looked after them. Whitney encouraged the family men to purchase their homes with the idea of having a stationary, satisfied group of employees. The village was operated for the betterment of the workers, with Whitney endeavoring to see that each man, woman, and child was properly cared for, both in sickness and in health. He definitely felt responsible for the financial, physical, and moral welfare of all, and the problems of his workers were his problems. Also, as he visualized his responsibility, their need for continuous employment imposed the duty on him to furnish it.

Whitney stayed in the village in a large farmhouse and with him lived, virtually as sons, several boys who were being trained as apprentices. One way to describe this first mill town in the United States is as a large family group, with the employer exercising a paternal influence over all and with every employee doing a day's work for a day's pay. Unskilled labor and capital in their initial joint effort at mass production by machine and division of labor were off to a good relationship in the United States. No such affinity existed between employer and employee in the older manufacturing areas of England and Continental Europe.

Samuel Slater (1768-1835)

Samuel Slater was born in Derbyshire, England. At fifteen he became an apprentice of Jedediah Strutt, a partner of Richard Arkwright, the famous British textile manufacturer who invented the yarn spinning-frame. He was the first to operate spinning wheels and looms by drive belts powered by a water wheel. The substitution of power, spinning-frame, and other labor-saving devices for hand work was the basis of Britain's eighteenth-century Industrial Revolution. Young Slater realized the principles which produced this change in the methods of manufacture and knew the machines in the Arkwright factory — how to build, operate, and repair them. At twenty-one, in 1789, he came to the United States. He brought no plans or sketches of machines with him as it was against the law to take them out of England, but regardless, early in 1790 at Pawtucket, Rhode Island, he was designing from memory machines for cotton spinning. By the end of the year he and his partners were turning out yarn and soon were establishing additional cotton and wool textile mills. Like Whitney, they had their troubles but overcame them.

Slater followed the English practice of using child labor in his factories. There was nothing complicated about the operation of the machines, the work was no harder than most youngsters did on the farm or at home, and parents welcomed the opportunity for their children to learn a trade which promised a good future. Slater did not adopt the treatment accorded children in the mills of England where they were underfed, poorly clothed, often beaten, and early frustrated. The English system was considered throughout Europe and America as a disgraceful exploitation of child labor and Slater would have no part of such an operation regardless of profits. Instead, the children in his mills were treated kindly, were provided with good food and good clothes, and conditions were made pleasant for them. For their benefit Slater started one of the first Sunday schools in America, and though there developed local opposition based on the belief that the Sabbath was being profaned, he continued with the school.

Again we see a wholesome relationship between capital and labor in the first true American textile mills. Slater has been called the father of American textile manufacture.

Francis Cabot Lowell (1775-1817)

Francis Cabot Lowell, of Boston, while traveling in England in 1811, carefully examined the textile mills at Manchester, and illegally smuggled out of the country sketches of important machines. On returning home in 1813 he, his wealthy brother-in-law, and Paul Moody, a machinist, planned a factory at Waltham, Massachusetts, for the manufacture of cloth from raw cotton by machines driven by water power. The factory was erected by the following year and was the only one in the world which machine-processed in one building all the steps from cotton to cloth. The machines were a vast improvement over the Manchester designs and, in addition, the mill was the best equipped in existence. Its products were an immediate success in spite of the strong preference for English cottons among American consumers. Lowell died in 1817, but the mill continued to prosper and by 1822 needed more water than Waltham could supply.

The Merrimack Manufacturing Company was organized and a cotton cloth manufacturing mill was located on the Merrimack River at the thirty-foot Pawtucket Falls where ample water was available. A town was later built and named after Lowell. The new factory had substantial production in 1823 (the first year after the company's organization) and in three years was turning out two million yards of cloth annually. Lowell was the textile center of the United States and proudly called "The Spindle City" and "The Manchester of America."

The Lowell Girls

The great majority of textile employees were women, which, after the foregoing background of industrial development in the United States, brings us to the purpose of this discussion. "The treatment of women is one thing, her legal status another; her opportunities for public activities still another, while the character and extent of her labors belongs again to a distinct category."[3] The availability of gainful employment at Lowell was opportunity itself for many of the early nineteenth-century New England girls. They came from Maine, Vermont, New Hampshire, Massachusetts, and other states. Most of them were single and in their late teens and early twenties, all were of good sturdy families, and many were from the farms.

The girl of this era who had to earn her own living usually hired out to some family for a dollar a week and "keep." To her Lowell's wage scale and other advantages were beyond fondest expectancy and the first pay envelope a thrill of a lifetime. Many a girl who came to Lowell wanted money for a particular purpose such as to pay her way through one of the seminaries for young ladies or to assist a brother in getting an education, and the differential in pay and expenses enabled her to save scarce dollars.

Wages were not the only inducement bringing girls to Lowell; it offered educational and cultural advantages of strong appeal. To this early mill town came well-known lecturers, educators, writers, and scientists, many from Europe. President Andrew Jackson in 1833 "reviewed" the girls all dressed in white, and with his known enthusiasm for beauty in the fair sex, exclaimed: "They are very pretty women, by the Eternal." Other visitors were Ralph Waldo Emerson, John Quincy Adams, Davy Crockett, Harriet Martineau (whose father was an English manufacturer), and Charles Dickens. Dickens, who criticized most of what he found in America, had only praise for Lowell.

Good books were on hand for the girls and they pored over their pages with a determination unknown to the average modern student. The company had to adopt strict rules to keep the girls from reading on the job, though most of them were on piece work, and some tried the Bible, thinking their foremen would be hesitant to prohibit its study. On the looms they pasted verses and in the dressing rooms pinned up mathematical problems. When not at work they attended educational societies, church gatherings and ladies circles, and even had a debating club. For five years, starting in 1840, they published a periodical, *The Lowell Offering,* which was widely read and praised at home and abroad. During the last three years it was edited by Harriot F. Curtis ("Mina Myrtle") and two of its contributors were Lucy Larcom (whose mother operated one of the company boarding houses) and Harriet Hanson.

Management soon realized there was a positive relationship between the education of its employees and their work efficiency:[4]

> Most of the New England girls attained a high degree of skill, and it was soon established that the amount of education they possessed bore a direct relationship to their efficiency as workers, operatives who had been schoolteachers, for example, earning 17¾ percent more in wages than the average, and 40 percent more than the few illiterates. One agent found that he could speed up the machinery from 12 to 15 percent without damage to the product by using better-educated girls, while another was obliged to return to the production of a coarser type of material when illiterate immigrants replaced them.

In Lowell's shopping district were the same styles found in Boston and New York – the merchants sent the best to this town of young ladies with cash in their purses. To the girl from the farm who wanted to learn how to dress, talk and act, to know what was going on in the world, Lowell was her opportunity. Also, there she could satisfy her craving for companionship with other girls: girls from different states, some from the cities, all eager to talk and be friendly, to help one another and to advance themselves. This socializing produced satisfaction, enthusiasm, and efficiency in work and without more was worth the hours of toil to the lonely rural New England girl. Her attitude toward Lowell was much the same as today's rural Spanish girl's regard for Madrid, where all wish to live, and which they call El Cielo, meaning heaven. "It is better to go hungry in El Cielo," they say, "than never to live there at all."

By 1840 there were 6320 female employees in the Lowell factories, and by 1849 Merrimack alone had built thirty-five boarding houses for its girls. The houses were not operated by the company but by responsible women tenants or "house mothers" under the company's supervision. The strict requirements appear from the following rules of about 1830:

> The Tenants of the Boarding-Houses are not to board or

permit any part of their houses to be occupied by any person, except those in the employ of the Company.

They will be considered answerable for any improper conduct in their Houses, and are not to permit their Boarders to have company at unseasonable hours.

The doors must be closed at ten o'clock in the evening, and no person admitted after that time without some reasonable excuse.

The keepers of the Boarding-Houses must give an account of the number, names and employment of the Boarders when required, and report the names of such as are guilty of any improper conduct.

Not only were the boarding houses regulated, but the off-duty activities of the girls were supervised by the company. Attendance at church services was required, regular hours were enforced, and the male employees were admonished under penalty of discharge to have proper respect for the female employees, one of the rules providing:

The Company will not continue to employ any person who shall be wanting in proper respect to the females employed by the Company, or who shall smoke within the Company's premises, or be guilty of inebriety, or other improper conduct.

The youthful French editor, Michel Chevalier, visited Lowell in 1834. His government had sent him to the United States to study water transportation at the request of influential friends who wished his release from jail where he was serving a sentence for advocating free love in his paper. Chevalier, upon questioning a factory director at Lowell — no doubt in further research of the subject which had caused his recent misfortune — learned that only three of Lowell's thousands of single female employees had become pregnant, and in each case the father and mother married several months before the baby arrived, hence no illegitimate child had ever been born in Lowell. Chevalier was surprised that young attractive girls could be trusted so far away from home unaccompanied by an elder protector, a risk which he said would not be taken in France.

He hastily concluded that the American girl's good conduct without chaperonage was due to her Protestant training. Unlike De Tocqueville, he had made no study of the underlying causes for the moral fiber of the young women of America. Only three years earlier De Tocqueville had observed no difference in the morals, social thinking, and general attitude of the American Catholic and the American Protestant, lay or cleric, and he had concluded that *democracy* was the factor which gave the American girl and woman her staunch morality.

At the time of Chevalier's visit Lowell was a show place, world famous, a factory town unique in the annals of industry where there was dignity in labor, enthusiasm in work, pride in effort. Chevalier never forgot the "Ladies of Lowell" and commended them during the rest of his life. (I mention that with maturity he abandoned his support of free love and became a prominent citizen of France.) The ladies too knew the role they were playing, that they were contributing to a national economic development, that the eyes of America and Europe were on them, and they did their job with heads high and with credit to their sex and to youth.

The impression must not be given that all was utopian at Lowell. The mills were not as sanitary or as well ventilated as modern mills, the working hours were long, there was no pay for overtime, and some persons considered the situation unsatisfactory for female labor. The girls did not object. Most of them wanted to save money as fast as they could, would work only two or three years, were healthy, trained to tasks, and little concerned with what others regarded as harsh working conditions. It is true that the boarding houses were usually crowded, and that the food was typical of such establishments, but the rates were low, there was plenty of the food, and the more boarders, the larger number of intimate friends to be remembered. The company regulation of off-duty activities was more annoying to the girls than the hard work and the full quarters. In spite of supervision and some discomforts, there has never existed more satisfaction between capital and labor than at Lowell, and women have never been more benefited by employment.

Several writers have compared the social position of the Lowell girl to that of the contemporary school teacher, and actually many former school teachers worked at Lowell and many Lowell employees became school teachers. The Lowell employee (as the average woman mill worker throughout the East) received better pay than the average woman school teacher. Also, working at Lowell had a romance which school teaching lacked. When the Lowell girl returned to her home she was a person who had been somewhere, who had been in contact with important people, who had something to talk about besides crops and neighbors, and who knew how to be somebody. She married well and her daughters and granddaughters were not mill hands. Her ambition and the country's prosperity gave her descendants a share of New England and of the domain to the West, and many became leaders in business, industry, politics, and the professions.

Female Labor in the National Economy

To appreciate the great contribution which women, including the Lowell girls, have made to the industrial development of our country, we must understand the national situation. When the factories were coming into existence late in the eighteenth century, there was a dearth of male labor, not only skilled but common, and this continued well into the nineteenth century. It was easy to acquire farm land to the West, and movement in that direction was a controlling factor in the economy. A man could have more for himself and family by owning a tract of land than by working for wages. Sons were also more valuable on the farm than in other occupations because of the extreme difficulty in finding hired hands. Daughters were of value too, but not to the extent as were teenage boys who could do heavy work in the fields.

Most economists were of the definite opinion that the national income would suffer by a shift of male labor from agriculture to industry; that there was more net profit to be derived from the application of a man's effort to raising crops and stock than to factory work. Still, a family with three or four girls could always spare one or two without noticeable reduction in the farm's products. Thus the stage was set for women to supply the labor for the textile mills, and that was what happened, not only at Lowell but throughout the East.

Female factory labor was used by the high-tariff advocates or Protectionists as an effective argument in support of their cause. During all this period the question of tariffs was an active economic and political issue. The manufacturers, wishing to protect their infant industries against competitive imports, extolled the benefits which flowed to their female employees with a zeal born of high profits. They proclaimed that factory work made women financially independent, improved morals, reduced idleness, saved thousands from becoming public charges, and was a boon to the sex. In spite of the dollar enthusiasm the Protectionists had sound reasoning on their side: women were benefited by earning money and, as a rule, so were their families. Many a daughter gave part, sometimes all, of her earnings direct to the family.

And there was no question that the nation needed manufacturing badly to round out its economy, even though perhaps agriculture had to be harmed temporarily. But it did not have to be and was not, since the established New England and Eastern areas had several thousand women who could quit the farms without detriment to agriculture. The Free-Trade Convention in 1831 stood by its position that labor in the United States was less productive in manufacture than in other occupations, but conceded one exception: female labor in the cotton and woolen factories. Such labor, the convention agreed, was much more beneficial than if applied to "the ordinary occupations of women." (In one sense textile factory labor was a mechanized extension of the work women had theretofore tediously performed in their homes with old-fashioned spinning and weaving devices.) Also meeting in 1831 was an industrial convention whose committee on cotton reported there were 39,000 females working in the cotton factories in the United States with total annual earnings of over $4,000,000. Obviously this was a gain for the country, both in national income and in the growth of an essential industry.

All agreed that capital's taking of female labor as a bride was fitting, and all recognized that their honeymoon resulted in the birth of the textile industry for the new Republic. Had it not been for the bride this industry would have lagged for years — some have estimated for half a century, almost a third of the time we have been an independent nation. Men with vision, among them Alexander Hamilton, knew what women, by their factory work, were contributing to the nation's future and openly commended their efforts. Even the determined Free Trader, Gallatin (mentioned in connection with De Tocqueville's visit), praised the cotton and woolen mills since agriculture could spare the female laborers.[5] Woman successfully launched a major industry in the United States, and history accredits her. A toast to the bride!

---

[1] All quotations from Alexis De Tocqueville's *Democracy in America,* are from the translation by Henry Reeve, published by Appleton-Century-Crofts, Inc., New York (1899).

[2] Mill was a staunch advocate of women's rights, and the author of *On the Subjection of Women.*

[3] Lowie, Robert H., *Primitive Society.* Liveright Publishing Corporation, New York (1920).

[4] Josephson, Hannah, *The Golden Threads: New England's Mill Girls* & *Magnates,* p. 77. Duell, Sloan & Pearce, Inc. (1949).

[5] Gallatin forcefully opposed war with France because war interferred with the free trade of the world which he considered essential to prosperity.

WOMAN SUFFRAGE

ONE OF THE GREAT ASSEMBLAGES OF THE WORLD, AND THE greatest for the United States, was the Constitutional Convention which met May 25, 1787, in the State House at Philadelphia. Most of the country's illustrious men were in serious attendance: eighty-one-year-old Benjamin Franklin, General Washington, Alexander Hamilton, James Madison, and other giants of the time. A state was to be created, and all were determined to draft a constitution under which it could survive, not another Articles of Confederation under which it could not. Thus differences large and small were adjusted and seemingly unsolvable problems were resolved. The constitution as finally adopted was truly, as it has so often been called, an instrument of compromises.

Yet one issue was so controversial it could not be compromised and was finally abandoned lest it disrupt the convention: the issue of woman suffrage. If this group of statesmen could not settle the question, who could? Many were disappointed at the convention's failure to adopt a clause permitting women to vote, feeling this new experiment in democracy should not be tainted from its beginning by a denial of suffrage on account of sex. The convention's throwing up of its hands on the problem meant each of the thirteen states could decide the issue for itself, which in turn meant nothing would be done. And nothing was. The average state legislator believed, as had his ancestors who settled the Colonies, that woman's place was in the home.

As a result woman suffrage was more or less dormant until 1820, when Frances Wright, of Dundee, Scotland, visited the United States and endeavored to channel thinking away from the old beliefs regarding women which she considered to have degraded them in society. She thought clearly on women's rights, slavery, theology, and politics, and advanced sound arguments for needed social reforms. She persuaded many but they were few compared to those who opposed any change in women's status. She was denounced in press and pulpit in words as strong as those media permit in propagandizing the public. Still her stay of several years was the forerunner of the movement in the United States for women's rights.

During this period the question of slavery was becoming of concern to many in the North. Soon that issue was to make two needed contributions to the movement for women's rights. First, it was a simple step for those who became convinced that slaves should have equal rights to conclude women should also. Why, they asked, should ignorant Negroes be given equality and intelligent women not? Second, slavery gave those women who were anxious to sponsor their own equal rights something to which they could anchor their cause, a needed impetus, and a training ground for their speakers.

By the 1830's the anti-slavery movement was well under way in the North, and many women of that section became so imbued with the belief that slavery must immediately and completely be abolished that they mustered the boldness to express publicly their views. As a rule these women were educated to a limited extent, which, with their otherwise acquired knowledge and native abilities, enabled them with practice to become plausible, often powerful, speakers.

There was general disagreement throughout the North as to the propriety and wisdom of the sudden innovation of woman's debating a moral and political issue in public. The Anti-Slavery Association was divided on whether or not it should permit them the use of its platforms. Only one group in the North was in agreement: the Quakers unanimously supported the right of the women to speak their piece publicly, for freedom of expression and additional rights for women were traditional policies with them. No group in the South was in disagreement as to the silencing of these fomenting female fanatics. Regardless of these sundry attitudes, within a short time numerous Northern women were playing a public part, even if a controversial one, in that section's anti-slavery movement, and with sound logic were applying to woman the reasons for the removal of the slave's legal disabilities.

The first outstanding example of this was Lucretia Coffin Mott, a Quaker, born in Nantucket, Massachusetts, in 1793. At the age of thirteen she attended a Friends' boarding school at Nine Partners, New York, where one of the teachers was James Mott, a strong opponent of the institution of slavery. The two were married in 1811 and together lectured extensively against slavery. In 1840 Mrs. Mott attended the World's Anti-Slavery Convention in London. Several delegates from anti-slavery organizations in the United States were women, but in spite of their delegate status they were excluded from participation in the proceedings, principally on the protest of the English clergy whose main objection was that Paul had denied women the right to teach.

It is not surprising that Sir Henry Maine, the nineteenth-century authority on the relation of ancient laws and societies to then modern thought, would soon write: "No society which preserves any tincture of Christian institutions is likely to restore to married women the personal liberty conferred by the middle Roman law." It would be well into the twentieth century before it appeared that women of Christian nations were to gain legal rights and liberties comparable to those of the Roman woman.

Mrs. Mott was incensed at the Convention's refusal to permit its women delegates to take an active part, and so was another American woman in attendance, Mrs. Elizabeth Cady Stanton. The two resolved that at the first opportunity after returning home they would sponsor a women's rights convention in the United States.

Mrs. Stanton was the daughter of Judge Daniel Cady, of Johnstown, New York, a member of a prominent American family, and from him and her study of law she had learned that women were denied many vital legal rights and essential privileges. She determined to do what she could to remedy their handicaps, and was much more interested in rights for women than for slaves. She worked successfully, along with many others, in support of the significant 1848 New York law which gave property rights to married women in that state and she never lost an opportunity to improve the legal status of her sex.

When she and Mrs. Mott met again at the 1848 Friends' yearly meeting in New York, they called for that year, at Mrs. Stanton's home in Seneca Falls, the women's rights convention they had planned in London. It was well and enthusiastically attended. Mr. Mott presided, since none of the ladies present was sufficiently versed in parliamentary procedure to chair the meeting. After two days' sessions at Mrs. Stanton's, the group adjourned to Rochester. Much publicity was given the convention and the action taken by it, particularly by Horace Greeley's *New York Tribune*. This gathering formally initiated the modern movement of woman suffrage in the United States and elsewhere in the world; and its importance lay principally in this initiation, in the publicity it received, and in the merits of the action taken.

No redress of woman's legal position followed directly as a result of the convention, but of forceful impact on the public was the essence of the Declaration of Sentiments, modeled after the Declaration of Independence, prepared by Mrs. Stanton and adopted by the convention. This woman's bill of rights set forth the injustice of her position in law, church, home, education, elective franchise, and society generally in the following effective tone:

Declaration of Sentiments

When, in the course of human events, it becomes necessary for one portion of the family of man to assume among the people of the earth a position different from that which they have hitherto occupied, but one to which the laws of nature and of nature's God entitle them, a decent respect to the opinions of mankind requires that they should declare the causes which impel them to such a course.

We hold these truths to be self-evident: that all men and women are created equal; that they are endowed by their Creator with certain inalienable rights; that among these are life, liberty, and the pursuit of happiness; that to secure these rights governments are instituted, deriving their just powers from the consent of the governed. Whenever any form of government becomes destructive of those ends, it is the right of those who suffer from it to refuse allegiance to it, and to insist upon the institution of a new government, laying its foundation on such principles, and organising its powers in such form, as to them shall seem most likely to effect their safety and happiness. Prudence, indeed, will dictate that governments long established should not be changed for light or transient causes; and accordingly all experience hath shown that mankind are most disposed to suffer, while evils are sufferable, than to right themselves by abolishing the forms to which they were accustomed. But when a long train of abuses and usurpations, pursuing invariably the same object, evinces a design to reduce them under absolute despotism, it is their duty to throw off such government, and to provide new guards for their future security. Such has been the patient sufferance of the women under this government, and such is now the necessity which constrains them to demand the equal station to which they are entitled.

The history of mankind is a history of repeated injuries and usurpations on the part of man toward woman, having in direct object the establishment of an absolute tyranny over her. To prove this, let facts be submitted to a candid world.

He has never permitted her to exercise her inalienable right to the elective franchise.

He has compelled her to submit to laws, in the formation of which she had no voice.

He has withheld from her rights which are given to the most ignorant and degraded men — both natives and foreigners.

Having deprived her of this first right of a citizen, the elective franchise, thereby leaving her without representation in the halls of legislation, he has oppressed her on all sides.

He has made her, if married, in the eye of the law, civilly dead.

He has taken from her all right in property, even to the wages she earns.

He has made her, morally, an irresponsible being, as she can commit many crimes with impunity, provided they be done in the presence of her husband. In the covenant of marriage, she is compelled to promise obedience to her husband, he becoming, to all intents and purposes, her master — the law giving him power to deprive her of her liberty, and to administer chastisement.

He has so framed the laws of divorce, as to what shall be the proper causes, and, in case of separation, to whom the guardianship of the children shall be given, as to be wholly regardless of the happiness of women — the law in all cases going upon a false supposition of the supremacy of man, and giving all power into his hands.

After depriving her of all rights as a married woman, if single, and the owner of property, he has taxed her to support a government which recognizes her only when her property can be made profitable to it.

He has monopolised nearly all the profitable employments, and from those she is permitted to follow she receives but a scanty remuneration. He closes against her all the avenues of wealth and distinction which he considers most honourable to himself. As a teacher of theology, medicine, or law, she is not known.

He has denied her the facilities for obtaining a thorough education, all colleges being closed against her.

He allows her in church, as well as state, but a subordinate position, claiming Apostolic authority for her exclusion from the ministry, and, with some exceptions, from any public participation in the affairs of the church.

He has created a false public sentiment by giving to the world a different code of morals for men and women, by which moral delinquencies which exclude women from society are not only tolerated, but deemed of little account in man.

He has usurped the prerogative of Jehovah himself, claiming it as his right to assign for her a sphere of action, when that belongs to her conscience and to her God.

He has endeavored, in every way that he could, to destroy her confidence in her own powers, to lessen her self-respect, and to make her willing to lead a dependent and abject life.

Now, in view of this entire disfranchisement of one half of the people of this country, their social and religious degradation; in view of the unjust laws above mentioned, and because women do feel themselves aggrieved, oppressed, and fraudulently deprived of their most sacred rights, we insist that they have immediate admission to all the rights and privileges which belong to them as citizens of the United States.

In entering upon the great work before us, we anticipate no small amount of misconception, misrepresentation, and ridicule; but we shall use every instrumentality within our power to effect our object. We shall employ agents, circulate tracts, petition the States and National legislatures, and endeavor to enlist the pulpit and press in our behalf. We hope this Convention will be followed by a series of Conventions embracing every part of the country.

This declaration drew the attention of many fair minded men and women to the harsh conditions imposed on woman.

The next woman's rights convention, sponsored primarily by Lucy Stone, was in 1850, at Worchester, Massachusetts, and two others soon were held in New York, at Rochester in 1853 and at Albany in 1854. Thereafter the feminist movement spread rapidly to other states and began to draw support from influential men who believed in equality for women. The Blackwell brothers, one of whom was married to Lucy Stone and the other to Antoinette Brown (the first woman minister in the United States), actively backed their wives. Still the average male opposed the suffrage movement. Mrs. Brown was ejected from the World's Temperance Convention in 1853 by the clergymen in control of the proceedings and a resolution was passed that "we recognize women as efficient helpers in the home, but not on this platform." Even Mr. Stanton was not always happy with his wife, and she would leave home from time to time to fight for her rights; yet their domestic relations must not have been too strained — they had seven children.

The early feminist movement should not be thought of as the work of a few dedicated women and a sprinkling of men. They unfurled the banner but underlying the movement were strong currents of progress and a new type of thought convincing to many persons. The medieval concepts of the church were being challenged on all fronts, not alone on its theory of woman's inferiority, and science was making it clear that truth and facts were often at variance with the pronouncements of those who arrogated the interpretation of scriptures.

> The Church ceased gradually to dominate mankind, for an age of reason proclaimed other laws, observable in nature and not merely expounded by men who claimed to speak for God; a Darwin could, in the nineteenth century, popularize his beliefs until only a few fundamentalists a century later still disputed his theory of the origins of man. Without this triumph of secular reason, women might never have thrown off the caveats which religious teaching had imposed on them.[1]

A fortunate development in the women's rights movement, and more important than the early conventions, was the meeting for the first time in 1851 of Mrs. Stanton and Susan B. Anthony and the following half-century's active cooperation between them. Miss Anthony supplied a forcefulness which the cause needed. She and Mrs. Stanton had a catalytic effect on each other and worked better as a team than separately. The length of their uninterrupted friendship and the smoothness of their joint operations were as efficacious as their dedication to the cause.

Miss Anthony was born February 15, 1820, at Adams, Massachusetts. She taught school for a number of years, but her restless desire to better the world was broader than the classroom and more immediate than the next generation. She soon proved her ability to work successfully with large groups of persons and over considerable areas: first as a temperance worker, then as a statewide agent of the American Anti-Slavery Society, and later as a nationwide advocate of women's rights. She was a vice-president of the National Woman Suffrage Association for twenty-three years and became its president in 1892. For three years she published, and Mrs. Stanton edited, a weekly called *The Revolution.* Its motto: "The true republic — men, their rights and nothing more; women, their rights and nothing less." Miss Anthony and Mrs. Stanton, with some assistance from others, also wrote a history of woman suffrage. Their views reached and influenced many.

Books, editorials, propaganda, lectures, and women's conventions did not satisfy Miss Anthony. She wanted amendments to state constitutions allowing women to vote. The ideal time for such overt action was thought to have arrived soon after the Civil War since women had performed admirable service during that conflict and were in high public favor. The suffragettes were able to get a proposed woman suffrage amendment to the Kansas constitution submitted to the electorate of that state in 1867. It was defeated by a landslide majority. At the same election also was submitted an amendment providing for Negro male suffrage. It, too, was defeated but not by the large majority as was the woman's amendment.

Amendments affecting male Negroes were submitted in other states but were also defeated as fast as voted upon. It was therefore obvious to any practical politician that the route of amending individual state constitutions offered little hope for male Negro suffrage and none for the less popular woman suffrage. The white male, the only one who could vote on the proposed amendments, preferred to retain his exclusive right of franchise. The Republican leadership, committed to equal rights for the former slaves, was disappointed; the suffragettes were disheartened.

The Republican Party, however, had a way to meet its commitment to give the vote to Negro men, which was to have Congress propose to the legislatures of the several states a Negro male suffrage amendment to the federal constitution. This would bypass the uncooperative white male voter. The procedure was set forth in Article V of the Constitution. Congress, whenever two-thirds of both Houses deemed it necessary, could propose amendments which would become a part of the Constitution when ratified by the legislatures of three-fourths of the states. The Party was in control of both Congress and the state legislatures, so no particular difficulty would be involved in passing the amendment. By this same procedure two other amendments had already been adopted for the benefit of the Negro.

In February, 1865, the Thirty-eighth Congress had proposed the Thirteenth Amendment, which by December of that year had been ratified, providing:

> Section 1. Neither slavery nor involuntary servitude, except as a punishment for crime whereof the party shall have been duly convicted, shall exist within the United States, or any place subject to their jurisdiction.

In 1866, the Thirty-ninth Congress had proposed the Fourteenth Amendment, popularly called the Reconstruction Amendment, which was ratified in 1868, and in part provided:

> Section 1. All persons born or naturalized in the United States, and subject to the jurisdiction thereof, are citizens of the United States and of the State wherein they reside. No State shall make or enforce any law which shall abridge the privileges or immunities of citizens of the United States; nor shall any State deprive any person of life, liberty or property, without due process of law; nor deny to any person within its jurisdiction the equal protection of the laws.

So in 1869, the Fortieth Congress proceeded to propose the Fifteenth Amendment, providing for Negro suffrage:

> Section 1. The right of citizens of the United States to vote shall not be denied or abridged by the United States or by any State on account of race, color, or previous condition of servitude.

It was ratified the following year. Thus the Republican leadership accomplished, nationwide, its aim to give the vote to the Negro male.

Prior to the submissions of the Fourteenth and Fifteenth Amendments, Miss Anthony had demanded in strong words that women be included in each, but she was turned down on both. Actually, she was not supported by many who favored the feminist movement because they feared dual submissions for women and Negroes would defeat the amendments; and no chance could be taken on obtaining the desired rights for the former male slaves merely to increase those of women. Besides, Susan Anthony was causing too much agitation in the opinion of the politicians and conservative suffragettes.

Also, in the public's mind the women's rights movement was associated with the unpopular perpetual temperance movement — a main reason was that most of the leading feminists at one time or another had crusaded for temperance, for the Cold Water Army. Miss Anthony and Mrs. Stanton even had organized a temperance society, and though the men they permitted to join immediately took over its control, the public nevertheless knew of their connection with it.

In view of these various unfavorable factors it was felt by the practical politicians that women would have to wait for a federal constitutional amendment on suffrage. And wait they did for another half a century.

Upon the adoption of the Fourteenth Amendment, Miss Anthony construed it to give women the right to vote. Her position from a legal standpoint was not untenable although the courts later held to the contrary. She registered to vote in 1872, for which she was arrested, tried, convicted and fined $100. She has not yet paid the fine.

Since women had been unable to ride the coattail of the erstwhile slaves on the way to the ballot box, certain of the suffragette leaders, including Miss Anthony and Mrs. Stanton, in 1869 organized the National Woman Suffrage Association with the avowed purpose of obtaining an amendment to the United States constitution giving women the right to vote. For the same purpose and in the same year Lucy Stone and others organized another national association, the American Woman Suffrage Association. The two associations merged in 1890 with the name National American Woman Suffrage Association.

Lucy Stone died in 1893, Elizabeth Stanton in 1902, and Susan B. Anthony in 1906 at the age of eighty-six shortly after attending a woman's suffrage convention. Their work was carried on by thousands including Dr. Anna Howard Shaw, Mrs. Carrie Chapman Catt, the Rev. Olympia Brown, Dr. M. Cary Thomas, Miss Alice Paul, and socialite Mrs. Oliver H. P. Belmont, formerly Mrs. William K. Vanderbilt, nee Alva Smith of Mobile. Mrs. Belmont formed the Political Equality League and with Miss Paul the National Woman's Party. Parades, harangues, sensational episodes and militant methods entered into the movement and quickly spread to Europe.

Perhaps the most publicized event occurred in London in May, 1914. One hundred suffragettes led by Mrs. Sylvia Pankhurst moved on Buckingham Palace. The Palace, previously warned, was defended by 1500 policemen and constables. The 100 lost the day but the 1500 suffered the casualties — they were splattered with eggs, stuck with hatpins, and bitten.

In the United States, Congress and state legislatures were constantly importuned and progress was gradually made. Wyoming, admitted as the 44th state in 1890, had a provision in its constitution granting women the elective franchise which was in keeping with its policy as a territory, and by 1918 fifteen states had granted them full franchise. In 1912, Teddy Roosevelt's Bull Moose party endorsed woman suffrage. The final impetus however was the valuable, patriotic, and unselfish work performed by women in World War I. Thereafter they could no longer be denied; and in 1920 their long fight was successfully ended with the ratification of the Nineteenth Amendment providing:

Section 1. The right of citizens of the United States to vote shall not be denied or abridged by the United States or by any State on account of sex.

What have women done with their vote during the four decades since this Amendment? In 1920, at the Victory Convention of the National American Woman Suffrage Association held at Chicago, there was organized the National League of Women Voters for the purpose of the political education of women regardless of party, the rationale being that such education is essential to the democratic processes. Has the granting of the elective franchise to women, politically educated or otherwise, outlawed wars, reduced crime, elected better qualified office holders, or done any of the things claimed it would do? We know the answer: No. Woman suffrage merely increased the quantity of the electorate without affecting its quality. Neither has it changed the complexion of the vote; the rural woman thinks as the rural man, the Southern woman as the Southern man, and the laborer's, banker's, and industrialist's wife as her husband.

It follows that the effect on the outcome of elections by women's vote is negligible; and when an election does turn on this rarity, it is still politics, not statesmanship nor morality nor any other factor to the credit of woman suffrage. Furthermore, woman often chooses candidate and cause, as does man, not upon their merits, but upon the factors of class, religion, and creed. Thus she finds herself in the low company of the harlot of democracy, prejudice at the polls.

Yet the purity of woman's vote is not the point, she is entitled to it regardless, as a matter of political equality. She has never been and probably never will be any better qualified than the male voter to exercise the elective franchise. That is immaterial. Also immaterial is that virtually all husbands and wives see eye-to-eye politically. It is a political absurdity to fancy an election in which it is man versus woman. As it should be in a two-party system of government, it is Democrat versus Republican, liberal versus conservative, "reform" versus "corruption"; or simply the *outs* versus the *ins*.

---

[1] Jensen, Oliver, *The Revolt of American Women*, p. 42. Copyright 1952, by Picture Press, Inc. Reprinted by permission of Harcourt, Brace and Company, Inc.

MODERN LAWS

Introduction — Community Property and its Source — Contrast Between Modern and Common Law Rules — Equal Rights Amendment — Equal Pay Legislation

PRESENT-DAY DISCRIMINATIONS IN THE LAW AGAINST women of the United States will be stressed in this chapter; but lest we lose our perspective, it must be kept in mind that these discriminations are minor relative to the total body of legal rights and privileges. Modern woman's equality in marriage, divorce, and the domestic realm is far removed from the husband's power to punish her, to discard her at will, to reduce her from the mistress of the household to the servant of a new and younger wife. Gone is the Golden Age when man's love was prostituted by its diversion from wife to courtesan, gone are the Dark Ages when woman's life was withered by man's interpretation of the Books of Moses. Woman of today, as seen in the panorama of the six millennia of recorded history, is almost the legal equal of man.

Near equality from a historical viewpoint is not full equality in an isolated period, however, and we now scrutinize the existing inequalities of our own time, remembering that they spring from influences of lands and ages not our own. As stated in the first chapter, it is a purpose of this book — written at a time when woman approaches full equality — to point out the nature of these underlying influences in present law and economy so that their perception will hasten their elimination, and in turn hasten the complete equality for woman.

First, we must understand the present stage of our law as it relates to woman. This presentation is limited to two subjects, both of general interest. The first is the ownership of property or assets acquired (other than by gift or inheritance) by either spouse during marriage. There exist in the United States two distinct legal systems as to this property: (1) the co-ownership thereof by husband and wife, called the community property system and derived from Spain; and (2) the individual ownership of such property by either husband or wife, known as the common law system and derived from England. Obviously, the ownership of property acquired during marriage is of utmost importance to women. The second subject is a comparison of major specific discriminatory laws against women as they existed in English common law and as they presently exist. (Chronologically women's rights at common law follow the chapter on Magna Carta, but the discussion of our common law was deferred until now, since both it and modern law best can be understood by comparing the two.)

After the review of the existing stage of our law, we will consider two needed future enactments: the proposed Equal Rights Amendment to the federal constitution and better and more widespread state and federal equal pay laws, the purposes and aims of which are indicated by their names. The passage of the Amendment and of such equal pay laws will accomplish the next stage in our legal development of women's rights.

COMMUNITY PROPERTY AND ITS SOURCE

The common law of England, rooted in militaristic feudalism, recognized the individual ownership of property acquired during marriage as distinguished from its co-ownership. This resulted in the husband's not only owning outright his own property, but in his gaining the ownership or possession of that belonging to his wife. As we know, all states in the United States, except Louisiana, have for the bases of their respective laws the English common law.

A notable exception is the property rights of spouses in the eight community property states where the Spanish theory prevails that what is acquired during coverture by the efforts, labor, skill, or savings of the husband and wife, or either of them, belongs half to the husband and half to the wife; and upon dissolution of the marriage for any cause, the "net profits" of the partnership are divided equally. If the dissolution is by divorce, the division is between the two partners; if by the death of one partner, between his heirs and the survivor. The eight states presently having the community property system are, from east to west, Louisiana, Texas, New Mexico, Arizona, Idaho, Nevada, California, and Washington.

This system originates from the Germanic tribal customs regulating the ownership of property. It is not traceable to Roman Law (though sometimes thought to be) as that Law at no time contained the community property concept. Modestinus' high-sounding definition of marriage, "a partnership of all life; a mutual sharing of laws human and divine," (and later pleasing ecclesiastic and Anglo-American definitions) must not be thought of as meaning common ownership of proprty during marriage with an equal division of profits upon its inevitable termination. The Germanic community property customs were grafted onto the Civil Law of Spain by the Visigoths in the fifth century, and late in the seventh became a part of their Code or *Fuero Juzgo*. Thus firmly established, community ownership continued as part of Spanish law, and through the Spanish Conquest was passed to New Spain, then to Mexico and the states in the United States subject to Spanish and Mexican jurisdiction or influence.

The Spanish law of community property gave co-ownership to the husband and wife on the legal theory that each contributed to the partnership all his time and effort. This co-ownership did not apply to property owned by either spouse at the time of the marriage or acquired during the marriage by gift or inheritance, since such property did not result from any integrant contributed to the partnership. However, the income from separately owned property belonged to the community, the theory being that it also was contributed.

During the marriage the husband was the exclusive manager of the community estate, which he controlled and handled as a joint ownership. It was only upon dissolution of the marriage that any division took place. The wife's separate property first was set aside, then the husband-manager's, and thereafter the remainder, or the community estate, was divided equally. If any separate property was not intact in its original form or could not be traced into other property, capital of an equivalent value was taken. If separate property could be traced — an easy example being where real estate was exchanged for other real estate — the spouse took the property which could be identified with his original separate asset. The tracing of ownership was kept within narrow limits. In case of question the construction was that the separate property had been put into the partnership and invested in partnership assets, and that the original owner had only the right to reimbursement of capital and not to ownership of the *new* asset.

The community property system presently exists in some form in most Western jurisdictions which do not follow the English common law as to marital property rights. In the common law states in the United States having the system, it necessarily exists by constitutional or statutory provisions since it is an exception to the common law of England as generally adopted by them. The eight named community property states either had the system when they became states or soon adopted it. For that reason they are called the "old" community property states. All follow the Spanish system. (Louisiana is no exception although community property was first established there by the French, but after its cession to Spain in 1763 the Spanish system became the law.)

It will be seen from the geographical location of the eight states that they were directly subject to Spanish-Mexican influence.

Texas was a part of Mexico until 1836, when it gained its freedom. During its nine years of independence it retained the community property system and continued therewith after becoming a state. In 1848, most of the area of New Mexico, Arizona, Nevada, and California was acquired from Mexico by the treaty of Guadalupe Hidalgo. Idaho and Washington, as a part of the original Oregon territory, were also subject to Spanish-Mexican influence.

Basically the community property laws of these eight states are the same as the old Spanish Civil Law although each has its own modifications and refinements, particularly California. The community property system in the beginning did not spread beyond these states, all other states and territories following the common law as to individual ownership; and neither did the individual ownership theory encroach on the community property area. While the two systems and their respective advantages and disadvantages furnished a subject for continual academic discussion, especially from the wife's standpoint, each state was satisfied with the system it possessed and gave no serious consideration to altering its set pattern in order to benefit the wife.

In the 1930's, however, it became generally recognized throughout the United States that a federal income tax advantage existed for the taxpayer in the community property jurisdictions where wages, salaries, dividends, interest, and other items on which an income tax was paid, were owned equally by the marriage partners. Since half the husband's salary, etc., was income to the wife, and vice versa, the total income of the two spouses could be split down the middle and half reported by each. This resulted in considerable saving, especially to those in the then surtax brackets, over having to report all or most of the income as that of the husband where he was the sole or principal money-maker, the ordinary situation in the non-community states.

In order to obtain the tax benefits of the community system, Oklahoma, in 1939, passed a statute permitting a husband and wife to file a written election to have their property rights determined by community property law, but the statute failed to accomplish its purpose. The elective or permissive feature caused the Supreme Court of the United States, in 1944, to hold that a true community property system had not been created within the meaning of the federal income tax laws. In 1945, Oklahoma enacted a second statute — this time taking no chances — which created a marital ownership system similar to those of the old community property states. In the same year Hawaii adopted a well-drafted compulsory community property statute. Oregon, which had followed Oklahoma's first enactment, repealed its permissive statute and passed another similar to Oklahoma's 1945 law. In 1947, Nebraska and Pennsylvania modeled statutes after Oklahoma's second law, and Michigan after Hawaii's. Community property bills were introduced in numerous other legislatures and were being considered generally throughout the nation.

Congress, which for repeated sessions had been importuned to pass a tax law equitable for all, finally incorporated in the Revenue Act of 1948 a provision permitting husband and wife to file a joint return dividing equally their combined income and to pay a total amount of twice the tax on each half. This put the married taxpayer of the non-community property states on the same basis as those of the community property states.

In 1948 Michigan and in 1949 Hawaii, Oklahoma, Oregon, and Nebraska repealed their community statutes. The Pennsylvania act was held unconstitutional by its Supreme Court. It would seem the "new" community property states had not adopted the system in furtherance of the principle that marriage is "a partnership of all life," but for a more prosaic reason.

It should not be overlooked that in the individual ownership states there is considerable voluntary co-ownership by husband and wife of specific assets acquired during marriage. Well-known illustrations are joint checking and savings bank accounts, stocks and bonds in the name of both spouses, and tangible personalty and real estate conveyed to both. The nature of the estate or ownership created by the conveyance of physical property to both husband and wife depends on the particular state, the wording of the instrument of conveyance, or both. In the common law states these estates can be tenancy by the entirety, tenancy in common, or joint tenancy. Both husband and wife, especially before buying real estate, and particularly a home, should know which one or more of these estates exist in their jurisdiction and the nature of those which do. Merely to instruct the lawyer to put both their names in the deed is not enough. If that creates a tenancy by the entirety, upon the death of one, the survivor owns outright the property. The couple may want this, or they may want the heirs of the deceased to inherit his half, or the survivor to have full ownership of the home but not of other real estate. The effect of title in both husband and wife should be ascertained and if that does not accomplish exactly the couple's preference, recitations which will accomplish it can be inserted in the deed or other instruments drawn.

In the community property states, title is of less importance. No matter in whom it is vested the property is jointly owned, although if title is put in the wife a presumption exists that the property was a gift to her, but this presumption is rebuttable if the facts are otherwise. Since the husband is the manager, no presumption of individual ownership arises in his favor if he alone is named in the conveyance. Of course, in all states the husband and wife live much the same during marriage, each sharing the economic fortunes of the other regardless of title and ownership as between them. It is when divorce or death comes that rights in property reveal their practical importance, often for the first and only time.

In all community property states today, the husband is the manager of the community estate as he was under the old Spanish Civil Law. However, there are numerous safeguards for the wife: in Louisiana she can have the community dissolved if the husband has shown himself to be an unfit manager; in other states she becomes the manager if he disappears; in Idaho and Washington he has no control over her earnings; and in all states the wife can obtain relief in the courts against the husband's purposefully wasting community assets or defrauding her under the guise of management. One objection to the community system, from the standpoint of full equal rights for women, is that the husband is the manager of the community estate. Actually this is of more significance in law than in practice, as ordinarily the husband and wife consult and arrive at a joint decision on any important economic step; but if they disagree, he has the legal right to exercise his own discretion.

Antenuptial agreements are valid in the community property states, but their scope is limited. The Texas courts have held that these agreements cannot change from community to separate the character of property acquired during the marriage. In Washington, an agreement was held unenforceable as unfair to the wife which provided that if title was taken in the name of either spouse the property would be his or her separate property.

I have practiced law approximately fifteen years each in a non-community property state (Tennessee) and in a community property state (Texas) and am persuaded the advantage is with the wife in the latter. The community theory recognizes the realistic part she plays in the couple's saving and having something. It is rare that a man's financial success is not attributable in large part to the wife's aid, efforts, and thrift. Often she earns substantial amounts herself, and, regardless, the rearing of children is as taxing and confining as any man's job. For the wife to own half of everything she and her husband accumulate gives dignity and reward to her labor, be it gainful or domestic, and the knowledge she has an equal financial stake in the marriage venture encourages her to endeavor and economy. It is gratifying for a woman in love to share in wedlock's joys, companionship, duties, and hardships; but it also comforts her to be a partner in its worldly assets as well. In a community state if her mate's heart wanders, she has the practical consolation of salvaging half of what they have saved. Also, if she is the one who prefers a change, she still receives her half.

CONTRAST BETWEEN MODERN AND COMMON LAW RULES

It was marriage which took from woman many fundamental legal rights under the medieval common law of England, the disabilities of the single woman being minor compared to those of the wife whose rights were transferred to the husband. As stated by eighteenth-century Blackstone in his *Commentaries*:

> By marriage, the husband and wife are one person in law: that is, the very being or legal existence of the woman is suspended during marriage, or at least incorporated and consolidated into that of her husband.

This concept prevailed well into the nineteenth century in all common law jurisdictions.

Existing individual laws in the various states of the United States are not only based on the common law of England, the civil law of Spain or France, or combinations thereof, but also on the Colonies' statutory law, judicial precedence, customs and experiences. Since most of the present legal discriminations against women come from the English common law, the comparisons in this chapter are mainly between its rules and modern rules. The so-called "married women's acts" and other statutes have removed or mitigated many inequalities against women but by no means all. The following comparisons of specific rules of particular interest to women, as they existed at common law and now exist, will show not only their present discriminatory features but also woman's advancement in law during the past two centuries. The rules are stated in most general terms, many have both common law and modern exceptions not here mentioned, and in addition most states have their own particular modifications. Thus few of the following rules are exact for all fifty jurisdictions, yet they correctly reflect, in a general way, the difference between common law and modern statutory law.

CONTRACTS. At common law the contracts of a married woman were void. Today in virtually all states she has broad contractual power independent of her husband, although if real estate is involved there are often limitations. It is only in about half the states that a wife can dispose of her own land the same as if she were a feme sole; in about a third she can make a valid conveyance of her title and interest, but the husband's rights are not affected unless he joins in the conveyance; and in a few states the husband must join for the conveyance to be valid. In all states except Georgia and Texas the wife has full power to contract as to her own personalty, physical or intangible. At common law an antenuptial contract between prospective husband and wife was voided by their subsequent marriage, but today these contracts are valid although, as stated in the preceding chapter, in certain of the community property states their scope is limited.

LAND. At common law during the period of marriage the wife had no separate estate, owning nothing except she did have what was called a general legal estate in her own land. This estate was subject to the husband's interest in the land, known as the freehold estate, which gave him the valuable rights of possession, control, rents and profits. The freehold terminated with the wife's death, but thereafter as long as the husband lived, provided a child had been born to the marriage, he had a courtesy estate in the land, with which also went the rights of possession, control, rents and profits. The husband was not permitted to sell or encumber the land, and upon his death his estate terminated and all rights in the land vested in the wife or her heirs. Succinctly stated, the husband, during his lifetime, enjoyed the wife's land as if it were his own but he could not deprive her or her heirs of it after his death.

Land, until modern times, was the main source of wealth and power. Laws relating to it are the slowest of all to change, and present-day rules are mainly a modernized common law real estate system. Nevertheless, in all states today a wife has unrestricted ownership of her separate real estate, except, as mentioned, for the contractual disabilities in certain states and the rule in the community property states that the income from separately owned property belongs to the community.

PERSONALTY. At common law any personal property owned by the wife at the time of marriage or acquired by her during marriage, even by gift or inheritance, belonged outright to the husband. She had no claim or interest of any nature in personalty, tangible or intangible, and the husband could sell, encumber, or do with it as he wished. If he died during the wife's lifetime, the personalty passed to his heirs. Only the wife's "paraphernalia" was an exception to this rule; if she outlived her husband, she did inherit her clothes, personal ornaments and jewelry to the exclusion of all other heirs. Still, during the husband's lifetime he owned this paraphernalia and it was subject to his debts. There is no state in the United States today which does not permit a married woman to own and possess her own separate personalty.

WAGES. Wages earned by a married woman now belong exclusively to her in all non-community property states and are in no way subject to the control of the husband or to the claims of his creditors. As stated, at common law the husband was the exclusive owner of all the wife earned, which was based on the mutual rules that he was entitled to her services and was obligated to support her. She could not maintain a suit to recover her wages, having no legal interest therein; but of course the husband could. Anything she made was subject to his creditors. The husband's ownership of the wife's earnings is one common law rule which has been completely obliterated. The community property states are not an exception since the rule never existed in them, the community (rather than the husband) always owning the wife's earnings as it did those of the husband.

BUSINESS. Since at common law a wife could not enter into valid contracts and her earnings belonged to her husband, she could neither conduct in her name any trade or business nor reap the benefits therefrom. Today virtually all states permit a wife to conduct a business in her name and to own exclusively the profits and alone be liable for the debts. Five states, California, Florida, Nevada, Pennsylvania, and Texas (called the "sole-trader" states) require some legal step to be taken by the wife to remove her disability of coverture before she can engage in business independent of her husband. The courts are lenient in removing this disability, done as a rule upon a joint petition of the husband and wife setting forth the reasons why she should be permitted to operate a business separately.

DAMAGES FOR PERSONAL INJURY. Damages for personal injury to the wife at common law belonged to the husband and the right of recovery was in him alone. Today they belong exclusively to the wife in most states, although in the majority of the community property states damages for the personal injury of either husband or wife goes into the community.

BREACH OF PROMISE. At common law a woman had a right of action for breach of promise of marriage, and this right still exists in most states, yet some have abolished the action altogether and others have considerably limited it.

SEDUCTION. At common law an unmarried woman as a rule had no cause of action for seduction although her parents did, based on their right to the daughter's services. A few states presently give a single woman a right of action for her seduction.

AGE OF CONSENT TO MARRIAGE. The age of consent for marriage at common law was fourteen for the male and twelve for the female. These ages have been increased in the fifty states to an average of about twenty years for males and nineteen for females. However, where the parents consent the minimum age is lower, and even though the male or female marries without the consent of the parents at an earlier age than provided by statute, the marriage is not necessarily void or even voidable. However, probably all states set an early age below which a marriage is void, regardless of parental consent or other factors.

COMMON LAW MARRIAGE. The so-called common law marriage, where there is no religious or civil ceremony but the couple merely start living together as husband and wife, was not recognized by the English common law although it was by the ecclesiastical courts which considered it best to support marriage regardless of formality. In the Colonies the common law quickly developed that these marriages were valid. This was to be expected because of the scarcity of clerical or civil officials authorized to solemnize marriages, and in many areas there was no one to perform the ceremony. Also travel was difficult and risky, thus it was often a choice between common law marriage and many couples' "living in sin" with the children illegitimate. Naturally the former became law.

These comparisons between common law and modern statutory law amply illustrate the nature of existing legal discriminations against women and the progress made in women's legal position since Sir William Blackstone, quoted at the beginning of this chapter to show that at common law the husband and wife were one — and the husband was the one.

Blackstone was highly influential in America. His *Commentaries* were widely read, and in many frontier areas this work was the only available textbook on law. While Blackstone is the best known of the many famous English jurists, he was unquestionably the least scientific. He saw no distinction in the source of the laws of England and of the law of gravitation, both being imposed from above, in his thinking. He never acquired what is called a "legal mind." His classification of rights in the *Commentaries,* when compared with Gaius' classification in the *Institutes,* is haphazard and vague. A major division by Blackstone was the rights of persons and the rights of things, stated as if things had rights. This awkward division is thought to be due to a mistaken interpretation of the technical wording of the Roman law which was studied by the English lawyer of Blackstone's time. (We will recall that Gaius said that every right which one exercises "relates either to persons, or to things, or to actions.") Blackstone's style was lucid and what he said, correct or erroneous, was — for a lawyer — stated simply, and in this respect his *Commentaries* were suited to America.

He plainly set forth the disabilities of married woman under the common law and thus lessened the effect of the growing spirit in the United States for the mitigation of her inferior legal status. The part he played was somewhat comparable to Gratian's spread of the Canon Law. Because of the old world legal background of the American woman, every gain for her has been an uphill struggle, an example of which we saw in her century of effort to obtain the right to vote in national elections. Still feudalism and Paulism could not shackle her forever. The American spirit of freedom, which almost has equalized woman of this country in the eyes of the law, has been the inspiration for, and has given hope to, women around the world in their struggle for equality. Yet much remains to be done at home.

An example is freedom-loving Texas, the fiftieth among the states in progress in women's legal rights. Even the double standard, insofar as divorce for adultery is concerned, is written in the Texas law. The husband can obtain a divorce "where his wife shall have been *taken in adultery*," but the wife can obtain one from the husband only "where he shall have *abandoned her* and *lived in adultery* with another woman." (Emphasis supplied in both quotations.) Thus one act by the wife permits the husband's release while he is allowed considerable latitude before she can obtain her freedom.

Also in Texas the "unwritten law" exists in written statutory form to the extent that it is justifiable homicide (which carries no punishment) if the husband kills a man committing adultery with his wife, provided the homicide takes place while the wife and her paramour are still together. The husband is not permitted later to track down the paramour and kill him, nor to kill the wife at any point. If the wife catches the husband, she is not allowed to kill anyone. As just said, she cannot even get a divorce on the ground of her husband's occasional adultery.

While various states of the United States may drag in the removal of the remaining legal disabilities against women, in the East progress is rapid and by major steps. In January, 1959, the South Viet Nam Assembly passed the "Family Bill" which, with one stroke, changed the basic legal position of the women of that country. Prior thereto a girl or a woman, regardless of age, could neither marry without the consent of her parents nor refuse the groom selected by them. After marriage she could be divorced for minor causes, as disobedience, at the discretion of the husband. She could even be made the servant of a new mistress taken by him. She was expected to remain faithful throughout marriage and at the same time to submit meekly to any infidelity in which her husband indulged, periodically or continually.

The Family Bill changed all this. The woman's consent is now a requisite to marriage, the wife can engage in business without the husband's permission, his illegitimate children can no longer be forced on her, she cannot be made to live with her in-laws; legally, she is a new woman. As to divorce, one can now be obtained only if the marriage becomes intolerable, and the President, not the husband, decides if this situation exists.

South Viet Nam is chosen to illustrate woman's advancement in Asiatic countries because of a historical oddity in the movement culminating in the Family Bill. This was the strong position taken by the women (particularly by the influential, young and attractive Mme. Ngo) that divorce be completely outlawed. The right of the wife to obtain release from a marriage which has become unbearable to her has been considered by most civilizations as essential to her happiness and well being. In South Viet Nam, divorce over the years, as exercised alone by the husband, had been such an evil from woman's standpoint that she wanted no more of it; and any desire or need for this right was overshadowed by her interest in depriving the husband of all opportunities to quit her.

Regardless of the divorce issue the Family Bill was one of Oriental woman's capital victories, and perhaps the momentum of woman's achievements in the East, originally spurred by the West, will react on the West to hasten full equality here.

EQUAL RIGHTS AMENDMENT

In order to remove at one stroke throughout the entire United States all remaining legal inequalities against women, there has been proposed what is known as the "Equal Rights Amendment" to the constitution of the United States. The adoption of this Amendment would follow the same procedure as did the amendments mentioned in the chapter on woman suffrage, in that it would have to pass both the Senate and the House of Representatives of the National Congress by a two-thirds vote and be ratified by the legislatures of three-fourths of the states. The Equal Rights Amendment has been introduced in every Congress starting in 1923, and in the 81st (1951) and 83rd (1953) it passed the Senate but died without action by the House. No doubt it will be introduced in all future Congresses until adopted by both chambers, and it is reasonably certain that if Congress will approve and submit the Amendment, the necessary state legislatures will ratify it in due time.

The material part of the Amendment, as introduced in the 87th Congress (1961) by Mrs. Katherine St. George, of New York, reads:

> Equality of rights under the law shall not be denied or abridged by the United States or by any State on account of sex. Congress and the several States shall have power, within their respective jurisdictions, to enforce this article by appropriate legislation.

The 1959 report on the Amendment of the Senate Committee on the Judiciary states that "the purpose of the proposed legislation is to submit an amendment to the State legislatures which, if adopted, would insure equal rights for men and women." Legally, the passage of the Amendment would make invalid any state constitutional provision, any federal or state statute, any regulation of a federal or state agency, or any type of law or rule[1] which denied equality of rights on account of sex.

The practical effect of such a law of the land can be seen by applying it to the previously mentioned common law rules as they have evolved into modern times; every discrimination not removed during this evolution would be completely eliminated. The wife in all states could handle her own or separate real property as she saw fit regardless of what her husband thought she should do with it; she could engage in business the same as he could; she would have full equal legal rights with man throughout the United States. And so would man with woman.

While the rationale of the Amendment is to give women legal equality, it should be noted that its wording prevents discriminations, not against women, but "on account of sex." What of a law granting maternity benefits to women? Would that be a discrimination against men on account of sex which would contravene the Amendment? Not in my opinion because such a law would be based on a justifiable classification, and legislation meeting this test, though applicable to one sex only, would be valid. The concept of *equal* rights does not necessarily mean *identical* rights.

The evils to be removed by the Amendment and their historical basis and present unfairness were succinctly stated by Senator John Marshall Butler in 1957 (who earlier in that year had introduced the Amendment in the Senate), as follows:

> The evils which this amendment seeks to cure are many. There are states in this Union where women are denied the fundamental right to serve on juries, where women cannot own property except with their husbands' approval, where women are denied the rights of natural guardianship, where women do not even have full control of their own personal earnings. These evils have an historical basis in the inferior position of women in medieval days and under the old English common law, but they have no sound and reasonable basis in twentieth century America.
>
> American women today do not deserve the stigma of inferiority and incompetence that those laws carry . . .
>
> Socially, politically and economically, American women have demonstrated their abilities and their potentialities.

Senator Butler's saying "these evils . . . have no sound and reasonable basis in twentieth century America" and "American women have demonstrated their abilities and their potentialities," harkens of Gaius who used this identical reasoning to reduce to a nullity from a practical standpoint various discriminations against Roman women of the second century.

The enlarging of woman's rights by the judiciary (as by the jurists of the Roman Empire) is not the answer today. It takes legislation to do this, and legislation in the sense used includes a constitutional amendment. (We will recall that the decisions of the great Roman jurists had the quality of legislation by imperial edict.) Today most of woman's disabilities are written into our state statutes or codes and constitutions, which leave little leeway for courts. At times a judge can be liberal, as mentioned in connection with the authorizing of a wife in the sole-trader states to engage in a separate business, but in each particular case the judge is limited to the removal of one disability of the one legal inferior before him; and that is done pursuant to authority vested in him by legislation. We are a government of laws, not of men, the significance of which we have seen in previous chapters.

Since legislation is the answer to full legal equality, and since it is the state constitutions and statutes which contain the discriminations, the direct approach would appear to be a change of the offending state laws. However, the chapter on woman suffrage shows this is an unrealistic approach. The sponsors of the elective franchise for women first endeavored to obtain relief from the states, and while progress was made, it was slow, tedious, and unsatisfactory. Not even the high public favor of women after the Civil War resulted in the carrying of a single election to amend a state constitution to give women the vote, and this plan was, in effect, abandoned in favor of the amendment to the federal constitution.

Action at the federal level is, of course, the method of the supporters of the Equal Rights Amendment, and it is the most practical one. I do not discourage efforts on the state level, but that is a rocky road, and it will take years to budge some state legislatures. The 1961 Texas legislature refused even to submit to the voters a proposed equal rights amendment to the Texas constitution in the face of a concerted drive, after months of tireless preparation, by those sponsoring the proposal.

What are the hopes for the national Amendment? Its passage appears likely within the foreseeable future. Since 1940 support for it has been written in every Republican Party platform and since 1944 in every Democratic Party platform. Many influential senators and congressmen of both parties advocate the Amendment as do a substantial number of high federal officials, governors, union leaders, business leaders, industrial executives, and thousands of voters. The United Nations Charter, in its preamble, reaffirms faith in the equal rights of men and women, and the United States is, of course, a signatory to the Charter. Nevertheless, we withhold from women citizens the constitutional guaranty of legal equality and thus lag behind such countries as Burma, Egypt, Greece, Japan, Pakistan, and West Germany.

EQUAL PAY LEGISLATION

Laws requiring equal pay for men and women must not be confused with the Equal Rights Amendment. Wages (except minimum) are not as a rule set by law and do not come within the scope of the Amendment as proposed. Equal pay is defined as the payment by a particular employer of the same salary or wage to both men and women performing the same or similar services. This does not mean one employer must pay the same as another to their respective employees with comparable positions or jobs; neither does it prevent pay differentials within the same organization resulting from seniority, incentive systems, merit ratings, bonus plans, and the like.

The equal-pay-for-women movement in the Modern Age is over a century old, probably the first organized demand therefor being in 1833 by a union of Glasgow spinners. In the United States during this period those who believed woman should be confined to the domestic circle justified her lower wages on the theory that it discouraged her from leaving this circle for gainful occupation, which promoted the "traditional" and "intended" relation between the sexes. The attitude of the American women workers themselves was rather passive, but agitation for their equal pay soon came from male organizations. In 1868, the National Labor Union Convention passed a resolution recommending that Congress and the state legislatures enact laws securing equal salaries for equal work to women employed in government. In the next decade the Knights of Labor, the first major labor organization in the United States, openly advocated equal pay regardless of sex. Still very little was accomplished during the nineteenth century even with the favorable attitude of male labor, although in 1891 the International Typographical Union did require equal pay for its women compositors.

The great step came in 1918 during World War I when the railroad industry gave equal pay throughout the nation pursuant to a general order issued by William G. McAdoo, director general of the railroads for the federal government. The order required that the pay of women employees, "when they shall do the same class of work as men, shall be the same as that of men." Women rendered most needed services to this essential transportation industry during World War I and deserved the equal pay order. They were even more active in railroad work during World War

II and ever since thousands of women have held peacetime positions and jobs at all levels of railroading.

The first woman railroad employee was Susan Morningstar who went to work in 1855 for The Baltimore & Ohio. Her job: scrubwoman. Since then women have occupied the executive positions of chairman of the board, president, secretary, purchasing agent, personnel supervisor, public relations officer, and others. Also, women work as section men, gang foremen, signalmen, signal maintainers, switchmen, flagmen, and at numerous similar jobs, even on the coal and ore docks as laborers. They also run the trains. In 1954, according to the Labor Department, women accounted for 352 conductors, 430 locomotive engineers, and 196 firemen. Women have indeed become "railroaders" in the traditional sense of that term. Allamore, Texas, is named for one: Mrs. Alla More, the first woman station agent of The Texas and Pacific, employed by that line about 1880.

The large number of women engaged in essential World War I work also precipitated the first state equal pay laws, those of Montana and Michigan in 1919. In 1923, the federal government recognized the equal pay principle in the Civil Service Classification Act which prohibited wage differentials on account of sex in the various grades and classifications of work under that act. During the last years of World War II, four states, Washington (1943), Illinois (1943), New York (1944), and Massachusetts (1945), passed legislation for equal pay. Noticeable is the gap of two and a half decades between the first two states and the second four. Since 1945 equal pay laws have been passed by fourteen states: Rhode Island (1946), New Hampshire (1947), Pennsylvania (1947), Alaska (1949), California (1949), Connecticut (1949), Maine (1949), New Jersey (1952), Oregon (1955), Colorado (1955), Arkansas (1955), Hawaii (1959), Ohio (1959), and Wyoming (1959).[2]

While the equal pay laws of the first two states may be attributed in part to World War I, and of the next four states in part to World War II, the passage of these laws since 1945 must be credited to "education, rather than emergency."[3] The coverage of the twenty state statutes varies from those of Illinois and

Michigan, which are limited to manufacturing, to those of Colorado and Montana, which are applicable broadly to both public and private employment.

In 1945, Senators Claude Pepper of Florida (Democrat) and Wayne Morse of Oregon (Republican at that time) introduced an equal pay bill in the United States Senate, and a similar proposal has been introduced in each succeeding Congress, but none has been enacted into law in spite of the pressing need therefor. Senator Morse recently expressed disappointment at the long time it is taking to get a federal equal pay law passed, but told me he had hopes that the need soon would be sufficiently apparent to insure its enactment. Senator Pepper also recently told me this need is now more patent than ever and that experience, since the introduction of the first federal equal pay bill, has confirmed that equal pay for women is essential to a wholesome economic pattern in a country such as the United States. Alice K. Leopold, former Assistant to the Secretary of Labor and Director of the Women's Bureau, who has given much study to salary and wage discrimination against women, states: "The principle of equal pay, or payment of a rate based on the job performed, is basic to the American free enterprise system."

Most governments (federal, state, county, city, districts of numerous types) and most private employers, still pay women less than men for the same or similar services. In this respect we give only lip homage to our two high-sounding theories of equality for all in our sacred democracy and of equal opportunity for all in our valued capitalistic system. The extent of unequal pay in government is small when compared to the remainder of the economy. The effect of the imposition of this policy by business and industry will be realized from the statistics in the following chapter showing the percentage of women in the work force and their incomes relative to men.

Less pay for women permeates every occupational level throughout the economy. Although governments are secondary to private concerns in number of employees and total pay, their role as an example or pace-setter is paramount. If only the federal government would adhere to the equal pay principle one hundred per cent, state and local governments and business and industry would follow suit. Since it is basically unfair and inexcusable for an employer to reward one person less than another for equal service, if an employer with the influence and widespread activity of the United States were to refuse to violate this rule of fairness, others would find the pressure too great to violate it. President Eisenhower, in his 1956 State of the Union message, declared that equal pay for equal work was "a simple matter of justice."

Those not concerned with simple justice may reason that women's loss from unequal pay, which runs into the billions of dollars annually, is the gain of the employer or of the male employee or of the consumer, and therefore the economy or the society as a whole does not suffer. Regardless of the merits of this theory, there are harmful results, not of a monetary nature and not always readily discernible, flowing from inequalities in pay. The same is true for inequalities in advancement and in other opportunities, a forceful illustration of which is our shortage of scientific personnel. I refer no more to top scientists than to the thousands of scientifically trained workers needed by a strong nation to maintain its position in the world of the present and of the future.

In most scientific fields men are definitely favored in both pay and advancement, and unequal advancement for a woman of the quality to become a good scientist can discourage her more than unequal pay. She turns from an endeavor in which she knows she will not be properly recognized and rewarded though she performs capable, efficient and loyal service for long years; and even if she enters a scientific field, her resentment to discrimination will materially lessen her worth. Democratic United States would do well to follow the example of dictatorial Russia where women receive equal consideration in scientific pursuits (as well as in the economy as a whole).

The potential abilities of our women have hardly been tapped for science, and in them lies a source for thousands of future contributors in this vital realm where rapid and sustained progress is now mandatory for leadership, even for safety and survival.

Some may minimize Russian space accomplishments and lull

in our discovery of Salk vaccine and other worthwhile achievements, pointing out that modern Russia has made no great scientific contribution in the humanitarian fields; but there is no way for us to keep pace with Russia in any field where science is a factor if she continues to take full advantage of the capabilities of her women and we continue to bypass those of our own. The odds are too unfavorable if we spot Russia this commanding lead. The Soviet is today giving a scientific education to many more boys and girls than are we, so we not only lag in this basic preparation for the future, but actually discourage it insofar as girls are concerned by their unfair treatment on becoming working women.

Discrimination within a class, such as those performing the same type of work, can be more demoralizing to effort than the mistreatment of the class as a whole. No woman of distinguishable qualities in her own right, seeing men of equal or less capabilities advanced over her, will remain content, day in and out, to wear the colorless and standard garb of mediocrity.

The reader who doubts that women treated fairly by an employer will make a needed contribution to a nation should again consider Lowell. And he who questions that the capable women of America can add to our strength should recall De Tocqueville: "If I were asked . . . to what the . . . growing strength of that people ought mainly to be attributed, I should reply — to the superiority of their women." And both doubters should be warned by Reich's observation of another society: "It was the failure of the Greeks to develop their women which proved their ruin in the end."

---

[1] Other than a subsequent amendment to the United States Constitution revoking or impairing the Equal Rights Amendment, which would be remote.

[2] This list does not include any states which may have passed equal pay laws since the 1959 legislative sessions.

[3] *The Long, Long History of Equal Pay,* 36 Business Woman 15 (1957).

WOMEN AT WORK

THE LOFTY IMAGE OF THE AMERICAN WOMAN IS NOT DEpreciated by women's working. The office, the counter, the assembly line do not detract from her rank as a lady. Neither do they require that she be less a woman — in mind, body or appearance.

The belief that women should not engage in gainful occupation has almost disappeared during the twentieth century. Even at the end of the last century, 1900, a period still affected by the narrow thinking of the Victorian era, the work force in the United States contained 5 million women, 20% of the 25 million women in the population fourteen years of age and over. Since the turn of the century there has been a large increase in the percentage of women who work: 36% by 1958, or 22.3 million of the 62 million women fourteen and over. Most women who do not work are engaged in caring for the family or come within the older age brackets. A high percentage of all single women work.

In 1900 there were 1.3 million more men than women in the United States. In 1942, for the first time, women outnumbered men; today we have approximately 3 million more women than men. This excess is expected to increase, both numerically and percentagewise. The great majority of these women will work. This and other factors will cause further increases in the percentage of women in the labor force. By the 1970's probably half of the women will be in the force. Already half work at some period during their lives.

We must become better acquainted with the working woman, with her contribution to the economy, her chosen fields, her income, her working years. How does she fare in comparison with the male worker in recognition, advancement and pay? What is her place and where is she headed in business and industry, this so-called "man's world"?

She is certainly rapidly reducing the ratio between male and female workers. The 5 million women working in 1900 comprised 18% of the total number of workers; the 22.3 million working in 1958 comprised 33% of the total.[1]

In the years from 1940 to 1958 women increased their ratio to men workers in all classifications of occupations except one. The highest increase was in the clerical group, where the ratio rose from roughly one-half to roughly two-thirds. The one group in which a decrease occurred was the professional; still in 1958 there were over 1 million more women in this group than in 1940. Professional men simply increased at a faster rate than did professional women. One cause is the emphasis in recent years on a scientific education, which boys find more to their liking than girls. (In the Soviet Union the young female is intrigued with science, understanding both its romantic appeal and practical value.)

Women are in the substantial majority in many occupations; in 1958 they comprised 97% of all secretaries, stenographers and typists (10% of the total of working women); 69% of all clerical and kindred workers (20% of the total); 75% of all teachers, except college (6% of the total); 98% of all household workers (11% of the total). On the other hand, women account for only 16% of all managers, officials and proprietors, except farm (5% of the total of working women); 37% of professional, technical and kindred workers (12.5% of the total); 3% of laborers, excluding farm and mine (.5% of the total). This partial list gives an idea of the type of work in which women engage and the ratio between them and men in particular work classifications.

An interesting statistic reflecting woman's changing preference as to type of work is that, although the actual number of private household women workers in 1940 and 1958 were approximately the same, their proportion to all women in the labor force dropped from 18% to 11%, a most substantial decrease. This did not result in any degree from replacement by men but from women's desire and ability to be something other than domestics, plus the factor that more and more housewives do their own housework, either by choice or from shortage of suitable help.

A recent and striking change in the marital classification of women in the work force is the increase in the number of wives. In 1957, 11.5 million, 53% of all women in the labor force, were wives. Of this 11.5 million, 10.8 million, almost 94%, had husbands also in the force. These husbands and wives comprised 28% of all married couples in the country. Only seventeen years earlier working couples numbered 3 million, a mere 11% of all married couples. And of all women in the labor force in 1957, nearly 7 million, or approximately one-third, had children under eighteen, with 2.5 million having children under school age. Criticism is heard of working wives and mothers, but the statistics indicate their reason is usually economic: in one-third of the families where both husband and wife work the husband's income is under $5000; in families where the husband is unemployed, two-fifths of all wives work; while among couples where the income of the husband is from $6000 to $7000 one-fourth of the wives work; and where his income is $10,000 or over, only one-eighth of the wives work. Among working mothers the largest proportion is in families in which the husband earns less than $4000.

Another interesting statistic is that 10% of American families are now headed by a woman (widow, divorcée or single) who supports other members of her family. These families number almost 4.4 million.

INCOME. The staggering sum of an estimated $45 billion was earned by women in 1957. About one-fifth of all salaries and wages for that year were paid to women. Since they comprised over one-third of the labor force, it is obvious that they did not receive as much proportionately as men. Less than 40,000 women earned $10,000 or more, yet 3.75 million came within the Census Bureau's classification of "professional workers, managers, officials and proprietors." The 1957 average income for all women was only $1199, almost exactly $100 per month, while for men the average was $4700, approximately $400 per month. However, this low average for women was mainly due to the large number who worked part-time and in part-year jobs, the average annual pay for full-time women workers being $3000 or about two-thirds that for men.

Of significance is that in 1957 the full-time, year-round women clerical help averaged $262 per month, while the full-time, year-round women professional workers, managers, officials and proprietors averaged $300. Thus $38 per month reflects the difference in economic value of women assigned to these two classifications.

To look at family income (comprised of wages, interest, dividends, social security benefits, etc.), the median income for 1956 for the 38 million husband-wife families was $4973. Where the wife did not work this income was $4645, while in the 10 million families where both she and the husband worked it was $5957. For the 4.4 million families of which women were the head, the median income was $2754. In the $7000-per-year bracket were one-third of the families in which both husband and wife worked, one-fifth in which the husband only worked, and one-tenth in which a woman was the family head.

EDUCATION. For women college graduates working full time and part time, the average income for 1956 was $3050. This was one and one-half times that of high school graduates with no college and three times that of elementary school graduates. For college graduates working full time the average was $3809.

In 1940, men in the labor force had an average of 8.8 years' schooling and women 10.2 years. In 1957 the averages were closer, being 11.3 years for men and 12.1 for women.

In 1957, of all women with college education, well over one-half were working. Of those who left school after the eighth grade, less than one-third were working. All working women averaged seven-tenths of a year more schooling than all women in the population.

Using figures to the nearest half million, of the 21 million women in the labor force in 1957, 1.5 million had four years of college and 2 million a less number; 7.5 million had four years of high school and 4 million a less number; 3 million had eight years of elementary school, 2 million had seven to five, and 1 million had less than five.

It is thus obvious that education has a positive relation to both work and pay: the more education, the more likelihood of working; the higher the education, the higher the pay. Furthermore, this is more applicable to women than to men. The main reason is found in the different types of work in which each sex concentrates. Women tend to the white collar jobs. Our present traditional educational system trains them for this, hence a majority planning to work finishes high school. Men, who in large numbers engage in technical, craft and manual work, often must get their training from their employer, so many quit school and go to work. Classic education is not so important for them as for the office worker, but aptitude and skill are vital from the employer's standpoint. He can supply the needed special training and education, but not the knack for the job.

WORK PATTERNS. Single women who enter the labor force young and remain single work most of their lives, the work pattern for them being comparable to that of men, married or single. These women continue in the force about forty years (three years less than men) and live thirteen years after retirement.

The married woman's work pattern is complex. A majority engage in gainful occupation at some time during their lives, but the work period or periods vary with many circumstances and combinations of circumstances. The working woman who marries, stays married, and has no children, will work about thirty-one years, nine less than the single working woman. The working girl who marries and has children naturally quits her job with her first pregnancy and she may or may not return to work between children, most likely not unless they are several years apart. Still the chances are that she will some day work again. Divorce, separation, widowhood, and increase in the age of her children are factors influencing her to resume work, and of course a compelling need for wages or salary can be controlling, regardless of children or other duties.

Some married women discontinue working as they get older because of the husband's increased income or the reduction in family expenses, the children being on their own. Also, part-time work for many married women is the rule, their household duties not permitting a regular, full-time job, though they are able to supplement their husband's income by intermittent work. The extent of this is reflected by the fact that during 1957 a total of 29 million women worked at some time, yet the average for the entire year was only 22 million.

EFFECT ON MARRIAGE. The vast increase percentagewise of working women has influenced the marital status of the population of the United States in two major respects: (1) a greater percentage of men and women are marrying than ever before and (2) at an earlier age. According to census figures, of the male fourteen years of age and over, 56% were or had been married in 1890, 75% in 1959. Of the females fourteen years of age and over, 66% were or had been married in 1890, and 81% in 1959. Since the percentages for married and once-married include widowed and divorced, when these two classes are deducted leaving only those actually married at a particular time, we have an 1890 figure of 52% for men and 55% for women, and a 1959 figure of 70% for men and 66% for women.

Surprising as it may seem for the decades at the turn of the century, little more than half the population fourteen and over was married. The increase in marriage was gradual over the last seven decades, except for a pronounced acceleration during the 1940's, the decade subject to the World War II influences. The percentage of single persons of course decreased during the same period: for males, from 44% in 1890 to 25% in 1959; and for females, from 34% to 19%. The following table reflects the above in more detail:

TABLE A

Unstandardized Percentage Distributions of Persons Fourteen Years Old and Over, By Marital Status and Sex, for the United States

(Civilian Population, 1960 and 1950; Total Population 1940 and 1890)

Year and Sex	*Single*	*Married*	*Widowed*	*Divorced*
MALE				
1890	43.6	52.1	3.8	0.2
1900	42.0	52.8	4.5	0.3
1910	40.4	54.2	4.4	0.5
1920	36.9	57.6	4.6	0.6
1930	35.8	58.4	4.5	1.1
1940	34.8	59.7	4.2	1.2
1950	26.2	68.2	4.0	1.7
1960	25.3	69.3	3.5	1.8
FEMALE				
1890	34.1	54.8	10.6	0.4
1900	33.3	55.2	10.9	0.5
1910	31.8	57.1	10.3	0.6
1920	29.4	58.9	10.8	0.8
1930	28.4	59.5	10.8	1.3
1940	27.6	59.5	11.3	1.6
1950	19.6	66.1	12.2	2.2
1960	19.0	65.9	12.5	2.6

Since the table is for population fourteen years old and over, it covers ages earlier than those ordinarily considered as within the marriageable age bracket, but nevertheless it reflects a positive relation between marriage and women's working when compared with the following table on women in the labor force:

TABLE B

Women in the Labor Force
(Selected Years)

Year	Women workers (fourteen years and over) Number	Per Cent of all Workers	Per Cent of all Women
1890 (June)	3,704,000	17	18
1900 (June)	4,999,000	18	20
1920 (January)	8,229,000	20	23
1930 (April)	10,396,000	22	24
1940 (March – Pre-World War II)	13,840,000	25	28
1945 (April – World War II peak)	19,570,000	36	37
1947 (April – Postwar)	16,320,000	28	30
1950 (April – Pre-Korea)	18,063,000	29	32
1953 (April – Korean war)	19,296,000	31	33
1958 (April)	22,254,000	33	36

While Table A shows marriage to be popular – even if only in recent decades – a truer indication of its present mass appeal appears from the mature male segment of the population, ages thirty-five to sixty-four. In 1958, among all men in the United States of this age group, 92.1% were or once were married, leaving only 7.9% who had never married.

Why has per cent of married persons increased as per cent of working women increased? The major reason is that the working woman makes a good wife. She not only contributes income to the family but better understands the needs, ambitions, and plights of another working person, her husband. She is not more restless in the evenings than he, her working has added another mutuality to the partnership. While the man is primarily interested in the quality of his spouse, some will not marry because they do not make enough to support a wife as they feel they should. For these men the working woman offers marriage, something they desire but fear on their income alone. Hence, insofar as these men are concerned, woman's working has a positive ratio to increase in marriage.

Census figures definitely show that low income is the primary cause preventing men from marrying: in 1958, 13.2% of the men who earned less than $4000 were single (i.e., had never been married), while only 3.1% of those who earned $6000 or over were single. I construe these two small percentages plus their pronounced 4 to 1 ratio to indicate marriage's high popularity with men. Those who are financially able to marry proceed to do so and the 3.1% who do not is so small that most of it can be accounted for by men who have relatives to support, who are in ill health, or who have reasons preventing them from marrying other than a distaste for that status. Also, the great majority of men who are barely able financially to take a wife (the $4000-and-under class), nevertheless marry; and by no means all of them choose working women. With these men the factors of ill health and outside financial obligations – which strongly derogate from marriage where income is low – can account for a large part of their 13.2% who never marry. Men no longer discommend the wedded state.

Those who carry a mental picture of the American bride of the late nineteenth century as a blushing child clinging to her almost-as-young groom will be surprised to learn that in 1890 the median age for first marriages for women was 22 years and for men 26.1 years. By 1959, this age for women had fallen to 20.2 and for men to 22.3, as appears from the following table:

TABLE C

Median Age at First Marriage
By Sex, For the United States
1890 to 1960

Year	*Male*	*Female*
1890	26.1	22.0
1900	25.9	21.9
1910	25.1	21.6

TABLE C (Continued)

Year	*Male*	*Female*
1920	24.6	21.2
1930	24.3	21.3
1940	24.3	21.5
1950	22.8	20.3
1960	22.8	20.3

An expected statistic which appears from a comparison of Table C and Table A is that the greatest increase in the percentage of married persons – which occurred during the 1940's – was accompanied by the greatest decline in the median age for first marriage, for men 1.5 years and for women 1.2.

CONCLUSIONS. From the statistics in this chapter may be drawn the following conclusions about the American working woman:

She comprises an essential part of the work force, both in number and work classification.

The substantial majority of all routine office, teaching, and sales positions are held by her, also, a majority of all medical and health and retail trade positions. Without her these enterprises could not exist in their present form.

Women occupy only a small proportion of professional, technical, craft, and managerial positions.

The woman worker earns about two-thirds as much as her male co-worker, yet she is as valuable and better educated.

Single, she may expect to work forty years; married and without children, thirty-one years; married and returning to the labor force at thirty when her children are of school age, twenty-three years.

Once a woman has worked, she is likely to return to work at a later age.

Marriages have increased in close ratio to the increase in working women.

---

[1] *1958 Handbook on Women Workers,* published by United States Department of Labor, Women's Bureau, Mrs. Alice K. Leopold, Director.

OUTSTANDING VERSUS AVERAGE WOMAN

A COMPARISON OF OUTSTANDING WOMEN OF THE UNITED States with all women in the country's population discloses consequential dissimilarities between the two groups. As representative of the outstanding group I take the 19,671 women appearing in the 1958-59 or first edition of *Who's Who of American Women,* by Marquis-Who's Who, Inc. They are, as stated in the book's preface, "*women outstanding as women,* without regard to their achievements or positions in relation to men; in other words, not confined to the woman who stood out from her sisters and brothers, but who did *stand out from her sisters.*" This group must not be confused with the women listed in Marquis' *Who's Who in America,* the 1958-59 edition of which contains approximately 2600[1] and who obviously averaged a higher level of accomplishment than did those in *Who's Who of American Women.* This does not mean the comparison group is not comprised of prominent women. Each is exceptionally capable in her own field; and mere wealth, social position, or physical powers alone did not qualify a woman for listing.

The criterion for the outstanding woman, as that term is being used, is entirely different than for the successful woman in the broad sense. No one denies success to the woman who gives her children training and habits of thought and action which develop into character of virtue, honor, and industry. That mother makes the preeminent contribution to society, the spark of greatness is within her, and she glimpses the future.

A historical study of morals shows that the world grows better, that there is evolving a highly moral man as the dominant type. One example. It was the sincere conviction of most ancient races, even of Rome after Christ, that slavery was entirely justifiable and that any treatment meted out to an individual slave was legal, the theory being that since the slave (or his ancestor) was captured in war or raid, the victor could have put him to death and anything less severe was mercy. Prior to an edict of Nero it was not illegal to inflict pain on a slave for purely sensual pleasure, yet insignificant rights of the citizen had been vigilantly protected for centuries. Today we consider slavery as wrong *per se*, as contrary to the laws of nature and of God, and as degrading to both slave and master — tenets of a different order than earlier views on man's subjugation by man.

In a thousand ways history verifies our moral advancement; and while the truly ethical may still be in the minority, they increase and strengthen from one civilization to another. Whether this is by God's will or nature's continuing law of survival of the fittest is for the philosopher to ponder, but regardless, the moral man eventually must rule the earth. Thus the woman who rears her children not to compromise with right, who instills benevolence and tolerance in those she leaves in the world, furthers society's great trend. If we are not invested with this urge towards betterment, why is the political morality of *The Republic* a dominant dream of mankind, and Magna Carta regarded as reflecting a moral law above earthly authority, a "law of the universe" guaranteeing justice to all?

Obviously, it is not necessary that a woman be outstanding in order to contribute to the improvement of the present or, through her offspring, to the enrichment of the future; and just as obviously, the fact she is outstanding does not detract from her ability and desire to make these contributions. Outstanding women have much to offer their contemporaries, much to impart to their children, and make exceptional mothers. They are alert, progressive, educated; and by nature woman shares her ways with the young. All men know that a bond exists between woman and child. Courts are actuated to award the custody of children to their mother, reasoning that a mediocre mother by nature does a better job of caring for a child than does a worthy father by effort. There is truth in the saying: "Educate a man and you educate an individual, educate a woman and you educate a family."[2]

The thinking, still current to an extent, that education is wasted on girls because after college they marry, have children and become housewives, is as nearsighted a view as one can entertain; yet a college professor was recently quoted by a large city newspaper as wondering why he was teaching girls the advanced subjects of learning since upon finishing college they marry and spend their time rearing children. It is true that children interfere with women's working and becoming outstanding (amplified later), but the simple answer is that children must come first with women, and this they do. In the preceding chapter we saw that 64%[3] of all women, most of whom are mothers, are not engaged in gainful occupation.

We also saw that of the 36% of all women in the labor force, the better educated hold the better positions, and that three-fourths of this 36%, though more educated than men, are in routine clerical, sales, service, household, and operative manufacturing jobs. The outstanding women, highly educated, present a different occupational structure. Marquis' classification by field of accomplishment for the 19,671 women, with the number and per cent in each, is as follows:

Classification	*Number*	*Per Cent*
Advertising Agency Executives	130	0.7
Artists	1,309	6.7
Association/Organization Executives	549	2.8
Banking/Credit Executives	167	0.8

(Continued)

Classification	Number	Per Cent
Biological Scientists	241	1.2
Book Publishing Executives	133	0.7
Business Executives (not elsewhere classified)	986	5.1
Club/Religious/Civic Leaders	2,918	14.8
Composers/Lyricists	140	0.7
Designers	60	0.3
Educators, College (not elsewhere classified)	1,666	8.6
Educators, Elementary/Secondary	742	3.8
Engineers	34	0.2
Entertainers/Commentators	227	1.2
Federal Officials/Executives	399	2.0
Home Economists/Dietitians	466	2.4
Insurance Executives	76	0.4
Language/Literature Teachers	559	2.8
Lawyers	714	3.6
Librarians	943	4.7
Magazine Executive/Writers	429	2.2
Municipal/County Officials/Executives	210	1.2
Musicians	352	1.8
Newspaper/Syndicate Executives/Writers	595	3.0
Nurses	507	2.6
Physical Scientists	119	0.6
Physicians	895	4.5
Radio/TV Executives	202	1.0
Religious Workers, Career	105	0.5
Retail/Wholesale Executives	53	0.3
Social Scientists	852	4.3
Social Workers	343	1.7
State Officials/Executives	365	1.7
Writers	1,359	6.9
Others	826	4.2
	19,671	100.0%

This classification discloses high level positions and worthy callings, and while diversified, noticeable are the small percentages for the groups requiring talent: a total of 9.5% for artists, composers, designers, and musicians. The great majority of outstanding women are in positions which are attained by the long and laborious efforts of the educated and reasonably capable person; and no doubt in the talent group training and effort played a major part.

Not only in work does the outstanding woman and the average woman go her individual way, but each group evinces a different pattern in the three family factors of marriage, number of children, and divorce.

Only 58% of the women listed by Marquis were or ever had been married, as compared to 89.4% for all adult women of the United States. This ratio of approximately 2 to 3 is sufficiently pronounced to reflect an underlying fundamental cause or causes. A cause is not that men prefer a wife who does not work – the evidence adduced in the chapter on "Women at Work" clearly disproves this fallacious assumption. And the outstanding women were not yet outstanding at the customary age for marriage, so that did not frighten youthful suitors. Neither is it a cause that men dislike intelligent females, although this threadbare view has been repeated so long that many women accept it. No man is really looking for a woman of low intelligence or with less sense than he has; he does not want to be bothered with such a companion and does not want children by such a mate.

If the foregoing did not keep 42% of the outstanding women from becoming wives, what did? The same sundry reasons which keep 10.6% of all women from becoming wives. Certainly many of the single outstanding women preferred marriage, but no doubt on terms agreeable to them, and when a suitable marriage was not at hand they went to work, became absorbed in a career, in the arts, in social work, and after two decades of capable effort attained a noteworthy level in their field. Thus the only proposition established by the fact that 42% of the outstanding women are single, is that the single status increases woman's opportunity to become prominent. Free from family responsibilities, she has a better chance to make a name for herself in her chosen work, actually more than twice the chance of the married or once-married working woman. Of the 5.5 million single women in the labor force, 15 in 10,000 are listed by Marquis as outstanding, while of the 16.5 million married or once-married women in the force, 7 in 10,000 are listed.

Of the approximately 11,400 married or once-married women, relatively mature, 32.4% are childless, while of all women of comparable age in the population, only 19% are. The outstanding married woman has an average of 1.4 children, all married women an average of 2.4, a ratio of roughly 3 to 5. Therefore, the 19,671 outstanding potential mothers produced only about 16,000 children, whereas 19,671 average potential mothers produced about 42,200, over two and one-half times as many as their prominent sisters. It is not that women with the quality to become outstanding – this is in most of them – desire children less, again it is that the less the family duties the greater the chance of prominence.

Another factor which must be considered in connection with the above statistics as to the childless married or once-married women (32.4% for outstanding women and 19% for all women), is that 10 to 15% of all married couples cannot have children because of the sterility of either the husband or the wife. (This is developed later in the chapter on artificial insemination.) Assuming 12.5% as the sterility factor and deducting it from the 32.4% and 19%, we have *voluntary* childless marriages of only 19.9% for outstanding women and of only 6.5% for average married and once-married women. This considerably modifies the percentages which at first glance might be construed as reflecting a desire or lack of desire for children.

In divorce the difference between outstanding and average woman is not as pronounced as in marriage and children, although there is a difference. Figures are not available on the *divorce rate* for the women listed in *Who's Who of American Women* but are for the *number divorced* at the time of publication. While divorced status is not as good a comparison as divorce rate for our purposes, the former nevertheless reflects the situation. Of all outstanding women 2.6% were divorcée as compared to 2.8% of the comparable age group in the population as a whole. However, since only 58% of the outstanding women were ever married as compared to 89.4% of the general population group, this means 4.48% of the once-married outstanding women and 3.13% of the once-married average women are divorcées.

This rough ratio of 3 to 2 again reflects an underlying cause which I believe is obvious: the outstanding woman wanting her freedom is likely to get a divorce and be in no haste to remarry, having an interest outside her home and an income independent of a husband, while the mature woman in the general population often has neither, so she either stays married though dissatisfied with her situation or after obtaining a divorce remarries at the first reasonable opportunity. Thus the actual desire or need for divorce within the two groups may be much closer than is indicated by the 3 to 2 ratio.

Education appears to be virtually a requisite for a woman to become outstanding. Using 1958 figures to the nearest whole per cent, of the entire female population eighteen years or over, 5% have college degrees and 8% one to three years of college; of working women 8% have degrees and 9% one to three years' college; and of outstanding women 69% have degrees and 23% one to three years' college. Thus 92% of the outstanding group are college-trained as compared to 13% for all women and 17% for working women. If a woman desires to make a name for herself, her chances to a large extent depend on a good education.

The husband's earning the living for the family is his traditional role, and, in the eyes of most Americans, the measure of a man's success is achievement, not as husband or father, but in his field of endeavor outside the home. This is also the criterion of success for the woman listed in *Who's Who of American Women*: achievement in extra-domestic activity, be it in business, the professions, civic work, the arts or charity; not achievement in her capacity as wife or mother (although many of the 19,671 women combined these roles with their work, 58% being married and 39% having children).

By comparing the total number of prominent men chosen

for *Who's Who in America* for 1958-59 (48,000) with the total of all working men (55,000,000), we see that about 9 men in every 10,000 achieved notable success. Comparing the 19,671 outstanding women in *Who's Who of American Women* with the 22,250,000 working women, the proportion is about 8 in 10,000, but we must remember these women are outstanding only among women, not among both men and women. To use the more nearly comparable 2,600 women in *Who's Who in America,* they represent about 1 in 10,000 who have achieved the same degree of success as the 9 in 10,000 prominent men. It thus appears that women in the United States are still, first and foremost, wives and mothers. Their upbringing, their education, and the mores of the society, combine with women's instincts to foster marriage and procreation, and this way of life will continue to be the most appealing and sought after for the vast majority of American women (although not necessarily to the exclusion of some form of work at various periods of their lives).

Since women outnumber men in every age group except those born in the war years of 1942-45, more and more women will not have the opportunity to marry. This growing percentage will join those who for various other reasons — a lack of interest in marriage, a vital need for some other pursuit, parental responsibilities, emotional unreadiness — comprise the sizeable group of women who never marry. These women, almost in their entirety, will work. Without the duties of home and family they will, as their male counterpart in the business world, devote their efforts to their jobs and professions.

Since the single status for women is conducive to prominence — close to half of the outstanding women come from their ranks — with thousands of unmarried women in the population who are capable and educated, the number of prominent women should be far greater. In addition to no family responsibilities, the single woman has another advantage — one of a subtle nature — in making a success in her chosen field, which is that she can go her own way, follow her own aptitudes, exercise her own judgment, without being affected by the opinions of a husband with whom she is in continual close contact. Individualism is an element of success in many endeavors. The unmarried woman can develop *her* ideas, talents, and capacities free of the easily acquired habit of subconsciously relying on and being influenced by the thinking of a spouse.

Before leaving outstanding women — whose intelligence is proven and known to their husbands and friends — I comment once more on the stultification that men shy at, tremble before, and forswear all love for a brainy female. Nothing could be further from truth. Actually a man seeks and hopes for intelligence in the opposite sex, certainly in the woman who shares his life and bears his descendants. The one sure and lasting way for a woman to impress a man favorably is to let him know she is smart — and the higher the intelligence revealed the more favorable the impression. Naturally the impression must be accomplished in a suitable way, and perhaps a better phrasing is that the woman should let the man discover how smart she is. I do not indicate she should get the best of every argument or should forcefully espouse her views at all times; she certainly can make her intelligence repellent to a man, but that relates to manner, not to any built-in male resentment of feminine cleverness.

It is as logical to say a woman prefers a dull man as to say a man prefers a dull woman. My advice to women is that they neither repeat to men nor rely to any degree on the theory that men resent, secretly, subconsciously or otherwise, female intelligence. The man who hears a woman say this thinks she is dupable, perhaps a little stupid, for not knowing better, and this is true whether or not he has given thought to the subject. He senses — male intuition — that such talk is a pretext for the woman who is uninformed, an apology for the wife whose mind idles while her husband progresses.

We saw in the first chapter that it was probably woman during the pre-record era, who initially perceived the connection between sex and birth, realized the benefits to the family of agriculture, and made other fundamental discoveries which altered man's basic environment. These discoveries came not from education or training but from inborn high-level thinking by woman; perhaps her mate called it woman's intuition. Still he recognized its value. Yet many women say that woman's natural ability to think creatively and abstractly should be purposefully repressed in the belief that this ability is unpopular with men; that woman's need for male love is so compelling that she should rein her intelligence so as not to repel the source of this love.[4] Women who think this do not doubt their own ability, they just do not know what to do with it.

The theory that men do not prefer intelligent women is positively disproved by recorded history. When the Grecian society of the Golden Age divided its female population into family women whose mental processes were arrested from childhood and into courtesans whose intellectual capacities were developed and openly displayed, it was the courtesans who got the male love, devotion and admiration. It was said of the Greek wife that there were only two occasions on which she pleased her husband: her wedding night and her burial day; and said of the Greek husband that he only came home at nights to sleep. This was the attitude which the society took towards women who vegetated mentally and who failed to realize that the male has an instinctive desire for and a rational need of an intelligent mate. The Greek man was informed, cultured, imaginative; only a woman of like quality could hold his interest and affection. While Greece, because of the division of its women, is the one society which furnishes proof, unadulterated by confusing social factors, that male devotion and female intelligence have an affinity, all great societies lend support to this truth. The Roman woman of the four centuries after Christ, carefully schooled and the intellectual equal of man, received more male consideration than did her earlier sister whose mental development was thought secondary to domestic virtues. It was during prior eras that a husband would treat his wife as he did his slave, not after woman gained intellectual equality with man.

It is unrealistic for women to believe that a man does not appreciate a smart woman; and it is not clever for woman to pretend helplessness, dependency, stupidity, and mediocrity. Our outstanding women, such as those named in *Who's Who of Ameri-*

can Women, are recognized by men as an asset to the society; and admiration for the fair sex does not dampen male ardor, inhibit his romantic pursuits, or lessen his devoted love.

---

[1] These 2600 women comprised about 5% of the total listings, approximately 48,000 being men.

[2] Who first said this is not known for certain, and it has been attributed to a number of persons, but Dr. Otto F. Kraushaar, President of Goucher College, believes it was originally said by a former Governor of North Carolina in defending the importance of education of women before the State Legislature.

[3] 64% of all women fourteen years old and over in the population in 1958.

[4] See Marya Mannes, "Female Intelligence: Who Wants It?" *The New York Times* Magazine, January 3, 1960, and letters commenting thereon published January 17, 1960, in the same section.

LIFE INSURANCE

The economic factors which distinguish twentieth-century women of the United States from those of former civilizations are fewer than generally thought. We hear much of the vast amount of money which women currently own and control, often spoken of as something modern. Women of most past societies enjoyed wealth. In Egypt they controlled the inheritance of a nation and brother married sister to protect his interest in the family estate; in Greece the courtesan, Phryne, acquired a fortune by her own ingenuity; and in Rome women amassed assets so great that on one occasion of national stress they were the ones on whom the state called for financial aid. Modern woman has no claim to uniqueness because of her favorable financial status.

Actually there is only one factor in our modern economy entirely unknown to the past which especially affects woman, and that is life insurance. The cash women presently receive each and every year from this source runs into the billions, and it is women, not men or children, who are the high percentage beneficiaries of this financial innovation which now reaches astronomical proportions. Every woman should have a basic understanding of life insurance.

It had its beginning early in the eighteenth century, but its widespread coverage has come only during the twentieth. Today a husband seldom leaves his family penniless. If he dies young with no assets, he usually has some insurance, and even though it be modest in amount, the widow can pay the last illness and funeral expenses and maintain herself and children for a year or so. This freedom from financial straits, even if temporary, gives her an opportunity better to adjust herself, and a stake until she can get a job or remarry. At times insurance leaves the widow almost as well off from a financial standpoint as she was during her husband's lifetime since some husbands carry a relatively high amount in order that their families' standard of living will not be impaired in case of their death. Of course, others carry too little or none.

Prior to life insurance, the family of many a man who had saved nothing found itself impoverished. In the rural areas neighbors fashioned the casket and dug the grave, and in the cities relatives or charity met the burial expense. The widow's panic and depression over the future was as acute and absorbing as her grief.

There are two basic elements in life insurance contracts (excepting term): the benefit payable in case of death and the cash value accumulated over the years — the protection and the investment elements. Life insurance is purchased for the protection, the investment is a by-product. Premature death and failure to accumulate an estate are the two principal risks against which policyholders wish to insure or to be protected. The young man with a family has no promise of another day, and though he lives and saves he has no assurance against the economic vicissitudes of depression and inflation. He is not completely convinced when he reads some economist's theory that the factors causing depressions have been sufficiently mitigated so that a serious one cannot again occur, and he takes with a grain of salt the periodic statements of the administration's spokesmen that inflation is curbed — while we lavish dollars around the world.

Omitting periods of depression (which devalues real estate and stocks, if those are one's assets) or of inflation (which devalues money and bonds, if those constitute one's savings), every man knows he will have his individual misfortunes not related to economic conditions. A bad transaction, sickness – a hundred things – can create a temporary period during which it would be financially unfortunate for him to die. There are few men who do not have such periods, often prolonged ones. Furthermore, a man endeavoring to make money cannot continually maintain his assets in a state of preparedness for death. If that philosophy motivates him he will get no more than interest on his capital, or a return thereon roughly equal to interest. Life insurance for many men is the answer.

The protection it offers should certainly be understood by the wife with children. The number of children, type of husband, his financial condition, how much she could earn, whether assistance from parents could replace her husband's income, and the like, are all personal factors which the wife and mother must relate to the benefits of insurance proceeds and the cost in premiums. Some husbands anxiously overload themselves with premium payments (which insurance companies discourage); others wait until it is too late to protect their families. The wife should guard against both. She should learn the family planning features of life insurance sufficiently to discuss the elements involved with her husband and to contribute to their joint decision. She should know something of herself, especially what she is willing to forego, if necessary, in order that the premiums can be paid.

Before a policy is purchased the wife should understand what part of the premium covers the cost of insurance and what part is in effect savings, or to state it another way, the difference between term – or temporary – and permanent insurance. In all permanent forms of life insurance, cash values increase slowly but steadily. This is due to the level premium system, by which the policyholder pays slightly more than the actual cost in the early years and less in the later years. Should reverses come to the family which make it impossible for them to pay a premium at the time it falls due, they can instruct the life insurance company to borrow from the cash value to pay the premium. Thus the cash value is a built-in margin of safety in the early years. Later it grows into an emergency fund available to the family from which they can borrow if the need arises.

The wife should know that names given to policies, such as "educational" or "mortgage," are not fundamental but that the benefits to be received, and when received, relate directly to the amount of the premiums. Names are of use in that they suggest a policy tailored to a particular anticipated need. For instance, the so-called educational policy is either a policy to guarantee the college funds if the breadwinner does not live to do so himself or — if the more expensive plan can be afforded — an income payable about the time a son or daughter will be going to college, with the life of the income producer insured in the meantime.

Recently a mother, who had already purchased a small educational policy for her son, telephoned me suddenly concerned over the possibility that her son might die before he reached college age, in which event she feared the company would not pay the insurance, there being no one to educate under the "educational" policy. Had she possessed the slightest understanding of the nature of the policy she would have known it was a policy on her life, and if the beneficiary died, that a new beneficiary could be named by her; or if all need for the policy ended, that she could terminate it and the cash value would be paid to her.

Two elements are often contained in one policy. The family income policy combines reducing term and straight life insurance, thus providing, in case of the breadwinner's death, an income during the years of the children's schooling and then the full face value of the policy. The retirement income life insurance policy combines a lifetime annuity with an endowment insurance policy, the latter ceasing to exist at the point the annuity begins to pay income to the owner. Of importance is that the premiums on any combination policy are less than the total premiums on separate policies for each element.

In life insurance one gets what one pays for. The policyholder need seek no bargains from the premium-versus-benefit standpoint, nor fear any overcharges. This, of course, applies only within a class of insurance. An example of high-cost insurance is an industrial policy (defined later) with the collector coming to the insured's house weekly to pick up a 25c premium. Within a class there can be temporary variations in costs as where a new hazard is insured and the actuaries initially figure the premium higher than later is proven necessary, but these exceptions are minor and soon adjusted, and are not of consequence to the policyholder. In life insurance the theory of large numbers works too well to give either the company or the policyholder an advantage, and experience and information are such that rates can be figured with remarkable accuracy.

Hence a purchaser can safely limit his study to the following: his need for protection against particular risks, his ability and willingness to pay for the protection, the type of policy best suited to his needs, the financial condition of the company, and the agent with whom he is to do business over the years and in whom he should have full confidence.

In all of this coordination, it should be remembered that "wife insurance" has become an important part of the family financial planning. More and more wives are being insured to cover the economic costs in the event of their death. As an added incentive to this ownership, there is a widening tendency among life insurance companies to offer women a policy cost advantage (usually three years' lower cost than for men) commensurate with their better mortality experience. And if a husband wants an idea of the money it takes to replace the deceased mother of two infant children, four months and sixteen months old, by a trained substitute mother, here are the minimum costs during the children's years of legal minority as estimated by Elliot H. Drisko, of the Yonkers Family Service Society, in a 1959 New York court case.[1]

Wages for substitute mother (combination nurse-governess):	
@ $80 a week for the first five years	$ 20,800
@ $75 a week for the next fifteen years	58,500
Wages for part-time housekeeper @ $1.50 an hour, 16 hours a week for 20 years	24,960
Wages for baby sitter @ $1.00 an hour 6 hours a week (48 weeks a year) for 5 years	1,440

Social Security for three employees (substitute mother, housekeeper and baby sitter)	4,149
Workmen's Compensation insurance for three employees	1,500
Liability insurance	240
Advertising for, interviewing, and screening applicants for position of substitute mother	1,200
Agency supervision and training for substitute mother[2]	1,980
Family counseling and psychological guidance for father	5,000
Total for 20-year period	$119,769

The following life insurance data are disclosing. The figures are for the United States (Alaska and Hawaii excluded) and are approximate.

At the end of 1958, 124 million individual policyholders were insured for a total of some $550 billion. This was over 70% of the population and an average of over $4,000 per policyholder. Six out of seven families had one or more members who owned some type of life insurance with an average of nearly $11,500 per family insured. Many families had coverage for all members.

According to 1956 statistics, there was little difference in the percentage of families covered where the occupation of the family head was professional, managerial, self-employed, clerical, sales, skilled, or semi-skilled; the coverage for all being roughly 90%. However, there was a difference in the amount of coverage, and therefore in the amount of premiums paid. The average annual premium was $140 for skilled and semi-skilled, $185 for clerical and sales, $290 for professionals, and $415 for managers and self-employed. Of families headed by unskilled laborers 72% were insured with annual average premiums of $95, and 57% of farm operator families with premiums of $130. About 60% of all others had coverage, with premiums of $105.

During 1958, a total of $7.2 billion was paid to beneficiaries and policyholders in life insurance and annuity benefits by the life insurance companies. How women shared in this sizeable sum can best be analyzed by examining separately the payments made under ordinary, group, and industrial policies – a major classification of insurance – identified as follows:

Ordinary insurance is, as indicated, the kind usually encountered: straight life, twenty-year pay, term, etc. It is issued to individuals, as a rule in amounts of $1,000 or over. Premiums are paid annually, semi-annually, quarterly, or monthly.

Group insurance, as its name suggests, provides life insurance protection to a particular group of persons, usually the employees of a business or industrial concern. This insurance gives low-cost protection but only while the employee remains with his company as a member of the group. However, individuals usually have the opportunity to convert their group insurance to permanent (but not to term) insurance within a month after leaving the job, and without a medical examination.

Industrial insurance is issued in amounts less than $1,000 and the premiums are collected weekly or monthly at the door, a service used by many policyholders. Obviously, this is the most costly of all insurance, mainly because of the method of premium collection.

A recent study of payments to beneficiaries following deaths showed:

Under ordinary policies, which account for most family insurance, 63% of the total was paid to wives, 10% to children, 9% to other relatives including husbands, and 7% to estates or trusts. Wives and children were the beneficiaries of most of the trusts and in some cases received benefits from the insurance paid to other relatives.

Under group life insurance polices, 75% was paid to wives, 8% to children, and 3% to estates and trusts.

Under industrial policies, 31% was paid to wives and 27% to children. Proportionately more women are insured under these policies than under ordinary or group. Since women usually name as beneficiaries their husbands, children, or other relatives, a lower percentage of total payments from industrial policies goes to wives.

The same study of death payments showed that 93% of the total amount paid by life insurance companies resulted from the deaths of men, also 84% of the total number of claims. This is to be expected. Most life insurance is owned by men, which is logical enough, since the man is usually the principal breadwinner of the American family and therefore has primary responsibility for its financial security. Nevertheless, as of December 1958, women owned life insurance policies totaling $70 billion. Of this amount, $47.5 billion was ordinary and industrial and $22.5 billion was group.

It is interesting that of the 22.5 million working women, over 5 million were covered by group insurance at an average of about $4500. Of the 5 million covered, 60% were married and living with their husbands while the remainder were either single, divorced, separated or widowed.

The young couple with no estate will wish to consider the following: during 1958, there were paid to beneficiaries in death benefits under ordinary policies $60 million where the policies were less than a year old, and nearly $300 million where less than five years old, which was over 15% of the total paid in these benefits.

Life insurance is presently having a sustained growth in the United States due to the expanding number of families, reasonable prosperity, and an increasing recognition by individuals and families of their responsibilities for their own financial security.

This review tells woman of a great gain for her in the economy, of a paramount progress of which she alone is the principal beneficiary. It also tells her of a significant not found in the impressive life insurance statistics, nor written into the policies, and of a quality different from material advantage: her husband wishes that she and her children be well cared for after he is gone, desires from his heart that they have the comforts and pleasures of life, though he shall not share in them.

---

[1] *Weiss, Adm. v. Rubin, et al.,* Supreme Court of the State of New York, County of Westchester (White Plains), Index No. 1064-

1959. This was a malpractice suit brought by the administrator of a deceased housewife, age twenty-five, against a surgeon, an anesthesiologist, and a hospital. The administrator alleged deceased had been given the wrong type of blood in a blood transfusion from which she died. The jury, by a vote of ten to two, returned a verdict in favor of the administrator, represented by Rosenman, Goldmark, Colin & Kaye of New York City, for $130,000 for the wife's death and $20,000 for her conscious pain and suffering. The trial court, Doecher, J., reduced the $20,000 to $5,000, considering any amount above that as excessive since there was little proof of actual conscious pain and suffering by the deceased. The court did not disturb the $130,000 for her death, which sum was based largely on the pecuniary value of her life as testified to by Drisko. This is thought to be the first time evidence was ever admitted in New York as to the monetary value of the life of a housewife and mother; and $135,000 is probably the largest judgment entered anywhere for the wrongful death of a woman not engaged in a gainful occupation. The case was appealed and the Appellate Division was of the opinion that the $130,000 award for the death was excessive by $40,000. (Memorandum opinion, July 1960.) The administrator accepted the reduction.

[2] According to Drisko, the average stay of a substitute mother is three years. The proper selection of such a person necessitates the triennial screening of an average of ten persons. Each successful applicant without prior experience should be trained and supervised by a child-care agency. This requires weekly visits to the substitute mother during the first two months of her employment, bi-weekly visits during the next four months, and monthly visits during the next six months.

ARTIFICIAL INSEMINATION

The Altar and the Cradle — Reversal of the Husband's Historical Privilege to Legitimate Issue Even Though the Wife is Barren — Inability of One Spouse to Have Normal Sexual Intercourse — History of Artificial Insemination — Current Terminology, Statistics, Use and Procedure — Future Uses of AIH-Semen Banks — Relative-Donor — Judicial Decisions.

THE ALTAR DOES NOT INSURE THE CRADLE. MARRIAGE and motherhood may mingle in the maiden's mind, but many must learn later that the two roles are unrelated for them. No girl can be sure she is fertile until her first pregnancy. Medical tests can determine the degree of fertility or infertility for the male in most cases, but not for the female. Neither does her failure to conceive prove sterility, regardless of the time involved, as the husband may be the sole cause of this failure.

There are 2,000,000 women in the United States today whose marriages are involuntarily barren. Joining them each year are 50,000 brides, 30,000 of whom are themselves sterile and 20,000 of whom marry husbands who are. The stork does not seek the home in which the bride is fertile and the husband sterile, yet it will come if invited, by artificial insemination – a process which offers the wife a child natural to her and the husband a child of his own for all practical purposes. This offer the couple may wish to accept or reject. To make a proper decision they must understand what is tendered.

There are also many couples where both the husband and wife are fertile but who cannot have children in the ordinary way because of some physical abnormality on the part of one of them preventing sexual intercourse or preventing conception after intercourse. Artificial insemination offers these couples a child natural to both husband and wife, but they too must understand what is tendered. There are benefits and objections where the child is natural to both partners in marriage as well as where it is natural only to the wife.

Reliable public information is therefore needed on artificial insemination, not of the sensational variety or ordinary news item type, but factual data on the background, progress, and social problems of this biological innovation for the conception of children. And where the husband is sterile and the wife is fecundated with the semen of another man, called a "donor," the legal aspects also need delineation and discussion, as the law is uncertain with no statute in any state in the United States declaring the rights and obligations of the various parties concerned and with no decision by the highest court of a state determining any of the numerous questions involved.

We will also see in artificial insemination a striking illustration of how the time-worn theories of woman's inferior sociolegal status still affect the thinking of modern man, even of doctors and jurists. Science and religion are again thought by many to conflict, and Moses speaks from the bench of the twentieth century.

REVERSAL OF THE HUSBAND'S HISTORICAL PRIVILEGE TO LEGITIMATE ISSUE EVEN THOUGH THE WIFE IS BARREN

The laws and customs of ancient civilizations were such that the fertile husband of a sterile wife could, by divorce and remarriage or by concubinage, have natural legitimate issue. A man's desire to perpetuate his kind and his family was regarded as laudable, patriotic, and controlling, but no such privilege or reasoning existed in favor of the fertile wife of a sterile husband. Actually, when the marriage failed to produce children, it was she who was assumed to be barren, and a sterile husband was likely to change wives several times or have numerous concubines, or both, before the realization of his own sterility penetrated his ignorance and ego. Even then there was no thought of allowing the wife or concubines to have children by another man. The husband's sense of equality was not that elastic. Also, blame was imputed to the wife bearing only daughters, and, as we have seen, she was likewise subject to divorce and censure although hope for a son naturally prolonged her status for a reasonable time, and prospective sons-in-law and grandsons might reconcile the husband.

In the Near Eastern civilizations of the Babylonians, Egyptians, and Hebrews, the husband of a sterile wife often chose concubinage to divorce and remarriage, the former being lawful and honorable though these societies were generally monogamous. In the later civilizations of Greece and Rome, strictly monogamous, the husband's only choice was divorce and remarriage. This could be harsher than concubinage on the wife, as the mere fact she was known to be barren made remarriage extremely difficult for her. Not only was she unable to bear the next husband children, but her sterility itself reflected something degrading about her, something to be ashamed of. The girl of all older societies, until her first pregnancy, lived in dread of barrenness — she learned early that it portended misfortune for her. Mohammedan tribes even cast out a barren wife though it often resulted in her death, and in India a wife was returned to her parents if she bore no children. Scorn for the childless wife was widespread.

While the wife of a sterile or impotent husband had no lawful way to have legitimate children of her own, there were always cases — infrequent however and then unrecorded as a rule — when a determined wife of a husband she realized was sterile would have an illegitimate child by another man. This, of course, was *sub rosa* and the secret guarded for life because of the legal and social penalties against the wife and the domestic disruption which would follow the discovery in a man's household of a child not his own, a child which could have been born only of his wife's adultery.

With the advent of artificial insemination the wife of a sterile husband can, with his consent, have lawful children of her own by another man. Usually the husband who thinks out this advantage for his wife, and for himself as well, will consent and actively cooperate, and often he is the one who has the idea and importunes his wife to let herself be artificially fecundated. Most sterile husbands wanting children prefer this to adoption, and virtually all wives do.

This modern reversal of the husband's long standing prerogative to beget natural issue is, from a historical standpoint, a crucial innovation. In our present society the sterility of one spouse is not a legal ground for the other to terminate the marriage; all frown on divorce where that is the real reason although another is invoked in court; and the fertile spouse rarely considers it justifiable to quit the partner merely because the latter cannot have children. Actually there often develops on the part of the normal spouse a magnanimity or loyalty toward the sterile partner, an attitude of "we have each other." Certainly no fault or shame now attaches to sterility, and the marriage union is considered in law as more binding, in morals as more deserving, and in religion as more sacred than the desire and need to produce offspring. Within this morale, artificial insemination offers the wife, but not the husband, the opportunity of having natural, lawful children.

The barren Sarah no longer presents Abraham with a concubine, but if the sterility is reversed, he takes her to a doctor so she may bear a child. As to be anticipated, and as we shall soon see, this recent advantage to the wife is too drastic a historical change to come without heated objections, regardless of the merits of the change.

INABILITY OF ONE SPOUSE TO HAVE NORMAL SEXUAL INTERCOURSE

Before proceeding we should know that the attitude and reasons for not ending a marriage because one spouse is sterile do not apply where one is unable to have normal sexual intercourse.

Impotency is the legal as well as the ordinary term used to express this inability and the term applies to both male and female, though it is often thought of as limited to the male, no doubt because impotent women are the exception. Also, impotency is sometimes thought of as denoting inability to procreate since prior to artificial insemination a completely impotent male or female could not conceive; but I will not use the word as meaning or in any way indicating sterility, only as inability to copulate. In the law of divorce a typical definition of impotency is "such incurable sexual incapacity of one of the parties at the time of the marriage as prevents true and natural copulation. It is such deformity or weakness as prevents a consummation of the marriage by sexual intercourse. It is not sterility or barrenness . . ."[1]

If at the time of the marriage either party is completely and incurably impotent, that is ground for divorce by the normal spouse in forty-seven of the fifty states, Connecticut, South Carolina, and Louisiana being exceptions.[2] Under existing state laws, the fact that the impotent husband has virile semen with which his wife can be artificially inseminated, or the fact that the impotent wife can be fecundated artificially with her husband's semen and bear children, does not remove the impotency of either as a ground for dissolution of the marriage. There are probably no states which are exceptions to this general rule; however, most have strict requirements for annulment or divorce based on a spouse's inability to have normal intercourse.

Regardless of legal strictness, where the impotency exists while the couple, or one of them, are young, the odds are they will not stay together very long. Periodic normal sexual relations are essential to the average marriage. The various so-called perversions, while they may be desirable and arousing aids to the usual act, are seldom alone satisfactory to the normal man or woman over an extended period of time, hence separation and divorce virtually always result when the customary sex relation cannot be performed. And society recognizes that an untenable situation exists if the couple's sex life is unsatisfactory.

In the English case of *R. E. L. v. E. L. (1949)*[3] – initials only of the parties are sometimes used as the style of a case where the court considers it proper not to name the parties – it was held that the impotency of the husband was a ground for annulling the marriage at the instance of the wife, even though a child had been born to the marriage as a result of the wife's artificial insemination with the husband's semen. The parties were married in 1942 and at the hearing in 1948 the husband was thirty-seven and the wife thirty-one. For the first three years of the marriage the husband made no effort to have intercourse. His trouble was considered psychological as he appeared to have no physical disability preventing normal sex relations. In June, 1945, the wife insisted that he "face the question" and make the attempt. This he did but without success, and subsequent attempts were also futile. In the autumn of 1945, a doctor found the wife's health had been affected and considered the situation serious. He dilated her to make intercourse easier for the husband, and the husband took treatment, both to no avail.

The wife was anxious to have a baby, and with the cooperation of her husband, who was not sterile, and following the directions of an expert, she inseminated herself with her husband's semen on numerous occasions, but without results. On December 1 and 31, 1947, an expert inseminated her with the husband's semen and she became pregnant. The latter part of January she left her husband, not knowing her condition at the time, and on learning it she did not return to him. A baby boy was born in September. She brought suit for annulment on the ground of the husband's impotency.

A decree nullifying the marriage would mean the child was illegitimate pursuant to the common law rule that an annulled marriage is void and of no effect from its very inception. (This rule was not changed in England until the Matrimonial Causes Act[4] of 1950 making legitimate any child born of a nullified marriage if such child would have been legitimate had the marriage been dissolved by divorce.) Nevertheless, the court, Judge Pearce, annulled the marriage on the ground of the husband's incapacity to have intercourse. As to the wife's having left her husband, he said: "In most nullity cases there comes a moment when the most forebearing wife becomes sickened by the role, so unnatural to a sensitive woman, of trying to stimulate an impotent spouse sufficiently to enable him to achieve penetration." As to her failure to return to her husband after learning she was pregnant, the court felt "she could never endure to go back"; and as to the child's being illegitimate he was of the opinion that the few who would know of the illegitimacy would also know the facts.

There are no American cases where a couple, one of whom is impotent, have had a child by the wife's artificial insemination with her husband's semen and thereafter the normal spouse has sought a dissolution of the marriage on the ground of the other's impotency, but, in view of our mentioned statutory provisions, it is apparent the rule of *R. E. L. v. E. L.* is applicable and the normal spouse is entitled to a dissolution in all states except those mentioned as exceptions.

HISTORY OF ARTIFICIAL INSEMINATION

Artificial insemination "cannot be traced back to Hippocrates"[5] as said by Alan F. Guttmacher, M. D., of New York City, an outstanding specialist in the field. The first reference in history to the process is that fourteenth-century Arabs artificially impregnated mares with the semen of stallions. During the eighteenth and nineteenth centuries there were successful experiments with fish eggs, insects, amphibians, and mammals, including humans. The first successful artificial insemination of a mammal was in 1780 by Lazaro Spallanzani, an Italian priest and university professor, who inseminated a bitch which gave birth in term to three normal puppies. The news of his discovery evoked much interest throughout the scientific world.

Soon thereafter, perhaps in 1793, Dr. John Hunter, of London, as reported by him in 1799, artificially inseminated a woman by the syringe injection into her vagina of the husband's semen, from which a normal pregnancy ensued. The husband could not impregnate by intercourse because of hypospadias, a deformity of the urethra causing the misdirection of his semen. Dr. J. Marion Sims, of Montgomery, Alabama, performed and, in 1866, reported the first successful human artificial insemination in the United States, again a wife with the husband's semen.

Dr. Sims was a pioneer, has been called the father of American gynecology, and made original contributions in that and other branches of medicine. His success with artificial insemination and the frank publication of his methods were sardonically condemned in both the United States and England by those imbued with the medieval religious attitude, which included most members of his own profession. Prominent doctors and leading medical journals caustically criticized him, indignant that a reputable doctor would stoop so low as to invade the privacy of marriage by assisting a wife to conceive with her husband's semen. Sims, decorous and deeply religious, considered it a doctor's duty to help his patients have children, but the United States and England of his day thought otherwise. (In both countries he had become a legend by the twentieth century.)

The use to any extent of the semen of a man not the husband has come only in recent decades, although there were a few known cases of such use as early as the latter part of the nineteenth century.

Since the inception of donor semen, there has been directed

against it the severe charges that it is illegal, that the wife is an adulteress, and that the child is a bastard. As said, there are no statutes saying one way or the other, and the court decisions are conflicting; hence the field is fertile for individual expressions unrestrained by authoritative pronouncements. A wide variety of opinions, both pro and con, is to be found in the legal, medical, and religious literature. Typical newspaper and magazine donor insemination headlines of the 1930's and 1940's were *Artificial Bastards?*, *Adultery? Blackmail?*, and *Breach of Marriage.*[6]

In spite of legal doubt and blemishing sensationalism, courageous, humanitarian and highly reputable members of the medical profession proceeded to give motherhood to thousands of fertile wives of sterile husbands with the everlasting gratitude of both. These doctors refused to subscribe to an unnatural biological dead end, to a useless termination of reproduction in fertile woman. Actually, the great majority of doctors specializing in the heartbreaking problems of sterility consistently and enthusiastically recommended donor insemination where indicated by physical examination and check of social qualification. The Assembly of the Eleventh Annual Conference of the American Society for the Study of Sterility at its conference at Atlantic City, in 1955, adopted by a vote of 79 to 8 a public statement endorsing donor artificial insemination; and, in 1959, the Council of the British Medical Association also approved the practice, finding that it does not contravene any accepted principle of scientific medicine.

From the beginning donor insemination has been disapproved by most churches of the West, the major exceptions being the Protestant and Jewish faiths in the United States, and they can only be said to be neutral in the sense that those clergymen and active members for or against are somewhat balanced. The Catholic Church's attitude on artificial insemination became fixed in 1897 when the Cardinals were asked if the artificial fecundation of women was permissible, and, with the approval of Pope Leo XIII, answered in the negative. They gave no reasons for their answer. Pope Pius XII on September 29, 1949, in addressing Catholic doctors did say artificial insemination was "illicit" and "immoral" except where it is an auxiliary to the natural act of union of the spouses and of fecundation.

The Anglican Church follows the Catholic view. In 1945 the Archbishop of Canterbury appointed a 13-member commission to study artificial insemination. Finally, in 1948, the commission reported that it found no objection to artificial insemination with the husband's semen, but condemned – with one dissent – donor insemination as "a breach of marriage." The term "adultery" was avoided in the report, although the two lawyers on the commission were of the opinion that donor insemination constituted adultery on the part of a married recipient and even on the part of a married donor. The lone dissenter on the commission was the Dean of St. Paul, who considered the reasoning of the majority as medieval. The Archbishop agreed with the commission's majority and publicly stated that artificial insemination by donor's semen was "wrong in principle and contrary to Christian standards."

The General Assembly of The Church of Scotland (Presbyterian) approved the May, 1959, report of the Committee on Church and Nation disapproving donor insemination, but stated positively that the process was not adultery, pointing out that adultery "suggests action which . . . debases and corrupts," while with donor insemination "the moral atmosphere is quite different. There is no intention of unfaithfulness, the motive may be one of compassion and consideration, and the alien and illicit human relationship is absent."

CURRENT TERMINOLOGY, STATISTICS, USE AND PROCEDURE

Artificial insemination with the husband's semen is designated as "homologous" and popularly called AIH, while artificial insemination with the semen of a donor other than the husband is "heterologous" and called AID. AI is used for artificial insemination without connoting whether the semen is the husband's or a third party's. Sophia J. Kleegman, M. D., of New York City, prefers the euphemism "therapeutic insemination," and many, especially doctors, have adopted that term. Artificial insemination, therapeutic insemination, and AI are used interchangeably in this book.

The primary uses of AIH[7] have been where, though both husband and wife are fertile, the wife cannot be fecundated by ordinary intercourse because of an abnormality on her part such as vaginal malformation, vaginal secretions unfavorable to the sperm, or other cervical hostility; or because of an abnormality on the part of the husband such as impotency, penile malformation, subnormal sperm count, defective sperm migration after intercourse, or improper deposit of sperm during intercourse. In certain cases of the wife's cervical hostility, as put by Dr. Guttmacher, it is often helpful to give the sperm "a three-inch boost on a six-inch journey."[8] There are also the exceptional cases where coitus cannot be accomplished for psychological reasons, in which case AIH is usually successful.

The primary uses of AID[9] (now much more extensive than AIH) are where the wife is fertile but the husband is sterile or has some dysgenic factor which makes it ill-advised for him to have offspring. And there are the rare cases of a sensitized Rh-negative wife and an Rh-positive husband who cannot have live babies. J. R. Ratcliff reports[10] such a couple who had four children each dead at the time of, or within a few hours after, birth. The birth of four consecutive dead or dying children is patently a frustrating experience for any parent. This particular couple turned to AID, an Rh-negative donor was selected, and the wife bore a normal baby. When chance brings together a couple with an Rh incompatability, AID can eliminate nature's twist of death at birth for the offspring.

The expert estimates are that in the United States and England 10 to 15% of all married couples are doomed to involuntary childlessness,[11] and that 30 to 40% of the time this is due alone to the husband's sterility.[12] These estimates reflect that from 3 to 6% of all married couples are potential beneficiaries of AID. No doubt a substantial portion of these couples in the future will have children by that method, thus considerably reducing the number of barren marriages. As said by J. Jay Rommer, M. D., and Claire S. Rommer, of Newark,[13] "Sterility is one of the major problems of Western civilization. The decreasing size of the average Western family, combined with the rising rate of sterility, is changing the population structure of the world." Yet the patent social problems of sterility and the statistics on barren marriages do not tell the whole story, as aptly expressed by S. Leon Israel, M. D., of Philadelphia:[14] "The oft-quoted statement that from 10% to 15% of marriages in the United States are involuntarily barren, while coldly accurate, does not sufficiently express the appalling degree of marital insecurity and the deep unhappiness which lies submerged in the statistics."

While the seriousness of a young couple's realization that one of them is sterile must not be minimized, nevertheless, if the husband is the one who cannot conceive, the couple should recognize that the situation can be ameliorated by the wife's therapeutic insemination with the semen of a donor. This enables them to have a child of their own, a child natural to the wife, and a child of the husband except for the biological relationship, thus fulfilling to a large extent their need and desire for offspring.

Nevertheless AID is strongly opposed, not only by those of sincere religious convictions, but by various pharisaic moralists, clergymen, doctors, and lawyers who bestir themselves to prevent the children, the happiness, and the benefits of this medical advancement mitigating the socially serious and individually heartbreaking problems of sterility. The average young couple themselves, where the husband unfortunately is incapable of fecundating his wife, see nothing wrong in their wish to have a baby natural to the wife by her therapeutic insemination with the semen of a carefully selected, anonymous donor. This in no way offends their legal, moral, religious, or sexual views; actually they consider the procedure a scientific blessing.

It is estimated that 100,000 children have been born by AID to couples in the United States alone.[15] Fortunately it is too late for anyone to stop this advancement. The widespread artificial insemination of wives of sterile husbands with the semen of third party donors is already a social reality. There are probably 200,000 children — fine children I will add — in the world today conceived in this manner.[16] Many couples have more than one such child, which is conclusive evidence that the method is satisfactory and gratifying to them. Often these couples, so pleased with their first child, and also desiring that it have a full brother or sister, request the doctor to use again the original donor.

The usual procedure for a couple considering an AID child is first to consult the family doctor, then a reputable specialist in the field. If the latter determines that the couple's failure to conceive is due to the husband's sterility and the wife is presumably fertile, AID is indicated. Next, he screens the couple to determine if they are socially fitted to have and rear an AID child, but with a humanitarian approach to their problem. In this determination the specialist should rely heavily upon the views of the family doctor.

If the couple is found eligible for AID, the next major responsibility of the specialist is to select a suitable donor, and in exercising this trust he proceeds with caution and discernment. Naturally a donor is chosen for his possession of good and absence of bad inheritable characteristics, physical and mental. A doctor is especially qualified to make this selection because of his medical knowledge, his general understanding of the laws of inheritance, his ability to examine the donor, and his acquaintance with the donor and his children, if any, and often with his parents, grandparents, and collaterals. Thus the likelihood of good donor qualities and the unlikelihood of bad are assured. Naturally the donor is of proven, often high, fertility, has no venereal or other disease, and no history of mental disturbance. Also, one is selected who is of the same race as the husband, and usually has comparable skin coloring, build, and other physical characteristics.

The next step is the therapeutic insemination or the operation, which in the ordinary uncomplicated AID case is the simple process[17] of injecting semen by syringe into the cervix or upper vagina. (The injection of some of the semen into the uterus generally has been abandoned for the normal patient.) If pregnancy results, its course with birth at term is no different than where fecundation is by normal intercourse. Inseminations usually number one to three per ovarian cycle and are made on the days when the patient is most likely to become pregnant.

Results not only depend on the fecundity level of the patient but on the skill of the doctor, including an accurate estimate of the optimal time for conception or for insemination, which in turn depends upon an accurate estimate of ovulation.[18] At the present time 60 to 80% of the women who persist in AID for several months become pregnant, and of the pregnancies about 40% come in the first month and about 80% in the first three.[19] As reported in 1958 by S. J. Behrman, M. D., Associate Professor with the University Hospital, The University of Michigan,[20] experience over the preceding six years at the Hospital shows that 75% of the patients receiving therapy became pregnant, over 50% of the 75% within the first three months and 90% of the 75% within the first six months.

These percentages reflect a substantial reduction during the past two decades in the number of months for accomplishing pregnancy. Also the number of inseminations per month has been substantially reduced. Dr. Behrman's report shows for successful pregnancies an average of only 6.01 inseminations and of only 3.3 months, therefore of only 1.8 inseminations per month. The high percentage of the pregnancies within six months caused Dr. Behrman cautiously to suggest that the medical profession may have to revise its concepts of fertility by shortening the commonly accepted 18-month waiting period.

Even though most women receiving therapeutic inseminations became pregnant within six months, an attitude of finality should not be attributed to this period. The value of perseverance is illustrated by a table of Dr. Kleegman in a 1958 report by Robert G. Potter, Jr., Ph.D.,[21] showing that out of five women trying for as long as twelve months, one became pregnant in the twelfth month, and another of the five, the only one still trying in the twenty-first month, became pregnant in that month.

FUTURE USES OF AIH – SEMEN BANKS

As previously stated, the primary use of AIH to date has been where either the husband or the wife, both fertile, had some abnormality preventing conception by intercourse. While the bypassing of abnormalities will continue, and actually will increase, I am persuaded the future holds many additional uses for AIH, uses which will be highly controversial and will give rise to complex social problems. The enlarged horizon for AIH results from the fact that spermatozoa can now be preserved over a considerable, perhaps indefinite, period of time. Techniques for its preservation have already been developed, and women have already been impregnated with semen which was frozen, stored and thawed.

This unlocks the future for a young army husband being sent overseas to leave sufficient semen for his wife to proceed with the having of children; for a husband who may be exposed to excessive radiation in war or peace to store ample semen for his wife's fecundation without fear of abnormalities in the offspring; for a wife to bear children by her husband conceived after his death. These are but illustrations of the untold situations where preserved semen of the husband, if needed, will be of irreplaceable value, situations not speculative but sure to occur.

Before proceeding with the future, it is interesting to note the present technique of preserving semen and some of the cases of women impregnated with the preserved fluid. Many organisms, including human and animal spermatozoa, survive exceptionally low temperatures, evidently without damage. Mantegazza, in 1866, reported the survival of human spermatozoa at -15° C., and Jahnel, in 1938, at -79° C., -196° C., and -269° C. There was considerable experimenting after 1938 with good fortune when it positively was established that better survival could be obtained with glycerol added to the semen before it was frozen. (The study and use of substances which will protect biological material, including spermatozoa, against low temperatures is in its infancy,[22] but nevertheless there is considerable present knowledge on the subject.) Glycerol-treated human semen with 64% of the spermatozoa living just before freezing, upon thawing has had 43% living, or 67% survival.[23] Of significance is that the survival percentage was the same for one, two, and three months' freezing, thus indicating that the period of preservation may not enter into the survival rate.

In the forefront of artificial insemination of women with preserved semen are doctors presently or previously connected with the State University of Iowa, Iowa City, Iowa, including R. G. Bunge, M. D., Department of Urology; W. C. Keettel, M. D., and J. T. Bradbury, Sc. D., Department of Obstetrics and Gynecology; and J. K. Sherman, Ph. D., formerly with the Department of Urology. A semen bank was established at the University in 1953 and in the following year Drs. Bunge, Keettel, and Sherman reported four successful cases of therapeutic insemination with preserved semen,[24] the first two of which are:

Case 1. The semen samples were preserved for six weeks at -70° C. (the temperature of dry ice) and had an average sperm survival of 58%. Insemination was on the 14th and 15th days of the ovarian cycle, which varied from 28 to 32 days. (The insemination was scheduled for the 12th and 13th days but a severe Iowa snowstorm delayed the patient.) A normal pregnancy resulted and a normal baby boy was born in nine months (274 days) weighing nine pounds (4082 grams).

Case 2. The samples were preserved for five weeks, and had an average survival of 56%. The ovarian cycle varied from 24 to 25 days. The first series of inseminations on the 10th, 11th, and 12th days was unsuccessful, but the second series on the same days of the following cycle resulted in a normal pregnancy. In eight months (246 days) a normal baby girl was born weighing seven pounds (3175 grams).

I mention the internationally publicized story of the woman biologist said to have had two children by her husband several years after his death by inseminating herself with his semen preserved in a 30% glycerol solution at 110° F. below zero. The report of this occurrence is usually ascribed to Dr. Rostand (mentioned in the first chapter) but it did not originate with him and so far as he knows may have been "invented by a journalist."[25] Regardless of the story's origin or accuracy, as the great doctor wrote me, "What seems important . . . is that posthumous insemination has now become a scientific possibility, thanks to the techniques for the conservation of semen, and may even be realized without great difficulty. Here by the way is one instance of the problems which the progress in biology may pose to lawyers; the number of these problems will not cease increasing."[26]

In 1958 a Japanese widow, who had lost her seven-year-old only son and who did not wish to remarry, requested donor insemination,[27] so strong was her desire for another child. The doctor refused, not for medical or economic reasons as the widow was young, healthy, and wealthy, but because the child would have been illegitimate under Japanese law. Where the husband's semen is available and a child conceived by it is legitimate, and the widow can easily support and properly rear the child, some difficulty may attend an attempted explanation to her that she should be denied motherhood because of the misfortune in losing her husband. To advise remarriage may not be the answer for her.

Wives in Japan frequently request donor insemination because they are separated from their husbands but nevertheless desire children. Also, according to the *Tokyo Weekly* of May 31, 1959,[28] (reporting on the tenth anniversary of the successful artificial insemination program of the Department of Family Planning of Keio University of Medicine) two other interesting reasons are given by wives desiring donor insemination: one, that they are related to their husbands and fear the passing on of an inheritable disease; and two, that the husband works in an atomic energy plant and they fear his sperm may be affected. Japan is especially conscious of atomic radiation because of Hiroshima, the fishing boat incident, the island's vulnerability to bombing, and the continual publicity on the subject. No doubt the storing of the husband's semen, when feasible for the public, will enjoy popularity in the ancient Land of the Rising Sun.

A husband about to have an operation with a high mortality rate, to take a prolonged voyage into space, or to engage in any hazardous undertaking, can first provide all the semen necessary for whatever size family he and his wife may want should his risk prove fatal. I do not suggest it will be the rule for widows to have children in this manner; such will be the exception within the foreseeable future. Also the semen of many more husbands who die prematurely will have been stored than will be used. The young couple may idealistically believe the wife will continue with their family after the husband's death, but there are practical and emotional problems which will cause the average widow to see things differently once she realizes her husband is gone and her grief has run its normal course.

Yet the exceptions will add up, and it is time to start thinking about the problems and legal complexities which will attend a child conceived after its father's death. The concept of wedlock has always been extended beyond the husband's death a sufficient time to include the birth of a child conceived during his lifetime so that the child will be legitimate, will inherit from him, and will be legally his for all purposes.[29] Should the concept be further extended to cover the husband's children conceived with his sperm after his death, perhaps long after his death, or should these children be illegitimate? There will be enough of them to necessitate an answer to the question. A young widow could have numerous reasons sufficient to motivate her to this course: financial benefits to herself and child, a desire to be firmly connected with the family of her deceased husband, persuasion from his parents where he was an only child and they desire the continuance of their strain and a grandchild to inherit from them, and if for no other reason, because the widow wants the child she and her beloved had planned to have.

More extensive than the storing of the husbands' semen for potential widows will be its storing for wives whose living husbands may incur some accident or disease which would render them sterile or dysgenic. Only a few will have such misfortune, but many will protect against it. And we will always have widowers and divorcés, who, as they begin to get older, will anticipate romantic marriage to a young woman and the rearing of a second family, the probability of which can best be insured by storing their semen at the earliest date. There are many reasons why semen will be preserved, and entrepreneurs will meet the demand with popular prices at the first economic opportunity.

Regardless of commercial aspects and personal reasons, the preservation of the husbands' semen in sperm banks will come as a means for protecting a people against future wars. It is definitely established that radiation adversely affects the genes of various forms of life and no doubt it does those of man. It is therefore unreasonable to assume that the United States, or any nation, when sperm banks are scientifically and economically feasible, will not take adequate measures to protect future generations. Surely we will not send young men to an area where they may be exposed to radiation sufficient to render them unfit to beget without first arranging for them to store semen so those who return can have descendants free of defects. These youthful war veterans and their wives will not have the problems arising from the conception of children after the death of the father, only the problem of whether or not his genes were damaged by exposure to radiation. There is no sensible reason why these couples should not have available to them spermatozoa of the husband which is known to be unaffected.

The problem of radiation, as all realize, is much broader than the limited example of sending troops to an area of hostility. There presently hangs over our heads the Damoclean threat of the sudden and direct atomic bombing of entire civilian populations. The preservation of spermatozoa and the protection at all costs of selected impregnable females could become necessary for the continuance of a nation. Today the ability of an enemy to terminate a people is a possibility, tomorrow this may be a reality, if measures are not taken to insure another generation.

RELATIVE-DONOR

Often a couple planning on AID want the child to be of the husband's family strain. They therefore request of the doctor that the donor be a relative of the husband. Usually a brother is the choice, though it may be any close male relative. In the United States these requests are virtually always denied. The present practice is to withhold the identity of the couple and of the donor from each other, primarily to eliminate any possible emotional attachment between the wife and the donor. If a relative were used, the wife would know who he was, so a stranger-donor must be selected under current thinking.

A child from the sperm of a brother or other close relative will have many characteristics and traits which a biological child of the husband would have had, will have features and resemblances which the husband can call his own.

Many couples intending to have an AID child become imbued with the idea that the child should be of the husband's family, and the possible emotional complications seldom worry such a couple. It has caused no particular harm in the Scandinavian countries where relative-donors are used, and where there exists a strong attitude that the couple are entitled to such a donor if that is what they want; even that they are entitled to select the donor when not a relative. (This is not the majority view in the Scandinavian countries, neither the view of one of their leading and internationally known exponents of artificial insemination, Jorgen Lovset, M. D., of Bergen, Norway, who has written me that he thinks secrecy is the best policy, but adds that he has had no experience with the relative-of-the-husband donor.) The relative-donor procedure, if given a fair trial in this country, could prove more beneficial and satisfying than the current anonymous donor practice.

Artificial insemination should remain solely in the hands of qualified doctors, but it will not do so if they deny children of the husband's family strain to couples wanting such children. The doctor may fear the donor-wife entanglement but the chances are that the couple will not, and that they will go to someone who will give them what they desire.

A comparable situation once existed for therapeutic abortion, which respectable doctors would not perform. (In emergencies, where the woman might die in hours or days, Protestant doctors would terminate the pregnancy, but they would seldom do so to prevent serious impairment of health, even though death might be hastened.) The result was that many pregnant mothers went to quacks, and the quacks did a fair job because of their experience with both warranted and unwarranted abortions. The medical and legal professions now recognize, and have for some time, that it is best that needed therapeutic abortions be performed by qualified, responsible members of the profession. Skill in artificial insemination is not as essential as in abortions, artificial insemination can be performed surreptitiously much easier, and the risk of complications and death is relatively minor, so, if the public went to quacks for abortion, it will go to them for relative-donor insemination.

Once quacks and peddlers of artificial insemination get started, business for them will increase — in addition to giving determined couples a child of the husband's family strain, they will draw the gullible by promise of offsprings from geniuses to blue-eyed blonds.

JUDICIAL DECISIONS

In all court cases involving the artificial insemination of the wife with the semen of a man not her husband, the primary issue relating to the insemination was whether or not it constituted adultery on the part of the wife. If so, it follows that the child is illegitimate and that there does not arise between it and the husband any of the father-child legal relations which exist where the child is born in lawful wedlock, such as the child's rights of inheritance from the father and the father's visitation rights in the event of divorce. It comes as a surprise when one first learns that the law can seriously consider an AID wife to be an adulteress even though no sexual intercourse is involved, yet a few trial courts have gone so far as to say that she is, since the purpose of AID is the conception of a child by a man not her husband.

In order to hold that the wife committed an adulterous act these courts have redefined and enlarged the concept of adultery so as to bring AID within its scope. In all past ages and civilizations, the gravamen of a wife's adultery has been her sexual intercourse with a man other than her husband; and that is still the law regardless of the few modern lower court decisions to the contrary. A majority of the court decisions, and certainly the better reasoned ones, are to the effect that AID does not constitute adultery.

Before proceeding with a discussion of the leading cases dealing with artificial insemination (which is limited to the cases in English speaking jurisdictions), it will be helpful if there is demarcated briefly the presently well-established legal concept of adultery. It is defined generally as the voluntary sexual intercourse between a man and woman not husband and wife, one or both of whom are married.[30] A few jurisdictions are exceptions to this rule in that if one of the parties is single, intercourse for the single party is fornication only.[31] If neither the man nor the woman is married intercourse between them is always fornication.[32] A completed act or emission by the man is not essential to adultery;[33] neither is full penetration, but the male and female parts must come together.[34] Sexual indulgences other than intercourse are not adulterous, as where a woman fondles a man with her hands only.[35] Pregnancy is not a necessary element of adultery although it may, of course, be a result. It readily appears from these short statements, for which there are literally thousands of supporting cases,[36] that AID is not adultery unless that concept is altered and restated specifically to cover AID. Also the popular conception of adultery would have to be revised as it is generally the same as the legal.[37]

The nature of the evidence required to prove a charge in court is of practical importance, and today adultery can be, and usually is, established by circumstantial evidence.[38] No longer applicable is the law of the early Semitic societies that the wife must be caught in the act before she can be adjudged guilty. Obviously, such a rule of evidence, because of the privacy of adultery, would eliminate conviction in the large majority of cases, and it long has been abandoned. Therefore, if AID is adulterous, the offence can be proved in court without a witness to the act of insemination. Actually, it is the wife herself who usually advances her AID, either defensively as the reason for her pregnancy, or affirmatively to obtain full custody of the child on the theory that the husband has no claim to it. Thus the insemination is conceded and only its legal consequences are in issue.

Seven of the best known cases on artificial insemination are:

Orford *v.* Orford, Ontario Supreme Court (trial court), Orde, J., January 5, 1921.[39]

The parties were married in Toronto in 1913, the wife having come there from England three years earlier. They went to England on their honeymoon, where the husband left his bride with her parents. The marriage had not been consummated as each attempt at intercourse caused the wife severe pain due to her having, as she later learned, a retroflexed uterus. After remaining in England approximately six years, she returned to Toronto but her husband refused to receive her as his wife, whereupon she brought suit for alimony. Before the trial the husband learned that his wife had given birth to a child while in England. At the trial the wife admitted the child and claimed it was born as a result of her artificial insemination.

She testified that she rented a flat in London, became acquainted with a man named Hodgkinson and told him of her lonely married life and why she could not have intercourse with her husband; that a doctor refused to operate on her without her husband's consent but told her she could be helped by having a child which could be done artificially; that Hodgkinson agreed to cooperate and brought a doctor (whose name she could not recall) to her flat; that she undressed, went to bed, was put under an anesthetic, and on regaining consciousness Hodgkinson told her she had been inseminated with his semen;

that she did not become pregnant on this occasion but the procedure was repeated and pregnancy ensued.

The husband took the position at the trial that his wife was guilty of having sexual intercourse with Hodgkinson in the ordinary way; but if not, and if the child was conceived as she claimed, this nevertheless constituted adultery. The wife's position was that she did not have intercourse with Hodgkinson and that having the child by artificial insemination without her husband's consent was not adultery. The court did not believe the wife's story and found the facts to be that she and Hodgkinson had indulged in the ordinary sexual relations. The court could have denied the claim for alimony upon this fact finding, but considered it proper to pass on the wife's legal position that AID is not adultery.

He held that it was on the theory that this process is the voluntary surrender of the wife's reproductive faculties to a man not her husband and that such an act comes within the concept of adultery regardless of whether or not the husband consents. The court referred to the laws of Moses and "the sanctity of the reproductive functions of the people of Israel," saying that had such a thing as artificial insemination entered the mind of the Israelite lawgiver "it would have been regarded with the utmost horror and detestation as an invasion of the most sacred of the marital rights of husband and wife." The court also pointed out that adultery "has never had an exact meaning, nor has its meaning been the same in all countries or under all systems of law." What the court did not mention was that no matter how adultery has been defined, no matter whom it has covered or not covered, at all times under all systems of law sexual intercourse has been a necessary element of the offense.

Hoch *v.* Hoch, Circuit Court, Cook County, Illinois (trial court), Michael Feinberg, J., February, 1945[40]

Frank Hoch, of Chicago, was in the army and away from home from November, 1942, to January, 1944. On being discharged and returning home he found his wife two months pregnant. She told Frank she had been artificially inseminated and that his only rival was a test tube. He sued for divorce, one of his grounds being that his wife had committed adultery. The court granted the divorce, but on another ground, stating that donor artificial insemination did not fit any definition of adultery and was insufficient to support a decree of divorce on that ground.[41]

Strnad *v.* Strnad, Supreme Court, New York County, New York (trial court), Henry Clay Greenberg, J., January 13, 1948[42]

Antoine Strnad and Julie Strnad, husband and wife, had an AID daughter, Antoinette, the husband having consented to the insemination. Thereafter, they legally separated (but were not divorced) and the husband was granted the right to visit the daughter on Sundays of each week. Mrs. Strnad brought legal action for the full custody of the daughter to the exclusion of the husband's visitation rights.

The court, assuming that the wife was artificially inseminated with the consent of the husband and that the child was not of his blood, held that the husband "is entitled to the same rights as those acquired by a foster parent who had formally adopted a child, if not the same rights as those to which a natural parent under the circumstances would be entitled." The court also stated positively that in his opinion the child was not illegitimate.

Strnad *v.* Strnad, Oklahoma, 1949[43]

After the above mentioned New York proceeding, Mrs. Strnad moved to Oklahoma, established her residence and domicile in that state, and sued for divorce. She asked for the exclusive custody of her AID daughter on the ground that her husband had no rights in the child. The Oklahoma court awarded her a divorce and exclusive custody.

Ohlson *v.* Ohlson, Superior Court of Cook County, Illinois (trial court), November, 1954[44]

It was testified that the child of the couple was conceived by AID, but the evidence was not sufficient in the court's opinion to overcome the strong legal presumption that a child born during wedlock is the child of the husband of the mother and is legitimate. Therefore, it was not necessary for the court to hold one way or the other on the legitimacy of an AID child, and he did not do so.[45] It follows that conception by donor insemination must be established with certainty before the courts will find that the child was conceived in that manner.

Doornbos *v.* Doornbos, Superior Court, Cook County, Illinois (trial court), Gibson E. Gorman, J., December 13, 1954;[46] Appellate Court of Illinois, First District, November 19, 1956[47]

The wife filed a complaint for divorce charging the husband with habitual drunkenness and asking for the custody of her five-year-old son and for child support. Before the hearing on the divorce she filed a petition in the case asking for a declaratory judgment that the husband had no rights in the child. In this petition she alleged that her husband was sterile, the son was born to her as a result of artificial insemination to which the husband consented, and the husband was not the donor or the father of the child. She further alleged that artificial insemination is a common practice in the United States, annually thousands are conceived in such manner, the practice is not contrary to good morals, and the act of permitting the insemination by donor other than the husband is not adultery.

The husband answered that artificial insemination is contrary to the natural law and is illegal, and that he should be declared the father of the child because of the legal presumption that a child born of a married woman is the child of the husband if he has access to the wife during the time the child was conceived.

At the hearing on the petition for the declaratory judgment, it was established definitely that the husband was sterile and that the child was born as a result of AID. A reputable gynecologist and obstetrician also testified as to the common practice of artificial insemination in the United States.

The court held that AID, "with or without the consent of the husband, is contrary to public policy and good morals, and constitutes adultery on the part of the mother. A child so conceived is not a child born in wedlock and therefore illegitimate. As such it is the child of the mother and the father has no right or interest in said child." This holding caused much comment, pro and con, in the national press and magazines. The case was the first on artificial insemination in the United States in which doctors testified as to the husband's sterility, the insemination of the wife, and the current practice of donor insemination.[48] Charles C. Cooley, a well-known Chicago attorney who represented the wife, characterized the court's holding as "harsh and arbitrary." He received numerous letters and phone calls commending him on his efforts in support of the legality of donor artificial insemination and expressing indignation over the holding that AID was adulterous and the child was illegitimate. On the other hand, Judge Gorman, a Roman Catholic, received favorable comments on his decision.

Approximately two months after the entry of the declaratory judgment, the court granted the wife a divorce on the ground of the husband's habitual drunkenness, awarded her the custody of the child on the finding that it was born by AID, and relieved the husband of all obligations to support the child. The wife did not appeal the court's decision in spite of the reasoning by which it was reached, since it gave her the exclusive custody of the child, which was what she wanted. However, the State's Attorney (at the court's suggestion)[49] filed a petition to intervene in the case (leave for which the court granted) and moved to vacate the divorce decree or so much thereof as affected the legitimacy of the child. The court overruled this motion and the State's Attorney appealed (which was welcomed by the court).

The appellate court held that the State's Attorney had appealed only from the trial court's denial of the motion to vacate the divorce decree, that this decree was silent on the question of legitimacy, and that the State's Attorney had not appealed from the declaratory judgment which adjudicated the question of legitimacy. Hence the appellate court dismissed the appeal without passing on the questions of adultery and legitimacy. However, the court did decree: "In any event the minor child was not represented in the proceeding, no guardian *ad litem*[50] was appointed to intercede in his behalf, and therefore he is not bound by the adverse judgment."

MacLennan *v.* MacLennan, Court of Sessions, Scotland, at Edinburgh (trial court), Lord Wheatley, J., January 10, 1958[51]

The husband, a citizen of Scotland, sought a divorce on the ground of his wife's adultery predicated on the two facts that they had not lived together since May 31, 1954, and that over fourteen months later, on July 10, 1955, she had given birth to a baby girl in Brooklyn, New York. The wife admitted the child and the long period of non-access, and interposed the defense that the child was not conceived as a result of sexual intercourse but by AID. She did not claim the husband consented to the insemination. Her legal position was that AID without the husband's consent is not adultery. Her pleading did not set out any of the facts as to the artificial insemination and for that reason was attacked as insufficient. Her attorneys recognized that the pleading would have to be more specific if at the trial she was to rely on her artificial insemination.

However, counsel for both parties persuaded the court that before requiring the wife to amend, he should pass on the question of whether or not AID constitutes adultery. In a well-reasoned and thorough opinion he held that while non-consent AID was a grave breach of the marriage, it was not adultery since no sexual intercourse was involved. He stated that in the Mosaic, Roman, and Canon Law sexual intercourse was essential to adultery, also in the law of France, Holland, and England. In reviewing several of the leading cases on artificial insemination, he ably refuted the theory that adultery is the surrender of the reproductive organs and that, therefore, sexual intercourse is not a requisite of the offense. He disagreed with the Chicago trial court's decision in the *Doornbos* case saying that decision could not be followed in Scotland.

After receiving this ruling favorable to the wife, her counsel later informed the court that she had declined to provide the necessary information to make her pleading specific as to the alleged insemination. Accordingly, the court granted the husband a divorce on the grounds of adultery, the only evidence before him being that the husband was not the father of the child. It can, of course, be assumed that had the wife actually been artificially inseminated, she would have plead and testified to the circumstances.

We have seen three cases — *Orford, Hoch,* and *MacLennan* — wherein the inference is unremitting that the wife was not artificially inseminated although she attributed her pregnancy to that process. In none of the cases did the claim influence the court. It is therefore indicated that artificial insemination will be used as an excuse by wives for extra-marital pregnancies but that an insemination cannot be established in court if it did not take place. This is obvious since in donor artificial insemination cases there is a doctor for a witness, perhaps records, and circumstances positive testimony as to which can be adduced in court.

It appears from the foregoing seven judicial decisions that the case law on artificial insemination is still in an early stage of development. Nevertheless, we see the trend from the 1921 *Orford* decision that AID is adulterous, even with the husband's consent, to the 1958 *MacLennan* decision that AID is not adulterous, even without the husband's consent. There is no decision indicating that AIH is illegal, and some of the foregoing cases affirmatively state that it is not.

I am of the definite view — after much more study than is reflected in this chapter — that AID is not adulterous and that the child is legitimate; also, where the husband consents to the insemination, that he is the legal father of the child and that the identical father-child legal relations exist between them as exist between a biological father-husband and the child. This certainly should be the law because it is the husband who, with the wife, causes the child to be brought into the world. They plan for the child, together bring about its conception, together share in the wife's pregnancy, and their joint actions are the *legal cause* of the child's birth. Can the husband participate to the moment of birth and his rights and obligations there terminate?

The fact he is not the biological father is immaterial, in morals and in law. From the legal standpoint the biological father is not *per se* the legal father. To be the legal father, the biological father must be married to the mother. Wedlock is the factor to which the law attributes significance. At common law the child of an unwed mother was *filius nullius* — the son of no one. An AID child is born in wedlock because the husband participates in causing its conception during and as a part of the marriage. Courts and lawyers may fret over whether the AID child is born in or out of wedlock, but the uncomplicated attitude of those having such a child is shown by the following expression, with its touch of pride, made by a young couple answering a questionnaire: "The child is a result of just our marriage."[52]

---

[1] Am. & Eng. Enc. of Law, 2d Ed., Vol. 10, p. 1165.

[2] 28 Indiana Law Journal 620, n. 23; Compiled Laws of Alaska, 1949, sec. 56-5-7; Revised Laws of Hawaii, 1955, Title 33, Ch. 324, sec. 1.

[3] R.E.L. *v.* E.L. (1949) P. 211 (English).

[4] 14 Geo. 6, C. 25, sec. 9.

[5] Guttmacher, Alan F., M.D., Obstetrician and Gynecologist-in-Chief, The Mount Sinai Hospital, New York City, *The Role of Artificial Insemination in the Treatment of Sterility,* 120 JAMA 442 (1942).

[6] *Time,* February 26, 1945, p. 58, and August 9, 1948, p. 49.

[7] Grant, Alan, M.D., *Cervical Hostility: Incidence, Diagnosis, and Prognosis,* 9 F & S 321 (1958); Shields, Frances E., M.D., *Artificial Insemination As Related to the Female,* 1 F & S 271 (1950).

[8] Letter dated June 25, 1959, from Alan F. Guttmacher, M.D., to Cyril J. Smith.

[9] *Ibid.,* n. 7.

[10] *Woman's Home Companion,* March, 1955; *Readers' Digest,* June, 1955, p. 77.

[11] Shell, Thurston A., *Artificial Insemination — Legal and Related Problems,* 8 Fla. L. R. 304 (1955); Israel, S. Leon, M.D., F.A.C.S., Professor of Gynecology-Obstetrics, Graduate School of Medicine, University of Pennsylvania, *The Scope of Artificial Impregnation in the Barren Marriage,* 22 Am. J. Med. Sc. 92 (1941).

[12] *Artificial Insemination — Legal and Related Problems, ibid.,*

n. 11; see also Pommerenke, W. T., Ph.D., M.D., *Artificial Insemination: Genetic and Legal Implications,* 9 Obstetrics and Gynecology 189 (1957), Paul B. Hoeber, Inc., New York.

[13] *Sexual Tones in Marriage of the Sterile and Once-Sterile Female,* 9 F & S 309 (1958).

[14] *The Scope of Artificial Impregnation in the Barren Marriage, ibid.,* n. 11.

[15] Schellen, A., M.D., *Artificial Insemination in the Human,* p. 2. Elsevier Press, Inc., Houston (1957).

[16] This is an estimate by the writer from such information as he has assembled.

[17] Lane, Frederick E., M.D., *Artificial Insemination at Home,* 5 F & S 372 (1954); *ibid.,* n. 7, *Artificial Insemination as Related to the Female,* p. 274; British Medical Journal, January 13, 1945, p. 40.

[18] Cohen, Melvin R., M.D., Irving F. Stein, Sr., M.D., and Bernard M. Kaye, M.D., *Optimal Time for Therapeutic Insemination: Spinnbarkeit as the Preferred Criterion,* 7 F & S 141 (1956).

[19] Guttmacher, Alan F., M.D., editorial entitled *Artificial Insemination,* 5 F & S 4 (1954).

[20] Behrman, S. J., M.D., M.S., Ann Arbor, Michigan. *Artificial Insemination,* 10 F & S 248, 254. (1959).

[21] Potter, Robert G., Jr., Ph.D., *Artificial Insemination by Donors: Analysis of Seven Series,* 9 F & S 37, 47 (1958).

[22] Polge, C. and A. S. Parkes, The National Institute for Medical Research, Mill Hill, London. *Possibilities of Long-Term Storage of Spermatozoa at Low Temperatures,* 20 Animal Breeding Abstracts 1 (1952).

[23] Bunge, R. G., M.D., W. C. Keettel, M.D., and J. K. Sherman, Ph.D., *Clinical Use of Frozen Semen: Report on Four Cases,* 5 F & S 520, 521-2 (1954).

[24] *Ibid.,* n. 23, p. 525-8.

[25] Letter dated June 5, 1959 from Jean Rostand to Cyril J. Smith.

[26] *Ibid.,* n. 25.

[27] 167 JAMA 1146 (1958).

[28] *Tokyo Weekly,* May 31, 1959. Information furnished by

JAMA through its correspondent in Japan.

[29] Ten calendar months.

[30] 2 CJS 474, sec. 3.

[31] 2 CJS 478, sec. 11.

[32] Peo. *v.* Stratton, 75 P. 166, 141 Cal. 604.

[33] Com. *v.* Hussey, 32 NE 362, 157 Mass. 415; State *v.* Haston, 166 P. 2d 141, 64 Ariz. 72.

[34] Rutherford *v.* Richardson, (1923) A. C. 1, 11 (English).

[35] Sapsford *v.* Sapsford, (1954) Probate 394 (English).

[36] Title on *Adultery,* 2 CJS 471 et seq.

[37] State *v.* Hart, 152 NW 672, 673, 30 ND 368.

[38] 2 CJ 22, sec. 44; 2 CJS 491-2, sec. 24; Cadle *v.* State, 235 SW 894, 895, 90 Tex. Cr. R. 464.

[39] 58 Dominion Law Reports 251, 49 Ontario Law Reports 15.

[40] Unreported.

[41] *Family Law – Legitimacy of Child Conceived by Artificial Insemination,* 30 NY Law Review 1016, 1017 (1955); *Time,* February 26, 1945, p. 58, col. 2.

[42] 190 Misc. 786, 78 NYS 2d 390.

[43] Unreported. See Milwaukee *Journal,* Aug. 6, 1949, p. 2, col. 3; 1950 Wisconsin Law Review 136; 8 Florida Law Review 304, 310 (1955); 30 New York Law Review 1016, 1017 (1955).

[44] Unreported.

[45] 8 Fla. L. Rev. 304, 309; 187 JAMA 1638, 1639.

[46] Superior Court No. 54 S 14981.

[47] 12 Ill. App. 2d 473, 139 NE 2d 844.

[48] *Medicolegal Aspects of Artificial Insemination; A Current Appraisal,* 187 JAMA 1638 (1955).

[49] *Ibid.,* n. 48.

[50] A guardian for the particular legal action or suit.

[51] 1958 S. L. T. 12, 1958 SC 105.

[52] *Artificial Insemination*: *The Attitude of Patients in Norway,* 2 F & S 415, 427 (1951).

EVE ENTERS EDEN

WOMAN OF TODAY ENJOYS A WELL-BEING HERETOFORE unknown, both in an absolute or isolated sense and relative to man. The benefits, advantages, comforts, and pleasures of our society are hers, equally with man in most things, in some less, in others more. This type of equality has seldom existed during recorded history for the average woman. I do not say for the well-to-do or influential woman — she has always had the best her land and time could afford — but the vast majority of women until modern times led a life chiefly characterized by toil, seldom had a day's respite, and was never caught up. "Man's work is from sun to sun, but woman's work is never done," was a familiar saying as late as early twentieth-century America. Compared to the past, the average modern woman's duties, though many, are light; and she is the best fed, best housed, best doctored, best cared for human ever to live.

She outlasts man by almost seven years and has replaced the elephant as the longest-lived mammal which inhabits the earth. In the chapter on life insurance we saw that mortality tables more favorable for women than for men are being adopted, so stabilized has become our way of life which enables the "weaker sex" to survive the male. There are roughly 8 million widows in the

United States as compared to 2.5 million widowers, a ratio of over 3 to 1.

Woman's comfortable living is apparent on all sides. Milk is delivered to her kitchen and entertainment and news of the world to her living room; water she no longer draws and carries; and the setting of a thermostat gives her heat with no chill morning fire to build and ashes to remove. An above-average income is not necessary for these conveniences, neither are servants; and the difference in daily living between the woman of wealth and the average woman is at a minimum except for luxuries. Certainly the wealthy matron and her daughters are favored in social life, expensive dress, jewels, and travel, still the average woman shares to a considerable extent in these pleasures. The single girl without independent income can work, keep her apartment, prepare two meals a day, and be fresh for a date in the evening; and she is as alert, as attractive, and as well informed as the girl of means. One-third of all women homemakers have time for gainful employment, and time for relaxation and enjoyment as well.

Even youth, the traditional asset of woman, has lost much of its relative value. "Life begins at forty" could be said only of twentieth-century women; those of prior eras upon reaching that age felt that their "best years" were past. No such frustrating thought now attaches to the forties, nor to the fifties and sixties, and these periods are of feminine charm and usefulness. Half the women in the work force are over forty as are virtually all outstanding women. These women, as well as thousands who devote their primary interests to their families, no longer measure youth in years alone, nor age by wrinkles, anxiety and despair, but by spirit, an appetite for the amazements of life, and courage to maintain an active purposefulness.

Woman sits in the Congress and on the bench and occupies high position in the executive branch of government; she offices on Wall Street and Madison Avenue; she is the courted darling of all who have something to sell; she vacations in Paris and Rome. Refinement is the essence of her tastes, quality her demand, and discernment her attribute; she escapes the bondage of the vulgar. As a person she is the equal of man, as a woman she understands his basic wants and needs, as a mate she knows the value of compassion and tenderness, and of artfulness and suspense. Her life is full, she lives in her time.

Yet the scales still balance against woman in our modern society in that she must submit to pestiferous legal discriminations and to unfair treatment in the economy. The reason? The reader knows the answer, found in the historical part of this book, which is the extension into our modern era of the age-old views that woman is somehow not man's equal. And man, as always, still finds facts which appear to support these views and, from them, rationalizes a justification for discrimination.

For a manifestation of this factor and for an example of a purported justification for discrimination, let us look at a single young man and a single young woman first entering the business world. Many elements make for success in that world: a variety of experience and information, confidence, a practical approach, the need to earn money, and dozens of other intangibles wherein the male usually has an advantage. These intangibles are in addition to such qualifications as intelligence and education which for our example we can assume are equally present in both the youthful working man and woman.

The young man by the time of his first job has had a thousand interests outside his formal education. Anything mechanical has aroused his curiosity; anything involving speed, from horses to jets, has intrigued him; anything developing power, as the motor in his car, has prompted him to consider its practical application. He knows how and why the engine turns the wheels. He has a nebulous idea of stock and commodity markets, has daydreamed of high finance, has earned some money during the summers, and the value of the dollar is becoming a pragmatic concept in his thinking. This boy has also scouted around some on his own, has been taken advantage of in small ways, and has developed an attitude to watch out for himself. He has gambled much more than his parents suspect, can lose without his feelings being hurt, and knows that luck averages out while skill pays off. He reasons that this same principle applies to business, that all risks should be calculated. He probably studied commercial law in school, but regardless, he senses the need for a general understanding of his legal rights. Thus he has a background of a few years, though they be haphazard ones, for business, and an attitude of a worldly quality. Also, he thoroughly enjoys girls and fishing.

The young lady getting her first job presents a different picture. She has been primarily interested in her education, looks, clothes, boys and a few other activities, but not in the great variety of subjects which has absorbed and seriously concerned the young man. She has thought much of marriage, but is not quite sure of the difference between a share of stock and a bond. If she rides, one image of the horse is that of an accessory to her riding habit, and she has never considered how the hair dryer dries her hair — that is not material to her looks. Her thinking, though penetrating, plastic and purposeful, is personal; her outlook lacks a business quality.

After the young man and young lady get jobs, if he is at all promising, management will encourage him, will switch him from one position to another or do other things for the very purpose of preparing him for advancement. He will not find himself in a rut; but the young lady probably will. Management reasons she will soon marry and depart, and even if her marriage does not cause her to leave, pregnancy will; therefore no effort is wasted in preparing her for the future. Hence the young man advances while the young lady, promising or mediocre, types and files. If he thinks his employer is not giving him a break, he will go elsewhere, yet she will not in a similar situation; she continues with her chores. It happens she, too, is planning on marriage and pregnancy, and within months, not years, so there is no reason why she should fret over advancement when she will not be on hand to be advanced.

Thus there is present in our society an attitude, reflected by this example of the young working man and woman — to which many other examples could be added — that derogates from woman's full equality in the economy. The apparent justification for this derogation is that nature has made woman and man different, has assigned to woman the role of bearing and rearing children while giving the male something which better qualifies him for business and industry.

Before considering further this "justification," let us look at Russia where we find a credendum dissimilar to our underlying social attitude towards men and women in the economy. There the belief is established and applied that the two sexes are and should be equal at all levels and in all phases of the society. This premise is considered basic to national planning and activity, and to a strong position in both the world of today and of tomorrow. The woman motorman is expected to operate a trolley as well as the male motorman, and she is paid the same wage and accorded the same treatment. "There seems to be complete equality between men and women," says the Report of the First Official U. S. Education Mission to the U. S. S. R. (1959). This attitude comes from Russian leadership, from a plan originating at the top; women did not have to fight, beg and ballyhoo to get equality.

Boys and girls grow up in Russia being treated the same; both sexes sit at the same desks during the primary school years, each is taught early to respect the other as an equal, and each completes its education and enters the economy without preconceived notions that the male will serve in one capacity and the female in another. Certainly the young lady will tend to certain occupations – she cannot swing an axe with the same force as the young male – but this tendency will come from her judgment and inclination, not from tradition which decrees for her one "place" in the economy and for the male another. In fact, the Russian young lady would take it as an insult to her sex and to her personally if she were relegated to an inferior post merely because she is a woman, and those in authority would consider it unrealistic and unpatriotic to permit such deviousness.

Women of the Soviet Union bear the children as do women of the United States, and nature has otherwise molded them alike, so if the female role in procreation and child care is a controlling factor in economic equality, obviously either the Soviet or our own attitude is amiss. Perhaps all now concede that motherhood with its family duties is a rather poor reason for denying women complete legal equality; but, to stay with our illustration, what of equal opportunities for advancement in business for the young man and woman? It is a statistical certainty that most girls who start work will one day announce that they are quitting in two weeks because they are getting married, or if married, because they are pregnant; and some will telephone that they were married last night and have already resigned. No one blames them and the employer understands with good will, but is he not justified in discriminating against young female employees because of this termination-of-employment factor? I say he is not.

In fairness we will examine the problem primarily from his standpoint. To elaborate on the reasons for discrimination is unnecessary, since obviously there are savings by not expending time, effort, and money in training for the future a group most of whom will work for a limited time only. On the other hand, an employer receives substantial gains by not discriminating against this group. All the young women he employs will not leave him, hence discrimination against them in the beginning will for thirty to forty years affect the quality and amount of their output, and in addition will lessen the benefits which flow to an employer from advancing junior personnel solely on merit. Next, all girls employed will work for some period, and while they do, discrimination will reflect itself in their work. Also, we have noted that the majority of women who once work and stop will one day return to the labor force. If their first employer was scrupulously fair to them, their return will be with the serviceable attitude that they are again to receive equitable treatment, not with the malignant attitude that their initial bad experience is to be repeated.

We know that a need for wages is the dominant incentive for wives who presently work, yet there are thousands of wives without financial problems who would obtain employment if conditions were encouraging, but not otherwise. They do not have to endure discrimination. Today the wife of the successful husband whose children are grown finds that her domestic duties require too little of her energies. She is past the "dinner, dishes, and diapers" routine of the young wife of the struggling husband. The woman, married or unmarried, who is needed at home remains there unless earning a living for herself or family is a necessity; but the woman with time to spare seldom desires to waste it, preferring accomplishment instead. The employer who does not discriminate will draw these women, and among them will be many who will not have to be trained to business but who are entering their "second working period," a period steadily increasing for women.

Employers recognize the advantages of not discriminating against women but no doubt many conclude that these advantages are outweighed in their particular business by the benefits of depending primarily on the advancement of males. Even so, there are to be considered the reasons on the national level for not discriminating, such as encouraging women to scientific pursuits, mentioned in a preceding chapter. If these reasons plus the individual benefits to an employer do not persuade him, he will have to continue with his policy of discrimination so long as he can get women to work for him; no Russian-type plan will be forced on him.

What of the element of the male's advantage in business resulting from his prework years, from his early development of a business outlook as against the young lady's personal outlook? While this advantage is not to be discredited, it must not be overrated. As said, the male's prework years are haphazard, are of scattered rather than of planned interests, and the business information he acquired intermittently over five years can be learned in five months while actually engaged in business. Thus if the young lady is given a little help and advice upon taking her first job, she will soon develop the proper thinking. In truth, the female's so-called personal outlook often gives her an advantage; if she is with a concern which caters to women the fact that she thinks as do the customers can be a surprising asset.

Discrimination in advancement and in recognition within the economy is not only of grave concern to women, but results in great loss to the nation and to social progress. The withholding of advancement to the meritorious women is but one of many examples of economic discrimination which could be elaborated upon. Equal treatment of both men and women in all aspects of the economy is the only sound policy. After all, one-third of the work force is women; it cannot benefit to discriminate against such a proportion. Too, there is no sound reason why a woman should be paid a third less than a man holding the same job, especially when she probably does a third more work than he.

Many concerns no longer discriminate in any particular and many more are eliminating inequalities as fast as practicable. The voluntary adoption by employers of a policy of identical treatment for both sexes is the remedy for the removal of the remaining economic inequalities against women, just as the adoption of the Equal Rights Amendment is the remedy for the removal of the remaining legal inequalities. Those in authority, be they employers or high government officials, must not only recognize woman's worth to our nation, but also that if she is to contribute her full worth she must not be discriminated against.

Unwarranted discrimination has evil effects of such force that it retards our economic and social efforts to an extent beyond our very comprehension. Its cancerous consequences cannot be evaluated, so insidiously do they undermine our progress. An American rebels at unfairness, and where it is forced on a class, all are losers. When every inequality against woman is removed, we shall see a vast increase in her contribution to society from which both living and future generations will benefit.

It is shameful to know that the substantial loss from discrimination results primarily from a tradition of woman's secondary status, a tradition to which we publicly deny validity but which we nevertheless let influence us, and a tradition the very bases of which we honestly discredit. No one would revive the Mosaic inferiority of woman in law, or the Pauline subjection of the female in society, or the medieval lowly rank of the wife in the family. Yet the tradition bred by these outworn theories, the assumption that women cannot equal men in business and industry, still reflects itself in discrimination. It is not my intent to magnify existing inequalities in this closing chapter, the main purpose of which is to direct attention to the high station of woman in the United States today. Yet in reviewing this station the social attitude harming woman must be stressed candidly lest it be overlooked among the many equalities which she so recently has obtained.

Woman may justly be proud of her present prominent position and of her praiseworthy participation in all activities of life. Her good fortune is not by chance or favor, she earned it; it came not from man's altruism, but from her own merit. This she must know; also, that man will take selfish advantage of her. Before the white man's arrival in Hawaii, its women were prohibited the eating of one of the staples of the Islands' diet, bananas — there were not enough for all. Woman must also know that romance and chivalry did not advance her to where she is. Marriage did not become popular in this country because woman is a creature only once removed from a goddess or because of any moonlight desire for the irresistible female — four or five women can supply all the sex which a hundred males need. "Whenever, in the history of civilization," writes Durant, "woman has ceased to be an economic asset in marriage, marriage has decayed."

To near the end of this book on woman in such a realistic tone is not my preference. Rather would I speak of altruism, romance, and chivalry, but woman knows these blissful traits will bloom forever in countless deeds and sentiments — such are the natures of male and female. These traits she will emphasize in her reasoning and in her imagination — and that is good. This will not prevent her from understanding that woman must stand on her own value, must open her eyes to reality, and must contribute her full capabilities to her society's betterment. This Eden which she so recently entered is not sufficiently cleansed; she cannot dwell in the Garden and only partake of its fruits, but with man must till its soil of morality, if truly she is to be equal and free.

As to those who in the past have cast their influence against woman's equal status, be they clergymen, lawyers, moralists or others, in the final analysis I am constrained to say that they have been sincere; that within their training, limits, environment, and perspective they believed themselves to be right. No doubt history forgives them. Furthermore, criticism of their views and theories, while necessary, is not the true remedy; that remedy, as always, is a knowledge of the truth. Surely the historical part of this book demonstrates that there is no intrinsic value in the beliefs supporting a secondary role for woman in any phase of our culture, including the economy and law, the phases of current concern.

Of these beliefs we know: they held woman in subjection during the era of Moses, chained her to abjectness in Greece's Golden Age, took from her the virtual equality she gained in the Roman Empire during the period of its great jurists, relegated her to inferiority throughout the Middle Ages, and retard her full and final equality in the Modern Age. These beliefs come not from true religion, but from rationalizations based upon the past; not from great advancing civilizations, but from ignorance and desolation. We are particularly influenced by the views of the rugged Hebrew nomads whose original monotheism, because of a severe environment, expectedly lacked both the fertility attributes of the goddesses of lands fortuned by nature and the sublimity of the sole god of the pharaoh-poet-philosopher. It was circumstance, not religion, which bred the Mosaic laws unfavorable to woman, and tradition which enabled their perpetuation through Paul, Tertullian, Augustine, Gratian, Blackstone, and thousands of others into the modern day.

Woman has been combatting the concept of her inferiority ever since records were kept, and no doubt long before. The harmful effects of this concept lessen as her society progresses, increase when advancement stops. Since the complete lack of value of this concept is apparent, it must no longer stand against the future gains for woman which should flow from our progressing society; it must be uprooted, no matter how aged the roots. And that soon comes. Within this very decade there will remain few men who will not be abashed to claim superiority to woman and to invoke religion or nature to support this attitude. Our society's progress is such that within a few short years woman will be on an absolute equality with man in law, economy, politics, science, and every aspect of life.

Any nation which does not achieve this goal and thereby allow its women to contribute their full talents and abilities is foredoomed. Woman's aid is especially essential to the United States if we are to continue as the stronghold of democracy, and our failure in this duty betides ill for the free world. There is none to take our place.

Those among us who continue to oppose woman's advancement to complete equality, who strain their ears to catch the now faint beat of the distant desert drums of her inferiority, know not what they do, but they can no longer be forgiven. Jesus did not listen to this beat, though it was loud in his day. And modern woman does not listen. She knows that tradition is but a guise for discrimination against her, that man wishes not to bare his petty nature but pretends to shroud it with the past. Woman at times may pretend with him, but the rebel in her prods her on her way, and her instinct and practical nature combine to prompt her:

> Vex not thy soul with dead philosophy,
> Have we not lips to kiss with, hearts to love,
>   and eyes to see![1]

---

[1] Wilde, Oscar, *Panthea.*

BIBLIOGRAPHY

Augustine, St. (Aurelius Augustinus). *The Confessions*. The Harvard Classics. Editor, Charles W. Eliot. P. F. Collier & Son Company, New York (1909).

Beard, Mary R. *America Through Women's Eyes*. The MacMillan Company, New York (1933).

Bible, King James Version.

Butler, John Marshall. *The Case for Equal Legal Rights*. July 1957 National Business Woman. The National Federation of Business and Professional Women's Clubs, Inc., Washington, D. C.

Chiera, Edward. *They Wrote on Clay*. The University of Chicago Press, Chicago (1938).

Churchill, Winston S. *A History of the English Speaking People: The Birth of Britain*. Dodd, Mead & Company, New York (1956).

Conant, James B. *On Understanding Science: An Historical Approach*. Yale University Press, New Haven (1947).

Contenau, Georges. *Everyday Life in Babylon and Assyria. Ed*ward Arnold, London (1954).

Costain, Thomas B. *The Magnificent Century*. Doubleday & Company, Garden City, New York (1951).

Dale, Laura H.; Harris, Laura H.; and Morrison, Alice A. *The*

Legal Status of Women in the United States of America. United States Government Printing Office (1958).

De Tocqueville, Alexis. *Democracy in America.* D. Appleton & Company, New York (1899).

Driver, G. R. and Miles, John C. *The Babylonian Laws.* Oxford University Press (1956).

Durant, Will. *The Age of Faith.* Simon and Schuster, New York (1950).

Eberly, Marion Stevens. Various brochures and articles relating to life insurance.

Edersheim, Alfred. *The Life and Times of Jesus the Messiah.* Longmans, Green, and Co., New York (1904).

Eisenhower, Dwight D. "*. . . A Simple Matter of Justice.*" 36 National Business Woman, No. 7, p. 12 (July 1957).

Emmerich, Andre. *Savages Never Carved These Stones.* American Heritage, February 1959, p. 47. American Heritage Publishing Co., Inc. (1959).

Encyclopaedia Britannica.

Gordon, Cyrus H. *Hammurapi's Code: Quaint or Forward-Looking?* Rinehart & Company, New York (1957).

Green, Constance McL. *Eli Whitney and the Birth of American Technology.* Little, Brown and Company, Boston (1956).

Hansen, Henry Harald. *Costumes and Styles.* E. P. Dutton & Co., New York (1956).

Harris, Seale, M. D. *Woman's Surgeon, The Life Story of J. Marion Sims.* The MacMillan Company, New York (1950).

Hecker, Eugene A. *A Short History of Women's Rights.* G. P. Putnam's Sons, New York and London (1911).

Huie, W. O. *The Community Property Law of Texas, Vernon's Civil Statutes of Texas,* Vol. 13, p. vii. Vernon Law Book Company, Kansas City, Mo. (1951).

Institute of Life Insurance. *Life Insurance Fact Book 1959.*

James, Marquis. *The Life of Andrew Jackson.* The Bobbs-Merrill Company, Indianapolis-New York (1938).

Jensen, Oliver. *The Revolt of American Women.* Picture Press, Inc. (1952).

Josephson, Hannah. *The Golden Threads: New England's Mill Girls and Magnates.* Duell, Sloan & Pearce, Inc., New York (1949).

Keller, Werner. *The Bible as History.* William Morrow and Company, New York (1956).

Langdon-Davies, John. *A Short History of Women.* The Viking Press (1927).

Lodge, Henry Cabot. *The History of Nations.* P. F. Collier & Sons, New York (1932).

Marcus Aurelius. *The Meditations of Marcus Aurelius Antonius.* The Harvard Classics. Editor, Charles W. Eliot. P. F. Collier & Son Company, New York (1909).

Marquis-Who's Who. *Who's Who of American Women: Geographical-Vocational Index* (1958-1959).

Mill, John Stuart. *The Subjection of Women.* J. M. Dent & Sons, London (1955).

Moynihan, Cornelius J. *Community Property,* Vol. II, *American Law of Property.* Little, Brown and Company, Boston (1952).

National Encyclopedia, The (1934).

Ottenberg, Louis. *Magna Carta Documents: The Story Behind the Great Charter.* American Bar Association Journal (June 1957).

Pellison, Maurice. *Roman Life in Pliny's Time.* The Chautauqua-Century Press, Meadville, Pa. (1897).

Plato. *Menexenux* and *The Republic.* B. Jowett, translator. Random House, New York (1937).

Reich, Emil. *Woman Through the Ages.* Methuen & Company, London (1908).

Rommer, J. Jay. *Sterility: Its Cause and Its Treatment.* Charles C. Thomas, Springfield, Illinois (1952).

Rostand, Jean. *Can Man Be Modified?* Basic Books, Inc., New York (1959).

——— *Science Fausse et Fausses Sciences.* Gallimard, Paris (1958).

Schellen, A. *Artificial Insemination in the Human.* Elsevier Publishing Company, Houston, Texas (1957).

Tiffany, Herbert Thorndike. *The Law of Real Property,* Third Edition, Vol. 2. Callaghan and Company, Chicago (1939).

Uttley, A. M. *Computers Promise Man a New Freedom.* The Houston *Post,* Houston, Texas. August 9, 1959.

Volume Library, The. Educators Association, Inc., New York (1942).

Wiener, Norbert. *Cybernetics.* John Wiley & Sons, Inc., New York (1952).

Wigmore, John Henry. *A Panorama of the World's Legal Systems.* Washington Law Book Company, Washington, D. C. (1936).

Williams, Glanville. *The Sanctity of Life and the Criminal Law.* Alfred A. Knopf, New York (1957).

Wilson, Mitchell. *American Science and Invention.* Simon and Schuster, New York (1954).

Wollstonecraft, Mary. *A Vindication of the Rights of Woman.* J. M. Dent & Sons, London (1955).

Zane, John M. *The Story of Law.* Ives Washburn, New York (1927).

INDEX

B

C

D

E

F

G

H

I

N

O

P

Q

R

S

T

U

V

W

Y

Z